Hiking Colorado's Summit County Area

Help Us Keep This Guide Up to Date

Every effort has been made by the author and editors to make this guide as accurate and useful as possible. However, many things can change after a guide is published—trails are rerouted, regulations change, techniques evolve, facilities come under new management, etc.

We would love to hear from you concerning your experiences with this guide and how you feel it could be improved and kept up to date. While we may not be able to respond to all comments and suggestions, we'll take them to heart, and we'll also make certain to share them with the author. Please send your comments and suggestions to the following address:

The Globe Pequot Press
Reader Response/Editorial Department
P.O. Box 480
Guilford, CT 06437

Or you may e-mail us at:

editorial@GlobePequot.com

Thanks for your input, and happy trails!

A **FALCON** GUIDE®

Hiking Colorado's Summit County Area

A Guide to the Best Hikes in and around Summit County

Maryann Gaug

FALCON GUIDE®

GUILFORD, CONNECTICUT
HELENA, MONTANA
AN IMPRINT OF THE GLOBE PEQUOT PRESS

Falcon and FalconGuide are registered trademarks of
Morris Book Publishing, LLC.

Maps created by XNR Productions Inc. © Morris Book
Publishing, LLC.
Spine photo © 2004 Michael DeYoung
All interior photos by the author.

Gaug, Maryann.
  Hiking Colorado's Summit County area: a guide to the
best hikes in and around Summit County/Maryann Gaug.
       p. cm.
  Includes bibliographical references.
  ISBN-13: 978-0-7627-3651-5
  ISBN-10: 0-7627-3651-8
  1. Hiking—Colorado—Summit County—Guidebooks. 2.
Summit County (Colo.)—Guidebooks. I. Title.
  GV199.42.C6G39 2006
  917.88'45–dc22

                                        2006010173

Manufactured in the United States of America
First Edition/First Printing

The author and The Globe Pequot Press assume no liability for accidents happening to, or
injuries sustained by, readers who engage in the activities described in this book.

Contents

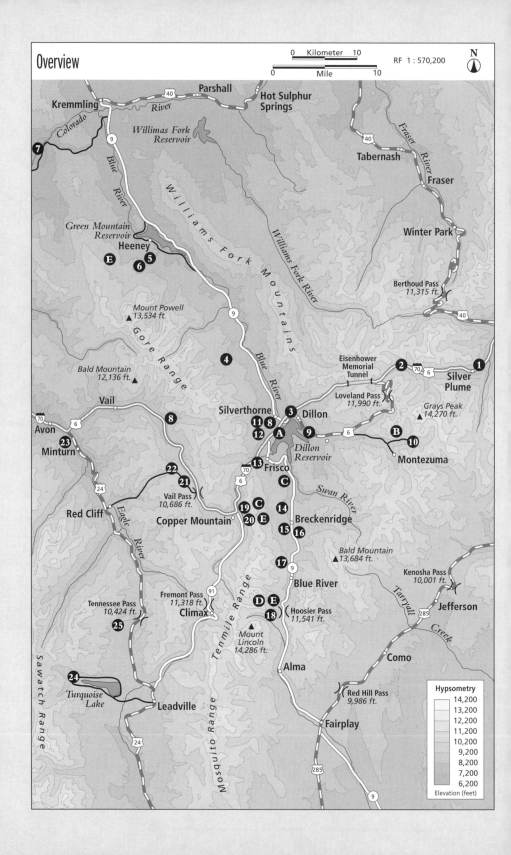

Overview

0 Kilometer 10

0 Mile 10

RF 1 : 570,200

N

Parshall

Kremmling

Hot Sulphur Springs

River

Colorado

Williams Fork Reservoir

Tabernash

Fraser River

Fraser

7

Blue River

Green Mountain Reservoir

Heeney

E

6 5

Williams Fork Mountains

Williams Fork River

Winter Park

Berthoud Pass 11,315 ft.

40

Mount Powell ▲ 13,534 ft.

Gore Range

Bald Mountain 12,136 ft. ▲

Blue River

9

Eisenhower Memorial Tunnel

2

70 6

1 Silver Plume

Vail

8

Silverthorne

11 8

12

3 Dillon

A

9

Loveland Pass 11,990 ft.

Grays Peak 14,270 ft. ▲

Avon

70 6

23

Minturn

4

Dillon Reservoir

6

B

10 Montezuma

22 21

Vail Pass 10,686 ft.

13

Frisco

C

Swan River

Red Cliff

Eagle River

Copper Mountain

19 C

20 E

14

Breckenridge

15 16

Bald Mountain ▲ 13,684 ft.

Kenosha Pass 10,001 ft.

17

9 Blue River

Tarryall Creek

Jefferson

285

Tennessee Pass 10,424 ft.

25

Fremont Pass 11,318 ft.

Climax

91

Tenmile Range

D E

18 Hoosier Pass 11,541 ft.

Mount Lincoln 14,286 ft. ▲

Como

24

Turquoise Lake

Leadville

Sawatch Range

Mosquito Range

Alma

Red Hill Pass 9,986 ft.

Fairplay

285

24

9

Hypsometry

14,200
13,200
12,200
11,200
10,200
9,200
8,200
7,200
6,200

Elevation (feet)

Acknowledgments

Many thanks to all my friends and new friends in the U.S. Forest Service, Town of Dillon, Town of Breckenridge, and the Bureau of Land Management for working with me on choosing the most appropriate trails for this book. Despite the "big brother" image federal and public employees often have, these people love the back-country and were eager to answer questions and help me. They took time from busy schedules to review the chapters and provide feedback. If I name everyone, I'll bore you to tears and would for sure accidentally forget someone.

Thanks to my good friends Keith Brown and Lance Masoner, and neighbor Doug Feely for helping me with transportation for three hikes. Because I hiked all of the trails by myself, Keith anxiously awaited my phone calls confirming that I was safe and not lost in the woods.

Thanks to Dr. Leon Chipman, the nurses, and Dr. Brian Maurer for fixing my knees and Achilles tendon after those body parts decided to hurt too much to hike the summer after I signed the book contract. Special thanks to my physical thera-pist, Della Crone, and massage therapist, Pegi Rapp. Because of their skillful hands, I hiked twenty-five trails in one summer instead of two. If you have knee problems, Summit and Eagle Counties have wonderful orthopedic surgeons.

Thanks also to all my friends and co-workers who put up with a year of "I have to work on the hiking guide" when they asked me to do things.

A special thanks and hug to my Mom, still living, and my Dad, long dead, for encouraging me to do what I want to do and strive for peace and happiness.

Last, but not least, thanks to you readers and fellow hikers for buying *Hiking Colorado's Summit County Area*. I hope you find it useful and interesting. May you enjoy many hours hiking the trails described between these covers.

Introduction

Rugged peaks reflected in high mountain lakes, sparkling streams tumbling through flower-filled meadows, high ridges where the view is forever, and a rich mining history make Summit County and the surrounding area a hiking gem. Today's hiking trails may have started when Native Americans followed game trails for their summer hunts. Miners scoured the area hoping to strike it rich after gold was found in the region's creeks. Railroads followed to move ore and bring supplies. Settlers arrived and worked the land, living here year-round through beautiful summers and snowy, cold winters.

I love hiking through the various ecosystems of this area in which I live, from the shores of Dillon Reservoir to the high alpine tundra which overlooks the valleys below surrounded by peaks reaching as far as the eye can see. Hiking to a lake then relaxing along its banks surrounded by wildflowers and listening to a chorus of birds is a great way to spend a day or weekend! Along the way you may see pine squirrels busily caching cones for the sure-to-be-long winter, deer browsing in meadows, or elk sunning themselves while chewing their cud in a high valley. Ospreys and eagles soar in the clear blue Colorado sky. A colorful carpet of wildflowers graces every nook and cranny along trails, attracting bees and other pollinators during the short summer. Although seldom seen, black bears and mountain lions patrol the area while moose munch on willows in wetlands. Little cascading rivulets born in high snowfields join together to create a creek that winds and tumbles to the river in the main valley below.

Some trails take me back to the mining boom days of the late 1800s. Only a few logs remain of cabins that once shared the happy times and sad tribulations of their owners. A mound of dirt and rocks by a hole in the ground is all that remains of a miner's dream.

Today the mining boom has gone bust but Summit County and surrounding Clear Creek, Lake, Park, Grand, and Eagle Counties are booming with recreation highlighted by eight ski areas, seven nordic centers, several reservoirs, gold-medal trout streams, and hundreds of miles of trails in the Arapaho, White River, Pike, and San Isabel National Forests and Bureau of Land Management (BLM) lands. For a more remote and primitive hiking experience, I spend many hours exploring three congressionally designated wilderness areas: Eagles Nest, Ptarmigan Peak, and Holy Cross. The towns of Dillon and Breckenridge own open-space parcels with hiking trails that lead to beautiful overlooks, back into mining history, or around special natural areas.

The majority of the hikes featured in this book are in Summit County and the White River National Forest, Dillon Ranger District. The northern part of Summit County has many hiking trails while the eastern area around Keystone has fewer hiking trails and more 4WD roads—a mining legacy. Many old mining claims just north of Breckenridge were purchased in summer 2005 by Summit County and the Town of Breckenridge. I had hoped to include a trail in that historic area but the purchase took longer than anticipated and trail planning has just begun. About one-third of the hikes lie in Clear Creek, Lake, Park, Grand, and Eagle Counties, which surround Summit. Most of the trails lie within 30 miles of Interstate 70.

The White River National Forest consists of approximately 2.3 million acres. Ten 14,000-foot peaks, eight wilderness areas encompassing more than 750,000 acres, and eleven ski areas can be found in this north-central Colorado playground. The forest started out as the White River Plateau Timber Reserve in 1891. In 1995, the White River ranked fifth in the nation for recreational visitor days.

Leave No Trace skills have become very important to the preservation of Colorado's wild lands and parks as the population grows and increasing numbers of visitors discover our magnificent state. We need to think about thousands of feet instead of just the two we each have. See the In Addition section on Leave No Trace and visit the Leave No Trace Center for Outdoor Ethics Web site at www.LNT.org for further information.

The featured trails described in this book are located at high elevation. The lowest trailhead is at 6,960 feet and most hikes start at over 9,000 feet. The high point is the 12,777-foot summit of Buffalo Mountain.

High elevation and winter snowpack means trails can be covered by snow into July. Here are some guidelines as to approximate times when trails dry out (from the U.S. Forest Service Dillon Ranger District).

Below 9,500 feet—mid-May

Between 9,500 and 10,000 feet—end of May

Between 10,000 and 10,500 feet—mid-June

Between 10,500 and 11,500 feet—July 1

11,500 feet and above—mid-July

Check with the listed land managing agency for current trail conditions.

Speaking of winter, when the snow flies, you can still continue to enjoy the backcountry on foot, snowshoes, or cross-country skies. Several trails are popular year-round and are often packed by many feet, so snowshoes are not necessary except after a large snowfall. I like to use Yaktrax on my boots for extra traction (www.yaktrax.com). These easy-to-slip-on coils provide great traction on firm snow and icy patches. (See Hike 12, Lily Pad Lake, for more ideas on winter fun).

This guidebook of twenty-five featured hikes is designed to take you on a hiking tour of Summit County and an encircling region. The Honorable Mentions add breadth and depth to the featured selections. Hikes range from easy to strenuous, from a 3-mile round-trip on a flat road along Dillon Reservoir to overnight backpacks. Some hikes are canine-friendly. I included some classic trails and found several new ones. Some trails travel through lesser-known and quieter areas.

Hiking is a great way to explore your surroundings and use all five senses to enjoy your journey. While walking around our public lands, you may learn a lot about yourself. Away from our motorized, mechanized, and electronic world, you may discover more about what your body needs, how strong you are both mentally and physically, or how little you know about the world around you. Hiking provides each of us many opportunities to grow and become more alive.

Free bus service by the Summit Stage gives hikers an extra bonus in Summit County. Several point-to-point hikes can be accomplished with just one car, because one or both trailheads are near bus stops. This service also makes trailhead access possible without a car. The chapters with trail(s) near bus stop(s) contain bus service information.

If you enjoy hiking on the trails described in this book, or other trails for that matter, consider volunteering for trail work at least one day each year. None of the land management agencies have huge budgets and are more and more relying on volunteers to help with basic trail work. A sampling of volunteer trail groups is listed in the back of the book. You'll meet some really great folks and gain the satisfaction of a job well done at the end of the day. One friend commented how much fun she had showing people the bridge that she helped to build.

A word about the details in this book. Featured trails were hiked during 2005. The information is as accurate as possible from that time frame. However, I actually discovered one change after I hiked the Shrine Mountain trail—when I drove over Shrine Pass to hike Bowman's Shortcut, the old rickety outhouse at the top of the pass was closed, and a new vault toilet had been built! Highway 9 is being rerouted onto North and South Park Avenues in Breckenridge (instead of Main Street), and mileages to the trailheads south of the reroute reflect the change.

Trail mileage, however, is as much an art as a science, even for land managers. I used a Global Positioning System (GPS) to obtain the mileage. In some areas, poor satellite reception may have provided less than accurate information. Please realize that trail locations and conditions, roads, and signage are subject to change over time. Even trailheads can move and some trails are rerouted to prevent environmental damage. Finding accurate historical information was sometimes interesting when different books contained conflicting information! I tried to find appropriate Web sites, only to discover URLs change rapidly.

Henry David Thoreau said, "In wildness is the preservation of the world." Aldo Leopold added years later: "When we see land as a community to which we belong, we may begin to use it with love and respect." My wish for you is to enjoy hiking and learn about yourself and the world around you to which we all belong. Remember, only we can preserve wild lands for ourselves and future generations.

As you hike around the beautiful Summit County region, capture part of nature's spirit and hold it close to your own. Leave a piece of your spirit as well, so that no matter where you travel or live, the peace and beauty of this wild country will remain with you forever.

Colorado Weather

Difficult to forecast and prone to change quickly, the Summit County area weather is a wonder in itself. Mountains often create their own weather. On the west slope of the Continental Divide, where Summit County is located, weather may be entirely different than in the Denver metro area on the east side.

Hiking season in the Summit County area is best from July through early October. I have noted trails that are hikable year-round or are popular for snowshoeing and cross-country skiing. Some trails disappear under winter's white mantle.

Summit County residents head to warmer climes during April and May for good reason—hiking is not very good! Snow still covers trails and you can sink in over your knees in the rotting snow even with snowshoes. When trails start to melt out, they can be quite muddy. If you do hike during "mud season," remember to get muddy—walk through the mud! Walking around muddy areas enlarges the size of the mess.

Summer attempts to begin in June, but winter's last gasp may still drop some snow. June also begins thunderstorm season. By July wildflowers bloom profusely. Be aware: Snowstorms do occur on July 4th above 8,500 feet! Colorado experiences a monsoon starting about mid-July and ending in early September. Afternoon thunderstorms are common. Two problems result from thunderstorm development. One is lightning, a killer from above; the second, more subtle, is rain. In Colorado rain tends to be cold, and unprepared hikers can become hypothermic very quickly, even in midsummer. Monsoonal rains can last for several days in a row.

Fall can be the best time to hike, with "fall" meaning mid-August to mid-September in the land above the trees and from September to about early October below treeline. Thunderstorms are less frequent, the air crisp and cool with dazzling blue skies. Aspen turn gold and red about the third week in September. By mid-October, snow tends to bring an end to most hiking in the region.

Winter travel typically requires snowshoes or skis. If you travel on backcountry trails during winter, take an avalanche awareness course at a minimum. Colorado often leads the nation in avalanche deaths with many occurring in Summit County! In spring and early summer, avalanches can still pose danger to hikers and climbers.

No matter the season, always bring layers of clothes and rain (or snow) gear. Check the local weather forecast before heading out. Weather changes quickly and a temperature drop of 10 to 20 degrees F in one hour is not unheard of. Be prepared!

Flora and Fauna

The Summit County area contains the montane (8,000 to 9,500 feet), subalpine (9,500 to 11,400 feet), and alpine (above 11,400 feet) life zones. Ecosystems, encompassing the physical environment and the organisms living within a given area, can vary within these zones.

Ecosystems include mountain grasslands and meadows, mountain wetlands, lodgepole pine, aspen, spruce-fir, limber and bristlecone pine, and alpine tundra. While hiking through these different environments, notice what plants and animals live where. For example, aspen grow in moist, protected areas. Bushes such as chokecherry, gooseberry, serviceberry, and snowberry provide browse for mule deer. Grasses and other plants offer good eats for elk, who also scrape the bark off aspen in winter. Black bears leave claw marks climbing their favorite aspen tree. Keep an ear open for the chick-a-dee-dee-dee call of the mountain or black-capped chickadee.

As you gain elevation, you can observe how animals and plants have adapted to shorter summers, less oxygen, wind, and colder temperatures. Above treeline, you can't miss the little pikas scurrying around with mouthfuls of grasses and flowers or the lazy marmots sunning themselves on rocks. Chipmunks, ground squirrels, and marmots will almost attack you expecting a handout. Please don't feed them as they may not forage for themselves. Crows, magpies, blue Steller's jays with their black crowns, and pesky Clark's nutcrackers and gray jays (nicknamed camp robbers) are easily spotted birds. Occasionally you might catch a glimpse of an eagle, osprey, or red-tailed hawk soaring above you.

If normal or greater precipitation has occurred during summer, mushrooms pop out in August and early September. Many mushrooms are poisonous while others are incredibly delicious and edible. Don't pick any unless you know what you're doing!

Bristlecone pines grow in Colorado roughly south of I–70, although those growing along the trail to the Griffin Memorial are just north of it. These incredible trees live 1,500 to 2,000 years in our state. Between the alpine tundra and spruce-fir or limber pine ecosystems, krummholz grow. These stunted trees, usually spruce, fir, or limber pine, form tree islands with a few flag trees sticking up. The deadwood on the windward side protects the rest of the tree organism, so please don't use it for firewood.

The most incredible plants grow above treeline: alpine forget-me-nots, sky pilot, moss campion, old-man-of-the-mountain, alpine avens, Parry's clover, and more. Each flower has its own particular niche, whether on windblown slopes or next to sheltering rocks. If you have a chance, learn about this incredible land above the trees and how you can protect it while hiking. (See Hike 3, Ptarmigan Peak, for more information).

Black bears, mountain lions, and moose live in the Summit County area, and if surprised, they can get downright nasty. See The Art of Hiking for good tips on avoiding or dealing with each of these fabulous wild creatures. Even deer, elk, bighorn sheep, and mountain goats can pose problems, especially if they think their young are threatened. Remember, they've been here for many years, and we're treading on their territory.

Wilderness Restrictions/Regulations

Hikes featured in this book include trails in three wilderness areas: Eagles Nest, Ptarmigan Peak, and Holy Cross. If you plan to hike or backpack in one of these wildernesses, please contact the responsible U.S. Forest Service office or www.fs.fed.us/r2/whiteriver/recreation/wilderness/index.shtml for up-to-date restrictions and regulations.

Eagles Nest Wilderness

The following acts are prohibited on National Forest System land within the Eagles Nest Wilderness:

- Entering or being in the area with more than fifteen people per group, with a maximum combination of twenty-five people and pack or saddle animals in any one group.
- Camping within 100 feet of all lakes, streams, trails, and any NO CAMPING or WILDERNESS RESTORATION SITE signs.
- Building, maintaining, attending, or using a campfire within 100 feet of all lakes, streams and trails, or within ¼ mile of tree line or above tree line, and within ¼ mile of all lakes.
- Storing or leaving equipment, personal property, or supplies for longer than seventy-two hours.
- Hitching or tethering any pack or saddle animal within 100 feet of all lakes, streams and trails.
- Possessing a dog, except working stock dogs or dogs used for legal hunting purposes, unless under physical restraint of a leash not to exceed 6 feet in length.
- Possessing, storing or transporting any plant material such as hay or straw. NOTE: Exceptions are allowed for livestock feed that has been processed through chemical or mechanical means in a manner that will destroy viable seeds. Examples of allowed material include: palletized feed and rolled grains.
- Possessing or using a wagon, cart, wheelbarrow, or other vehicle including game carts.
- Shortcutting a switchback in a trail.

Ptarmigan Peak Wilderness

The regulations for the Ptarmigan Peak Wilderness are the same as for Eagles Nest except for the restriction about fires near lakes because there are no lakes in the Ptarmigan Peak Wilderness.

Holy Cross Wilderness

Regulations for the Holy Cross Wilderness are similar to Eagles Nest regulations, except for a slight difference in the campfire regulation (see the Web site) and the addition of a regulation prohibiting "entering or being in the Holy Cross Wilderness without a valid wilderness permit." The regulations are listed on the back of the wilderness permit.

As of 2005, a free self-issue mandatory wilderness permit is required. The purpose of the permit is to measure the number of visitors in the wilderness and also to educate wilderness visitors about minimizing impact. The permit system continues to evolve. Contact the Holy Cross Ranger District, (970) 827–5175, or the Leadville Ranger District, (719) 486–0749, for current information on wilderness permits.

How to Use This Book

To aid in quick decision making, each hike chapter begins with a **hike summary.** These short summaries give you a taste of the hiking adventure to follow. You'll learn about the trail terrain and what surprises the route has to offer. Next, you'll find the quick, nitty-gritty details of the hike: where the trailhead is located, the nearest town, hike length, approximate hiking time, difficulty rating, best hiking season, type of trail surface, what other trail users you may encounter, trail contacts (for updates on trail conditions), elevation gain, and usage fees. The **Finding the trailhead** section gives you dependable directions from the closest I–70 exit right down to where you'll want to park your car. The **hike description** is the meat of the chapter. Detailed and honest, it's the author's carefully researched impression of the trail. While it's impossible to cover everything, you can rest assured that we won't miss what's important. In **Miles and Directions,** we provide mileage cues to identify all turns and trail name changes, as well as points of interest. The **Hike Information** section at the end of each hike is a hodgepodge of information. In it, you'll find such things as local information resources with which you can learn more about the area, nearby campgrounds, where to eat, and what else to see while you're hiking in the area.

Lastly, the **Honorable Mentions** section at the end of the book details the hikes that didn't make the cut, for whatever reason—in many cases it's not because they aren't great hikes, but because they're overcrowded or environmentally sensitive to heavy traffic. Be sure to read through these. A jewel might be lurking among them.

How to Use These Maps

For your own purposes, you may wish to copy the directions for the route onto a small sheet to help you while hiking, or photocopy the map and cue sheet to take with you. Otherwise, just slip the whole book in your pack and take it all with you. Enjoy your time in the outdoors and remember to pack out what you pack in.

Elevation Profile: This helpful profile gives you a cross-sectional look at the hike's ups and downs. Elevation is labeled on the left; mileage is indicated on the top.

Route Map: This is your primary guide to each hike. It shows all of the accessible roads and trails, points of interest, water, towns, landmarks, and geographical features. It also distinguishes trails from roads and paved roads from unpaved roads. The selected route is highlighted, and directional arrows point the way. Some trail junctions are marked by pins but the intersecting trail is not shown. These side trails are user-created trails neither recognized nor maintained by the U.S. Forest Service. Some dead-end in private property. Please stay on the main route to avoid damaging the environment or getting lost!

The maps in this book that depict a detailed close-up of an area use elevation tints, called hypsometry, to portray relief. Each gray tone represents a range of equal elevation, as shown in the scale key with the map. These maps will give you a good idea of elevation gain and loss. The darker tones are lower elevations and the lighter grays are higher elevations. The lighter the tone, the higher the elevation. Narrow bands of different gray tones spaced closely together indicate steep terrain, whereas wider bands indicate areas of more gradual slope.

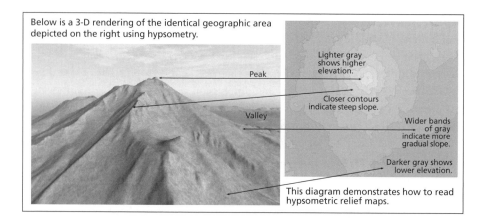

Below is a 3-D rendering of the identical geographic area depicted on the right using hypsometry.

Peak

Valley

Lighter gray shows higher elevation.

Closer contours indicate steep slope.

Wider bands of gray indicate more gradual slope.

Darker gray shows lower elevation.

This diagram demonstrates how to read hypsometric relief maps.

Trail Finder

Number	Hike	Best for Backpackers	Best for Children	Best for Great Views	Best for Lake Lovers	Best for Waterfalls	Best for Peak Baggers	Best for Geology Lovers	Best for Wildflowers	Best for History Buffs
1	Griffin Memorial									●
2	Herman Lake			●	●				●	
3	Ptarmigan Peak			●			●		●	
4	Kettle Ponds	●						●		
5	Surprise/Eaglesmere Loop	●			●					
6	Lower Cataract Lake		●		●	●			●	
7	Gore Canyon Trail									●
8	Mesa Cortina to East Vail	●		●				●	●	
9	Dillon Peninsula		●	●						●
10	Chihuahua Lake				●					
11	Buffalo Mountain			●			●			
12	Lily Pad Lake		●		●					
13	Masontown		●							●
13	Mount Royal						●			●
14	Iowa Hill		●							●
15	Cucumber Gulch							●		
16	Barney Ford Trail									●
17	Mohawk Lakes	●		●	●	●				●
18	Wheeler Lake			●	●	●			●	●
19	Wheeler Trail			●			●			●
20	Colorado Trail from Wheeler Flats to Guller Creek	●								
21	Shrine Mountain		●	●				●	●	
22	Bowman's Shortcut Trail			●						
23	Grouse Lake	●			●					
24	Bear Lake	●			●					
25	West Tennessee Lakes	●			●					

Trail Rating

Number	Hike	Easy	Moderate	More Difficult	Most Difficult	Strenuous
1	Griffin Memorial		●			
2	Herman Lake			●		
3	Ptarmigan Peak				●	
4	Kettle Ponds		●			
5	Surprise/Eaglesmere Loop			●		
6	Lower Cataract Lake	●				
7	Gore Canyon Trail	●				
8	Mesa Cortina to East Vail				●	
9	Dillon Peninsula	●				
10	Chihuahua Lake			●		
11	Buffalo Mountain					●
12	Lily Pad Lake	●	●			
13	Masontown		●			
13	Mount Royal					●
14	Iowa Hill		●			
15	Cucumber Gulch	●				
16	Barney Ford Trail		●			
17	Mohawk Lakes			●		
18	Wheeler Lake			●		
19	Wheeler Trail				●	
20	Colorado Trail from Wheeler Flats to Guller Creek			●		
21	Shrine Mountain		●			
22	Bowman's Shortcut Trail		●			
23	Grouse Lake				●	
24	Bear Lake			●		
25	West Tennessee Lakes			●		

Map Legend

Boundaries

▨▨▨▨	National Wilderness Boundary
▨▨▨▨	National Forest Boundary
—·—··	Continental Divide

Transportation

══70══	Interstate
══40══	U.S. Highway
══9══	State Highway
──────	Primary Roads
─709─	Other Roads
═709═	Unpaved Road
= = = = =	Unimproved Road
▬▬▬▬	Featured Unimproved Trail
▬ ▬ ▬ ▬	Featured Trail
············	Optional Trail
- - - - - -	Other Trail
—┼——┼—	Tunnel
┼┼┼┼┼┼	Railroad
— — — -	Ski Lift

Hydrology

∿	River/Creek
⌇ ⌇	Intermittent Stream
ℓ	Spring
∥	Falls
⬭⬭	Lake
≈≈	Marsh/Swamp

Physiography

×	Spot Elevation
)(	Pass
▲	Peak

Symbols

🚶	Trailhead
❷	Trail Locator
↻	Trail Turnaround
🅿	Parking
🚻	Restroom/Toilet
⛷	Ski Area
🚏	Bus Stop
▲	Campground
⬧	Cabin/Lodge
†	Cemetery
⊼	Picnic Table
○	Town
👁	Viewpoint
▪	Point of Interest
⚒	Mine
🐾	Nature Preserve
●━●	Gate
≍	Bridge
↖	Intersection with Unmaintained Trail

1 Griffin Memorial

The old wagon road (nonmotorized) to the 7:30 Mine climbs steadily above Silver Plume, past relics of the silver boom of the 1880s. Bristlecone pine, lodgepole pine, and aspen line the trail. After 1.5 miles the trail becomes narrower, and occasionally you'll have to duck under bristlecone pine branches while negotiating a side-sloping slippery route. The Griffin Memorial obelisk stands on a rock outcropping below the 7:30 Mine Road near the upper mouth of Brown Gulch. A tad farther up the narrow trail are two rusting boilers from the 7:30 Mine, the remains of which lie across the creek.

Start: At the trailhead at the top of Silver Street on the north side of town
Distance: 3.7 miles out and back (add 0.25 mile out and back for an optional hike to the 7:30 Mine)
Approximate hiking time: 1.5 to 2.5 hours
Difficulty: Moderate
Elevation gain: 1,180 feet
Trail surface: Dirt trail
Seasons: Best from mid-June to mid-October
Other trail users: Mountain bikers, equestrians
Canine compatibility: Dogs must be on leash.
Land status: County right-of-way and historic-district public lands

Nearest towns: Silver Plume
Fees and permits: No fees or permits required
Maps: USGS map: Georgetown; National Geographic Trails Illustrated: #104 Idaho Springs/Loveland Pass
Trail contact: George Rowe Museum, 315 Main Street, Silver Plume; (303) 569-2562 (summer season)
Other: Be sure to bring water with you. The trail, which is a county right-of-way, crosses numerous private mining claims, so please stay on the trail.

Finding the trailhead: Silver Plume and the 7:30 Mine Trail are along Interstate 70 west of Denver and about 12 miles east of the Eisenhower Tunnel. From I-70 exit 226, Silver Plume, turn right (north) by Buckley Bros. General Store (or if you're coming from the west, turn left, or north, under I-70) then go straight about 0.1 mile to Main Street. Turn right (east) on Main Street and drive about 0.1 mile to where you can park between Silver Street and Jefferson Street. The trailhead is 0.1 mile uphill (north) on Silver Street from Main Street. Look for the 7:30 Mine Road Historic District Public Lands sign which marks the trailhead. Additional parking is available at the I-70 exit. *DeLorme: Colorado Atlas & Gazetteer:* Page 39 C5

Special considerations: The trail crosses at least one avalanche path (Cherokee Creek). Hunters use this area during hunting season.

The Hike

Some people say you can still hear the sounds of his violin from the lofty rock outcrop 1,250 feet above Silver Plume. While hiking up the 7:30 Mine Road to the Griffin Memorial, listen closely. Do you hear the sweet violin playing of Clifford Griffin's ghost, or is it just the wind?

Several legends surround Clifford Griffin and his obelisk-shaped memorial. One tells the sad tale of the Englishman whose fiancé died the night before their wedding. Heartbroken, he traveled west to work in Colorado's mines, where he became the manager of the 7:30 Mine. Another version says he discovered the 7:30 Mine and became the wealthiest mine owner in the area. At night he played his violin from a rock outcrop above Brownville, just west of Silver Plume. One night when the music stopped, a gunshot rang out. Miners rushed to see what happened and found Clifford dead with a bullet through his heart, suicide note in his hand.

Another report claims that his brother, Heheneage (Henry) M. Griffin, owned the 7:30 Mine. He summoned his alcoholic brother, Clifford, to manage his mine in hopes that a responsible position would temper Clifford's drinking problem. Still another tale reports that the brothers co-owned the mine, and Henry shot Clifford to gain full ownership.

▶ Avalanches still occur although the hillsides are mostly forested. On March 23, 2003, after several days of heavy snows, an avalanche roared down Pendleton Mountain, destroying Silver Plume's water treatment plant and reaching the edge of I-70.

The trail to the Griffin Memorial switchbacks up past various mines and tailings. In 1859 when miners heard about gold discoveries in the Pikes Peak area, they swarmed to Colorado and spread out across the state in search of their fortunes. The mountains north of Silver Plume contained rich veins of silver. The first vein discovered was reportedly so rich that silver flakes broke off in the shape of feathers. The Silver Plume Mine started in 1863 and produced $500,000 in silver ore. The town, incorporated in 1880, probably took its name from the mine. The remains of the old Silver Plume Mine are about 800 feet above the first switchback in the trail. The 7:30 Mine, an optional short walk past the turnoff to the Griffin Memorial, produced $2 million and employed one hundred men.

With mines dotting Sherman and Republican Mountains, trees disappeared quickly for use in mine tunnels, houses, and heating. Mud and snow slides became a major problem for Silver Plume and its neighbor Brownville. Newspapers of the time reported five to ten avalanches each year. One in February 1899 destroyed miners' cabins and killed ten Italians. A granite memorial in their honor is located in the Silver Plume cemetery. Spring brought rock and mud slides, loosened by snow melt and rain. A series of slides from the tailings of the 7:30 Mine literally wiped out Brownville.

Peak production in the Silver Plume area came in 1894. By 1904, the seventy-two working mines had produced over $60 million in silver ore. By 1907 silver had lost value, but tourism became popular. Between 1907 and 1914, the Sunrise Peak

◀ *Griffin Memorial*

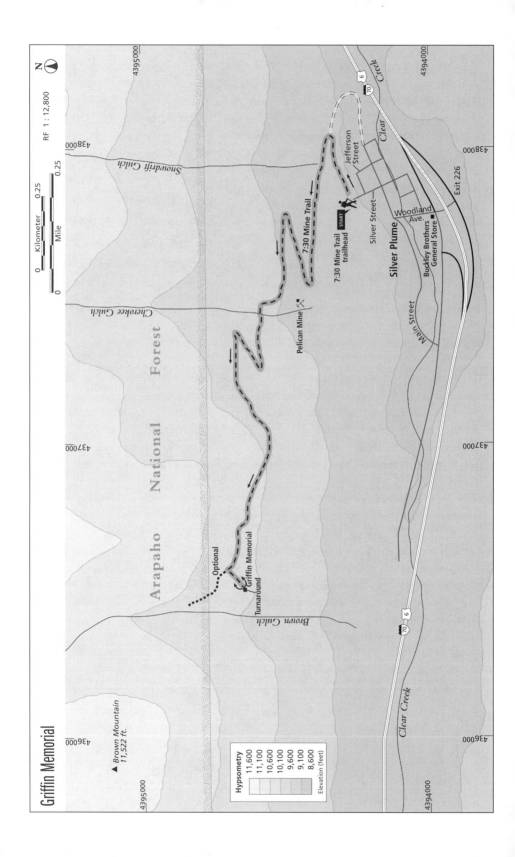

Griffin Memorial

Brown Mountain
11,522 ft.

Arapaho National Forest

Snowdrift Gulch

Cherokee Gulch

Brown Gulch

7:30 Mine Trail

7:30 Mine Trail trailhead

Pelican Mine

Griffin Memorial
Turnaround

Optional

Silver Plume

Jefferson Street

Silver Street

Woodland Ave.

Buckley Brothers
General Store

Main Street

Exit 226

Clear Creek

Clear Creek

START

N

RF 1 : 12,800

Kilometer 0.25

Mile 0.25

Hypsometry

11,600
11,100
10,600
10,100
9,600
9,100
8,600

Elevation (feet)

Aerial Tram took people from Silver Plume to the top of Pendleton Mountain. From the Griffin Memorial, you can see the remaining buildings on the peak on the other side of I–70. A train trip from Denver up Clear Creek Canyon and over the Georgetown loop, including the tram ride, costs $3.00 on weekends and $4.00 on weekdays.

While hiking up the trail, notice the pine trees with five needles grouped together covered with droplets of "sap." These bristlecone pine can live over 1,500 years in Colorado. As you walk by these long-lived trees, think of all that they have seen during the mining boom, bust, and today's world. Maybe they know the true tale of Clifford Griffin.

Miles and Directions

0.0 Start at the 7:30 Mine Trail trailhead at the top of Silver Street. 437849mE 4394283mN Elevation 9,175 feet.

300 ft. A trail comes in from the left (west). Do not turn here. Continue straight ahead (east) and uphill on the trail. 437926mE 4394309mN

0.5 The trail switchbacks by the tailings of the old Pelican Mine. 437520mE 4394411mN

0.7 To the right is a nice view down to town and the train station for the Georgetown Loop railroad. (**Note:** Along the trail check out the bristlecone pine trees with five grouped needles.) 437813mE 4394483mN

1.0 The trail crosses Cherokee Gulch. Note the avalanche debris across the trail. A little past the gulch, cross the downed cables from an old mine tram. 437461mE 4394593mN

1.6 The trail becomes narrower beyond this point. Watch for low tree branches across the trail! Grates cover several old mine shafts.

1.8 A little cairn (pile of rocks) on the left (south), across from a grate to the right of the trail, marks the trail to the Griffin Memorial. 436566mE 4394692mN Follow the left trail downhill. Where the trail splits, take your pick—both trails lead to the memorial.

1.85 Griffin Memorial. 436528mE 4394654mN Elevation 10,285 feet. Return the way you came to the 7:30 Mine Trail.

1.9 Back on the 7:30 Mine Trail. Return the way you came.

3.7 Arrive back at the trailhead.

Option: Back on the 7:30 Mine Road, turn left (west) at the turnoff for the Griffin Memorial and walk a little over 0.1 mile one way to where the trail crosses the

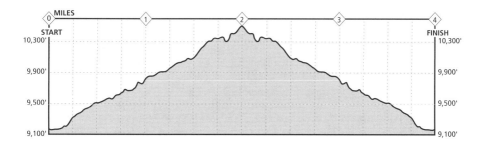

creek in Brown Gulch. Two old boilers from the 7:30 Mine lie in the creek bed. Elevation 10,500 feet.

Hike Information

Local Information
Gateway Visitor Center, I-70 exit 228, Georgetown; (303) 569-2405
George Rowe Museum, 905 Main Street, Silver Plume; (303) 569-2562

Local Events/Attractions
George Rowe Museum, 905 Main Street, Silver Plume; (303) 569-2562 (summer season)

Georgetown Loop Railroad, (888) 456-6777, www.georgetownlooprr.com

Restaurants
Silver Plume Antique Shop and Tea Room, 940 Main Street, Silver Plume; (303) 569-2368
Sopp & Truscott Bakery, 1010 Main Street, Silver Plume; (303) 569-3395

2 Herman Lake

The popular hike to Herman Lake starts on an old sawmill road through thick forest. The trail then wanders through fields of colorful wildflowers with spectacular views of the Continental Divide. Most of the trail doubles as a section of the Continental Divide National Scenic Trail. A last steep pitch takes you to treeline where the trail mellows on the final stretch to Herman Lake, nestled in a bowl at 12,000 feet below Pettingell Peak.

Start: At the Herman Gulch Trail #98 trailhead
Distance: 6.7 miles out and back
Approximate hiking time: 2.7 to 4.5 hours
Difficulty: More difficult
Trail surface: Dirt trail
Elevation gain: 1,700 feet
Seasons: Best from July to early October
Other trail users: Anglers, mountain bikers, equestrians
Canine compatibility: Dogs must be on leash.
Land status: National forest

Nearest towns: Silver Plume and Georgetown
Fees and permits: No fees or permits required
Maps: USGS maps: Loveland Pass, Grays Peak; National Geographic Trails Illustrated: #104 Idaho Springs/Loveland Pass
Trail contact: Arapaho National Forest, Clear Creek Ranger District, Idaho Springs; (303) 567-3000; www.fs.fed.us/r2/arnf
Other: Herman Lake is above treeline with danger of lightning from thunderstorms.

Finding the trailhead: The trail to Herman Lake is just off Interstate 70 exit 218 (no name). Turn right if coming from the east or left if coming from the west. Make a sharp right turn onto the dirt frontage road. Drive about 0.2 mile into the big parking lot. A vault toilet is available, but no water. *DeLorme: Colorado Atlas & Gazetteer:* Page 38 C3.5

Special considerations: Several avalanche paths cross the trail. Be aware of avalanche danger if skiing or snowshoeing this trail during the winter. The trail is neither marked nor maintained for winter use.

Herman Lake in early July

The Hike

Herman Hassell, an early timber operator in the area, supposedly named Herman Gulch after himself. While timber may have been Herman's ambition, today wildflower aficionados consider this trail a "100 wildflower" or "century" hike because of the possibility of seeing about a hundred different flower species during peak bloom in late July.

After the junction at mile 0.2, the Herman Gulch Trail climbs through lodgepole pine, spruce, and fir above the creek in Herman Gulch. Buffaloberry bushes, willows, common juniper, various berry bushes, strawberries, fireweed, and dandelions line the trail. After about 0.6 mile the trail levels a little with white geraniums, arrowleaf senecio, monkshood, little red elephants, and cinquefoil blooming in the moist area by a little creek.

As the summer sun rises higher in the sky and warms the ground, more wildflowers appear. In late June blue Colorado columbines burst forth in the meadows. Various members of the gentian family; purple fringe; paintbrush in different hues of yellow, magenta, and red; daisies; Jacob's ladder; lousewort; clover; Parry primrose; sky pilot; chickweed; sage; and chiming bells are among other flowers gracing the trail. The path is generally well maintained with stone steps in places, although an

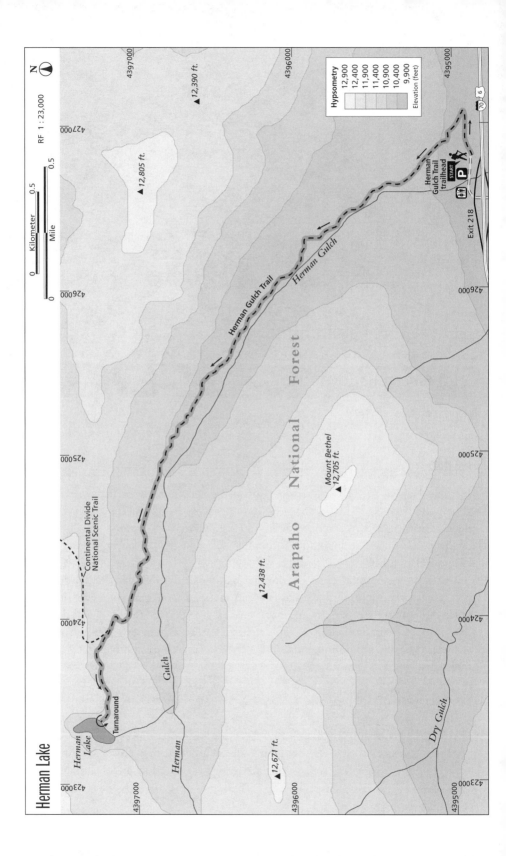

Herman Lake

RF 1 : 23,000

Hypsometry

Elevation (feet)
12,900
12,400
11,900
11,400
10,900
10,400
9,900

Continental Divide National Scenic Trail

Herman Lake

Turnaround

Herman Gulch Trail

Herman Gulch

Herman Gulch

Arapaho National Forest

Mount Bethel 12,705 ft.

▲ 12,805 ft.

▲ 12,390 ft.

▲ 12,438 ft.

▲ 12,671 ft.

Herman Gulch Trail trailhead

START

P

Exit 218

70 6

Dry Gulch

occasional boggy area makes for mucky walking. Please walk through any mud instead of around it to avoid trampling trailside vegetation which widens the bog. A nice feature of Herman Gulch is that the trail climbs then levels out so you can catch your breath before the next climb.

After about 2.5 miles, the trail climbs steeply for the next 0.5 mile. The trail splits, with the Continental Divide National Scenic Trail (CDNST) climbing to the right to a saddle on the Continental Divide. The CDNST was designated by Congress in 1978. The trail travels 3,100 miles from the Canadian border to the Mexican border through challenging and primitive areas of Montana, Wyoming, Colorado, and New Mexico. The scenic route uses existing trails whenever possible. Although many sections of the trail are completed, others need to be maintained, created, or rerouted.

▶ **The Herman Gulch Trail crosses several avalanche paths which descend from unnamed peaks to the northeast. Skiers and snowshoers need to be aware of avalanche danger. Two skiers triggered a hard-slab avalanche here in December 2003. One person rode the slide to the bottom and luckily was not trapped.**

The trail to Herman Lake heads northwest and continues steeply before it turns west on a bench and passes a little pond. You may find a snowbank still covering the trail in early July. The trees are small and twisted up here. They tend to grow in a row in the direction of the prevailing winds. Known as krummholz, German for crooked wood, they survive strong winds, blasts of ice crystals, and about a two-month growing season. The windward side of the organism protects the rest of the tree from the elements. Krummholz generally sprout via roots from existing branches, the summers being too short to produce many seeds. Because any dead branches protect the rest of the tree, please do not use any wood from krummholz for campfires.

Plants and flowers are smaller at this elevation, too. Miniature willows, blue forget-me-nots, pink moss campion, bright yellow alpine avens, grayish green sage, alpine phlox, and white death camas bloom among the rocky soil.

Herman Lake finally appears, nestled in a bowl beneath 13,553-foot Pettingell Peak. The Continental Divide rises over 1,000 feet above the lake. Water from melting snow cascades down to the lake in shimmering ribbons between willows and

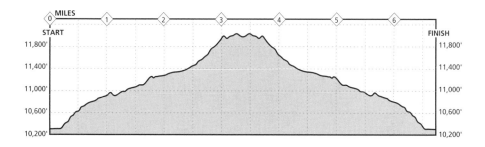

rocks. A few trails wander down to the right, but one in particular heads to a large rock slab, a great place to sit in the sun and enjoy a picnic.

Miles and Directions

0.0 Start at Herman Gulch Trail trailhead. 426810mE 4394877mN Elevation 10,300 feet.

0.2 The trail Ts. Turn left (northwest) onto Herman Gulch Trail #98. 427090mE 4394942mN

0.8 The trail crosses the first of several avalanche paths. 426489mE 4395587mN

1.1 The trail crosses a meadow. Look ahead for a view of Pettingell Peak and the trail above the trees. 426216mE 4395956mN

2.5 The trail crosses a little creek. A nice log provides a rest stop before the trail starts climbing steeply. 424417mE 4396952mN

2.9 Arrive at a trail junction. Turn left (northwest) to climb to Herman Lake. The Continental Divide National Scenic Trail (CDNST) heads to the right (northeast). 423948mE 4397163mN

3.3 Arrive at a trail junction. Turn right (northwest) down the trail to the lake.

3.35 Herman Lake. Elevation 12,000 feet. The big flat rock is a great place for a picnic. 423389mE 4397225mN Return the way you came.

6.7 Arrive back at the trailhead.

Option: You can take a side trip on the CDNST to the top of the Continental Divide. Turn northeast at the junction of Herman Gulch and the CDNST and hike for about 1.9 miles one way gaining about 1,065 feet in elevation to a saddle. The trail may not be well defined.

Hike Information

Local Information
Gateway Visitor Center, I-70 exit 228, Georgetown; (303) 569-2405

Local Events/Attractions
George Rowe Museum, 315 Main Street, Silver Plume; (303) 569-2562 (summer season)
Georgetown Loop Railroad, (888) 456-6777, www.georgetownlooprr.com

Restaurants
Red Ram Restaurant, 604 6th Street, Georgetown; (303) 569-2300

Organizations
Continental Divide Trail Alliance, P.O. Box 628, Pine 80470; (888) 909-CDTA; www.cdtrail.org
Continental Divide Trail Society, 3704 North Charles Street (#601), Baltimore, MD 21218; (410) 235-9610; www.cdtsociety.org

3 Ptarmigan Peak

The Ptarmigan Trail climbs steadily through various ecosystems including sagebrush meadow, lodgepole pine, aspen, spruce-fir, and alpine tundra—the land above the trees. While thick forest envelops the trail the first 4 miles, a few open spaces provide great views of the Gore Range or the lower Blue River valley. As you hike above treeline, keep your eyes open on the north ridge for the resident elk herd. The long hike is rewarded by beautiful vistas from the top, including four 14,000-foot peaks, much of the craggy Gore Range, the Tenmile Range, and Dillon Reservoir.

Start: At the Ptarmigan Trail #35 trailhead
Distance: 12.0 miles out and back
Approximate hiking time: 6 to 10 hours
Difficulty: Most difficult
Elevation gain: 3,407 feet
Trail surface: Dirt road and dirt trail
Seasons: Best from July to early October
Other trail users: Mountain bikers (outside of wilderness), equestrians, joggers
Canine compatibility: Dogs must be on leash in wilderness. Dogs must be under voice control elsewhere.
Land status: National forest and wilderness area
Nearest town: Silverthorne

Fees and permits: No fees or permits required
Maps: USGS map: Dillon; National Geographic Trails Illustrated: #108 Vail, Frisco, Dillon
Trail contact: White River National Forest, Dillon Ranger District, 680 Blue River Parkway, Silverthorne; (970) 468-5400; www.fs.fed.us/r2/whiteriver, www.dillonrangerdistrict.com
Other: The first part of the trail is on an easement through the Ptarmigan subdivision. Please stay on the designated trail and road. Water is very sparse on the Ptarmigan Trail. Make sure to bring plenty. Because the trail crosses about 1.7 miles one-way of open tundra, start early to avoid thunderstorms and lightning.

Finding the trailhead: From Interstate 70 exit 205, Silverthorne/Dillon, head north on Highway 9 about 0.2 mile to Rainbow Drive by Wendy's and across from the 7-11 store. Turn right (northeast) onto Rainbow Drive. In less than 0.1 mile, turn right (east) onto Tanglewood and twist up past restaurants and motels for approximately 0.2 mile. Turn right (east) onto Ptarmigan Trail and head uphill. The road turns to dirt about 0.6 mile from Wendy's. Continue straight ahead on the dirt road approximately another 0.6 mile to the trailhead parking on the right. The trailhead bulletin board is on the left. No facilities are available at the trailhead. Be sure to set your parking brake—the south side of the parking lot is a cliff! *DeLorme: Colorado Atlas & Gazetteer:* Page 38 C2

Special considerations: Hunters use this area during hunting season. The lower part of the trail is used by snowshoers, winter walkers, and cross-country skiers. The trail is neither marked nor maintained for winter use. Wilderness regulations apply starting at mile 4.3.

The Hike

The first 0.6 mile of the Ptarmigan Trail is a grunt, a 15 percent grade up Ptarmigan Trail (dirt road) then through an open sagebrush meadow where the sun can

View of Dillon Reservoir and Tenmile Range from the sagebrush meadow

beat down mercilessly. In June, the meadow becomes a colorful palette of white Mariposa lilies and yarrow, pale purple pasque flowers, golden stonecrop, yellow sulphur flowers, blue lupine, and scarlet gilia. The higher you climb, the better the view of Dillon Reservoir and the Tenmile Range to the south and west.

At the top of the grunt climb, the trail mellows and winds through aspen groves filled with blue columbine, Colorado's state flower, and pink Woods rose. Aspen and lodgepole pine take turns lining the trail. Watch for elk tooth marks in the aspen bark. The cambium layer just beneath the bark provides a nutritious winter snack. Notice how the vegetation differs dramatically between the lush aspen groves and the drier lodgepole ecosystem.

After you cross two teeny creeks, keep an eye open to the left near mile 2.4 for a scenic view and nice log to sit on. This spot is a good turnaround for a shorter hike or a winter walk. From here the trail climbs and switchbacks through lodgepole pine and spruce-fir forest. Just before the wilderness boundary, the trail heads south through more open forest with fields of red paintbrush, blue lupine, and yellow cinquefoil and dandelions.

After the wilderness portal sign, the trail climbs steadily through the ecotone where subalpine forest and alpine tundra meet. The trees grow sparser and smaller where the winds blow harder, creating lower temperatures: A mean summer temperature here

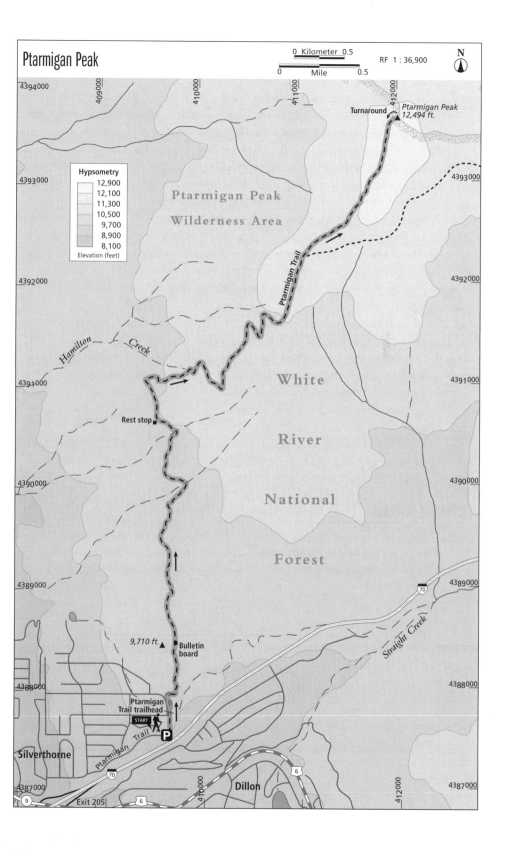

averages less than 50 degrees F. Speaking of wind, a chilly breeze usually blows over these open spaces and rare is the day when you can sit on the summit without wearing a jacket. Finally you are in the land above the trees, with its miniature plants and flowers that somehow survive where summer may only last for six weeks. One wet area with miniature willows provides a small dribble of water.

The flowers bloom brilliantly after the Fourth of July. Patches of blue forget-me-nots grow along the trail, accompanied by grayish green stalks of sage, the bright yellow of alpine avens and cinquefoil, pink moss campion, white alpine phlox, yellow paintbrush, and bistort. Plants such as the moss campion grow in cushions for protection against wind and ice particles. Their taproots may reach 4 to 5 feet underground to find moisture and anchor against the winds. The moss campion grows slowly—about one-quarter inch a year. The big golden sunflowers that tower over the smaller plants are old-man-of-the-mountain or Rydbergia. These giants take several years to gather and store enough energy to bloom. Once the flower fades away, the plant dies.

For all their seeming toughness, alpine plants are quite fragile. Frequent trampling by boots can destroy them. A piece of paper covering a small cushion plant may deny it the energy needed to make it through the winter. If no trail exists and you walk across alpine tundra, walk on rocks as much as possible, and spread out so no two footsteps land on the same plant.

Gentle Ptarmigan Peak has a false summit stick about 0.6 mile from the wilderness boundary. The summit is really another 0.9 mile. When you reach the top, it's easy to think that the other spot over there is a tad higher! A large elk herd spends the summers grazing nearby. They can often be seen along the ridge to the north or down by the little lake to the southeast.

Miles and Directions

0.0   Start at the Ptarmigan Trail trailhead. 409647mE 4387597mN Elevation 9,090 feet. The trail heads through a sagebrush meadow and aspen and ends up on a dirt road. Walk up the road (north) to the brown trail post that reads Ptarmigan Trail on the right (east) side of the road.

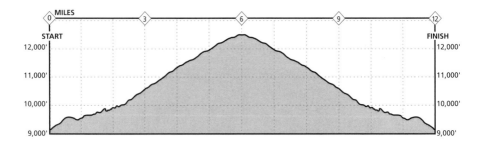

0.2 At the Ptarmigan Trail trail post, leave the road and walk on the trail through the open sagebrush meadow. The flowers are fabulous in May and early June! This part of the trail is steep and can be slippery with loose rocks and gravel.

0.6 The trail passes an old bulletin board. 409708mE 4388454mN

1.8 The trail crosses the first of two little creeks. 409847mE 4390045mN

2.4 To the left of the trail is a log that provides a nice rest and great view of Silverthorne, the Gore Range, and over to the Tenmile Range. Elevation 10,050 feet. 409562mE 4390649mN

3.9 An opening in the trees provides a nice view to the north of the lower Blue River valley. 410477mE 4391602mN

4.3 The trail reaches the Ptarmigan Peak Wilderness boundary. 410798mE 4391620mN

4.8 You're now in the land above the trees by a trail sign. 411092mE 4392336mN The faint trail to the right leads to Ptarmigan Pass. Go straight ahead to reach the peak. Sometimes the trail disappears, but just continue along the left (north) side of the ridge and you'll find the trail again.

5.9 A trail sign marks a good place to turn right to reach the summit cairn. 411974mE 4393770mN

6.0 You've made it! The Ptarmigan Peak summit cairn has a lot of rocks on the bottom which support a wooden pole. Elevation 12,498 feet. 412044mE 4393748mN Enjoy the 360-degree view to the Mount of the Holy Cross, the Gore Range, over to Longs Peak, Grays and Torreys Peaks, and the valleys below. Return the way you came.

12.0 Arrive back at the trailhead.

Option: For a shorter hike with beautiful views or a nice winter snowshoe, hike up to the overlook bench at mile 2.4. This part of the trail can usually be hiked year-round, but watch out for icy patches when snow covers the trail. This shorter hike is 4.8 miles out and back and a moderate hike.

Hike Information

Local Information
Summit County Chamber of Commerce, (800) 530-3099, www.summitchamber.org
Summit Visitor Information Center, Outlets at Silverthorne, 246 Rainbow Drive, Silverthorne; (970) 262-0817
Town of Silverthorne, www.silverthorne.org, (970) 262-7300

Local Events/Attractions
Blue River Festival, Town of Silverthorne, (970) 262-7390

Restaurants
China Gourmet, Highway 9 and Annie Road (by Target), Silverthorne; (970) 262-6688
Fiesta Jalisco, Summit Place Shopping Center, Silverthorne; (970) 468-6663
Sunshine Café, Summit Place Shopping Center, Silverthorne; (970) 468-9552

Organizations
Friends of the Eagles Nest Wilderness, www.fenw.org, or call the Dillon Ranger District, (970) 468-5400, for the current contact.

PTARMIGAN PEAK WILDERNESS

The Ptarmigan Peak Wilderness is just a sliver of protected area along the ridge and west side of the Williams Fork Mountains. Originally part of the Williams Fork Further Planning Area, environmentalists had requested designation of a 74,770-acre wilderness area that started farther down on the west side and continued east into the two drainages of the South Fork and Middle Fork of the Williams Fork and to Bobtail Creek, Pettingell Peak, and Jones Pass. The area ranked as one of the highest in Colorado in the U.S. Forest Service's Wilderness Attribute Rating System in the 1980s. But the Denver Water Board owned easements in the area and wanted to be able to divert water from the South and Middle Forks to their growing consumer base in the Denver area. The Federal Timber Purchasers Association also opposed wilderness designation for the larger area. By the time everyone took a bite, the Colorado Wilderness Act of 1993 proposed the Farr Wilderness Area with 13,175 acres. When the Act was approved in August 1993, it created the 13,175-acre Ptarmigan Peak Wilderness and renamed the Granby Pumping Plant the Farr Pumping Plant.

The Farr Pumping Plant is part of the Colorado–Big Thompson Project, which diverts water from the upper Colorado River from Grand Lake to Mary's Lake near Estes Park. The pumping plant lifts water from Lake Granby to Shadow Mountain Reservoir, which then goes into Grand Lake. The Farr family, in particular W. D. Farr, was honored for its contributions to water development, agricultural innovations, and conservation in Colorado.

In Addition

What Is Wilderness?

Ten of the hikes in this book are in congressionally designated wilderness areas. What is wilderness? What makes wilderness different from any other part of national forest or Bureau of Land Management (BLM) land?

Wilderness areas are very special places. The American people, through acts of Congress, designate certain pristine and primitive sections of undeveloped federal land as wilderness. The Wilderness Act of 1964, which created a National Wilderness Preservation System (NWPS), gives Congress the authority to designate lands as wilderness.

First a little history. Back in the 1870s, people became alarmed at the rapid rate of development in America and the overuse of natural resources on public lands. Efforts were made to conserve and preserve certain areas. Yellowstone became our first national park in 1872. The first primitive area, a forerunner of wilderness, was designated in 1930. Concerns about development and abuse of public lands didn't stop then. Some believed that certain areas should be saved in their pristine condition. In 1955 the first draft legislation outlining the NWPS was written. After nine years of negotiations and rewrites, the Wilderness Act became law.

The purpose of the NWPS is to assure that Americans now and in the future have the benefits of a wilderness resource. Those benefits include "outstanding opportunities for solitude or a primitive and unconfined type of recreation" and "the public purposes of recreational, scenic, scientific, educational, conservation, and historical use." The Wilderness Act specifically states "A wilderness, in contrast with those areas where man and his works dominate the landscape, is hereby recognized as an area where the earth and its community of life are untrammeled by man, where man himself is a visitor who does not remain . . . an area of undeveloped Federal land retaining its primeval character and influence, without permanent improvements or human habitation, which is protected and managed so as to preserve its natural conditions and which . . . generally appears to have been affected primarily by the forces of nature . . ."

The Wilderness Act prohibits certain uses in wilderness such as motorized equipment, landing of aircraft, nonmotorized mechanical transport (like mountain bikes), roads, and structures except in emergencies or administrative necessity. However, Congress allowed other uses to continue, such as grazing, hunting, and fishing. Since the end of 1983, new mining claims are prohibited, but patented claims existing prior to 1984 may be worked under certain restrictions. Water in wilderness is a very touchy issue, especially in Colorado, where most of its major rivers originate within the state and flow outward. The state has historically held authority over water rights. Occasionally a wilderness area surrounds private or state lands. The Act assures these landowners "reasonable access" that is consistent with wilderness preservation. As a result you might see a building in the middle of a wilderness area!

Wilderness can be designated in national forests, BLM lands, national parks and monuments, and national wildlife refuges. The agency responsible for the land administers the wilderness. Designation of new wilderness areas on national public lands is still ongoing. By late 2005, Colorado contained forty-one wilderness areas: thirty-seven areas managed by the U.S. Forest Service and/or the BLM and three managed by the National Park Service. The National Fish & Wildlife Service helps manage Mount Massive Wilderness.

Public lands managers face an interesting challenge in trying to provide solitude and a primitive and unconfined type of recreation while preserving the wilderness character of the lands "unimpaired for future use," lands that are primarily affected by natural forces. Human visitation is bound to leave scars on the land and impact other visitors unless each of us is very careful. Wilderness managers therefore strive to manage human behavior, mainly through education, access limitations, and regulations. Several wilderness areas require dogs be on leash to minimize harassment of wildlife and other visitors. A self-issue free permit system has been implemented in the Holy Cross Wilderness to obtain accurate wilderness visitor data and to educate visitors. Land agencies alone can't preserve and protect wilderness areas. Each of us plays an important role.

As you hike or backpack in a wilderness area, remember you are in a very special place. Keeping groups small, understanding the ecosystems enough to make good decisions about where to hike and camp, keeping water clean, minimizing traces of your presence (for example preventing fire rings and scars), and respecting wildlife and other visitors is extremely important. One hiker may not make a huge impact, but we are now hundreds of thousands of hikers each year. By understanding what designated wilderness is and taking the responsibility to act appropriately, we can preserve these special areas for ourselves and future generations.

For further information, check out

Leave It Wild, www.leaveitwild.org

White River National Forest, (970) 945–2521, www.fs.fed.us/r2/whiteriver/recreation/wilderness/index.shtml

The Wilderness Society, (800) The–Wild (843–9453), www.wilderness.org

Wilderness Land Trust, (970) 963–1725, www.wildernesslandtrust.org

www.wilderness.net, an Internet-based tool about wilderness

4 Kettle Ponds

This gentle, uncrowded hike follows an old mining road then travels on the Gore Range Trail (GRT), climbing a lateral moraine left by two epochs of glaciers. The GRT wanders around the top of the forested glacial debris, past many small ponds, some covered with lily pads. The moraine is covered with conifers—mainly lodgepole pine interspersed with a few aspen, spruce, and fir. Dropping down to cross South Rock Creek, the trail crosses a few boggy areas, then climbs to an unnamed lake. The peaceful destination provides views of Red Peak with its craggy ridge, and the Thorn.

Start: At the North Rock Creek Trail #46 trailhead
Distance: 6.4 miles out and back
Approximate hiking time: 2.5 to 4.5 hours
Difficulty: Moderate
Elevation gain: 600 feet
Trail surface: Dirt trail
Seasons: Best from mid-June to mid-October
Other trail users: Equestrians
Canine compatibility: Dogs must be on leash.

Land status: National forest wilderness area
Nearest town: Silverthorne
Fees and permits: No fees or permits required
Maps: USGS map: Willow Lakes; National Geographic Trails Illustrated: #108 Vail, Frisco, Dillon
Trail contact: White River National Forest, Dillon Ranger District, 680 Blue River Parkway, Silverthorne; (970) 468-5400; www.fs.fed.us/r2/whiteriver, www.dillonrangerdistrict.com

Finding the trailhead: From Interstate 70 exit 205, Silverthorne/Dillon, drive about 7.8 miles north on Highway 9 to Rock Creek Road just past mile marker 109, across from Blue River Campground, and turn left (west). Follow the dirt road about 1.3 miles to the Rock Creek trailhead sign. Turn left (south) onto Forest Development Road (FDR) 1350. The road narrows and becomes bumpy here. Dispersed camping sites are available along the road. The road deadends at the North Rock Creek Trail trailhead in 1.6 miles. No facilities are available at the trailhead. *DeLorme: Colorado Atlas & Gazetteer:* Page 37 C1

Special considerations: This area is very popular during hunting season. The winter parking lot (small) is at the junction of Rock Creek Road and FDR 1350, 1.6 miles from the summer trailhead. The Rock Creek Road is popular for cross-country skiing and snowshoeing. The Gore Range Trail is neither marked nor maintained for winter use. Wilderness regulations apply.

The Hike

Between 150,000 and 12,000 years ago, two periods of glaciation (Bull Lake and Pinedale) deposited thick sheets of ice in this area. As the glaciers crept forward, they eroded the land underneath and pushed the resulting sediments out of the way, creating ridges known as lateral moraines. Hunks of ice sometimes became embedded in the moraine then melted creating small ponds. Geologists call these depressions kettle ponds or kettle holes.

Red Peak and the Thorn reflected in destination lake

This hike starts on the old Boss Mine Road (Rock Creek Trail) then turns south onto the Gore Range Trail (GRT) #60. The GRT descends to a nice bridge, which replaced a rickety log bridge over North Rock Creek. A local group, Friends of the Eagles Nest Wilderness, provided the labor to help the U.S. Forest Service build the new bridge and a good horse crossing. From here the GRT travels through lodgepole pine forest to switchback steadily up the side of a moraine. Once on top, the trail undulates along the moraine. Various kettle ponds appear along the trail—some are filled with green goop, some contain lily pads or grasses, while others have dried out. Some ponds hide in the forest not far off the trail.

The lodgepole forest has sparse under story including buffaloberry bushes, heartleaf arnica, yellow paintbrush, whortleberry, and harebells. Occasionally a large boulder, probably left by a glacier, sits near the trail, watching history march on. Pine squirrels scold hikers passing too close to their favorite trees.

The GRT eventually drops down and crosses sparkling South Rock Creek on a fancy bridge complete with handrails. A quick climb out of the drainage brings you to a ditch that takes water from South Rock Creek to Maryland Creek. In a few more steps, the trail comes to a small lake, the destination of this hike. Take some time to enjoy the scenery of the Gore Range and its reflections. The peak to the left is on the ridge of Red Peak. Spindly spires form the ridge to Red Peak's

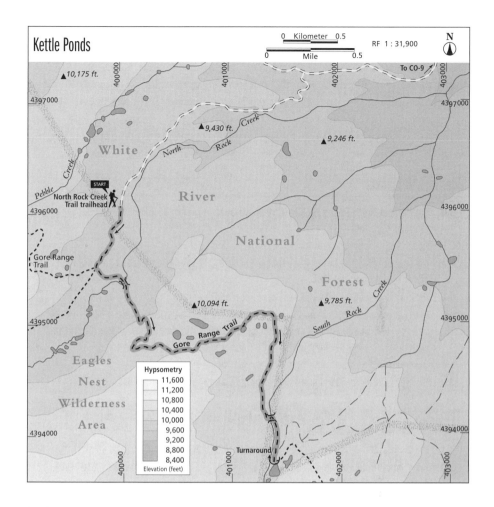

RF 1 : 31,900

N

0   Kilometer   0.5
0   Mile   0.5

▲10,175 ft.

4397000

▲9,430 ft.   Creek

▲9,246 ft.

White

North   Rock

Creek

START

Pebble

North Rock Creek
Trail trailhead

4396000

River

National

Gore Range
Trail

Forest

Creek

▲10,094 ft.

▲9,785 ft.

South   Rock

4395000

Gore   Range Trail

Eagles

Nest

Wilderness

Area

Hypsometry
11,600
11,200
10,800
10,400
10,000
9,600
9,200
8,800
8,400
Elevation (feet)

Turnaround

4394000

To CO-9

4397000

4396000

4395000

4394000

high point to the west. On the other side of the rounded ridge lie Salmon and Willow Lakes. The craggy peak above is known locally as East Thorn or the Thorn. The peak to the right of East Thorn is unnamed, as are many in the Eagles Nest Wilderness.

The Gore Range was uplifted with the present Rocky Mountains starting about seventy million years ago in an episode called the Laramide Orogeny. These mountains lifted along the Blue River Frontal Fault, and the lower Blue River valley dropped as a block.

A regional uplift occurred between five and two million years ago, raising the Rockies and the Colorado Plateau as much as 5,000 feet. The climate changed and snow remained year-round, growing deeper with each season. Eventually only the tops of the highest peaks poked above the glaciers. The Gore Range is unusual in that both sides of the range were glaciated. In other mountain ranges only the east slopes, which filled with snow blown by west winds, developed glaciers. The sharp arêtes of the Gore Range were created as the ice stripped away rock and dirt, leaving behind sharp ridges and points.

While a few mines were discovered and worked in the Gore Range, like the Boss Mine, the mountains and creeks did not contain the wealth of minerals found in other parts of Summit County. The Eagles Nest Wilderness is therefore less disturbed by human activity than areas that were mined.

This section of the GRT is lightly traveled except during hunting season and provides a pleasant escape from the more crowded trails in Summit County.

Miles and Directions

0.0 Start at the North Rock Creek Trail trailhead bulletin board. 399996mE 4396074mN Elevation 9,470 feet.

500 ft Eagles Nest Wilderness boundary.

0.4 The trail intersects with the Gore Range Trail (GRT). 399748mE 4395512mN Turn left and hike south on the GRT.

0.6 The trail crosses North Rock Creek on a nice bridge.

0.9 The trail crosses a boggy area with a little foot bridge. 400108mE 4395139mN (**Note:** Look back as you cross this area because the trail is not as obvious on the return trip. Remember to take the right branch of the trail here.)

1.6 The trail reaches the top of the moraine. High point 10,070 feet.

2.0 The trail passes several kettle ponds with grass and one with lily pads. 401013mE 4394941mN

2.9 The trail crosses South Rock Creek on a bridge with handrails. On both sides of the creek, the trail traverses boggy areas.

3.1 The trail Ys at a ditch. Cross the ditch and head uphill to the left.

3.2 Arrive at an unnamed lake with beautiful views of the craggy Gore Range. 401379mE 4393760mN Elevation 10,060 feet. Return the way you came.

6.4 Arrive back at the trailhead.

Option: At the junction of the Gore Range Trail and North Rock Creek Trail, you can continue straight on the North Rock Creek Trail to the Boss Mine, 2.1 miles (one way) from the trailhead. Mine tailings elevation 10,220 feet. Elevation gain 750 feet and moderate difficulty.

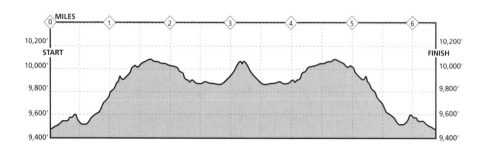

Hike Information

Local Information

Summit County Chamber of Commerce, (800) 530-3099, www.summitchamber.org
Summit Visitor Information Center, Outlets at Silverthorne, 246 Rainbow Drive, Silverthorne; (970) 262-0817
Town of Silverthorne, www.silverthorne.org, (970) 262-7300

Local Events/Attractions

Blue River Festival, Town of Silverthorne, (970) 262-7390

Accommodations

Blue River Campground entrance is almost opposite Rock Creek Road. For more information contact White River National Forest, Dillon Ranger District, 680 Blue River Parkway, Silverthorne; (970) 468-5400; www.fs.fed.us/r2/whiteriver, www.dillonrangerdistrict.com.

Restaurants

China Gourmet, Highway 9 and Annie Road (by Target), Silverthorne; (970) 262-6688
Fiesta Jalisco, Summit Place Shopping Center, Silverthorne; (970) 468-6663
Sunshine Café, Summit Place Shopping Center, Silverthorne; (970) 468-9552

Organizations

Friends of the Eagles Nest Wilderness, www.fenw.org, or call the Dillon Ranger District, (970) 468-5400, for the current contact.

MOUND FIRE HOW-TO

Many people enjoy an evening campfire for camaraderie, warmth, storytelling, and even security. From other perspectives, fires can damage the vegetation underneath as well as leave ugly scars on ground and rock. However, there are ways to "have your fire and prevent damage, too."

A mound fire is an ecological and aesthetic way to build a fire and prevent both environmental damage and ugly scars. First, make sure no fire bans are in effect and that you are below treeline. Next, find either a big level rock imbedded in the ground, make a rock base out of "flat" rocks, or find exposed soil with less than three inches of plant remains. Be sure not to build your fire right under tree branches. Find some "mineral soil" along a creek or by an uprooted tree. Mineral soil is dirt and/or sand that has minimal organic matter such as pine needles, leaves, or twigs in it. Put enough soil on a large plastic garbage bag to make a flat-topped mound about 6 to 8 inches thick and about 18 inches or less in diameter. Carry the garbage bag and soil to your chosen spot and shape the mound.

To gather firewood, spread out and pick up downed and dead wood that's no larger than your wrist. Gather the wood from various places on the ground so as not to remove all dead wood in an area. Birds use dead branches on trees, so please don't break any off. Build your fire on the mound within 1 inch of the edges. Enjoy!

When finished, let the fire cool to white ash. Scatter the cold ash and any unused wood over a large area. That way no one will see that you had a fire. Return the soil to where you found it. If the garbage bag has no burn holes, you passed the mound fire test!

5 Surprise/Eaglesmere Loop

This loop trail, which visits four lakes, can be hiked in a long day, broken into shorter segments, or done as a backpack. The farther into the Eagles Nest Wilderness you travel, the more primitive the area seems. Various features along the trail highlight the glacial past. Lower Cataract Lake, far below most of the trail, forms the hub of the loop. Several views of craggy Eagles Nest, the peak after which the Eagles Nest Wilderness was named, treat the eye along the way. At 13,400 feet, Eagles Nest is the second-highest peak in the Gore Range.

Start: At the Eaglesmere Trail #61 trailhead (see Options for other possibilities)
Distance: 12.3-mile loop hike
Approximate hiking time: 5.5 to 8.5 hours
Difficulty: More Difficult
Elevation gain: 1,845 feet
Trail surface: Dirt with a short stretch of dirt road
Seasons: Best from mid-June to early October
Other trail users: Equestrians
Canine compatibility: Dogs must be on leash.
Land status: National forest and wilderness area
Nearest towns: Heeney and Kremmling
Fees and permits: Daily fee required during the summer

Maps: USGS map: Mount Powell; National Geographic Trails Illustrated: #107 Green Mountain Reservoir, Ute Pass
Trail contact: White River National Forest, Dillon Ranger District, 680 Blue River Parkway, Silverthorne; (970) 468-5400; www.fs.fed.us/r2/whiteriver, www.dillonrangerdistrict.com
Other: The trail goes up then down then up then down. The elevation gain listed is between the low point on the road and a high point on the way to Eaglesmere Lakes. Some sections of the trail have water while other sections are dry. Camp fires are prohibited at all four lakes.

Finding the trailhead: From Interstate 70 exit 205, Silverthorne/Dillon, drive north through Silverthorne on Highway 9 16.6 miles to Heeney Road (Summit County Road 30). Turn left and drive on Heeney Road for 5.5 miles to the Cataract Creek Road sign. Turn sharp left (southwest) and follow Cataract Creek Road 2.2 miles to the road to Eaglesmere Trail trailhead. Turn right and drive 0.3 mile to the trailhead. Please park only in the few designated spaces. An outhouse is available near the trailhead. Self-pay fee stations are available at both the Eaglesmere and Surprise Lake trailheads. *DeLorme: Colorado Atlas & Gazetteer:* Page 37 B7

Special considerations: Hunters use this area during hunting season. The road is closed in winter about 1.3 miles from the trailhead. The Cataract Creek Road is nice for cross-country skiing, walking, or snowshoeing from the winter closure to Cataract Lake. These trails are neither marked nor maintained for winter use. Please comply with wilderness regulations.

View of Eagles Nest from mile 6.9 ▶

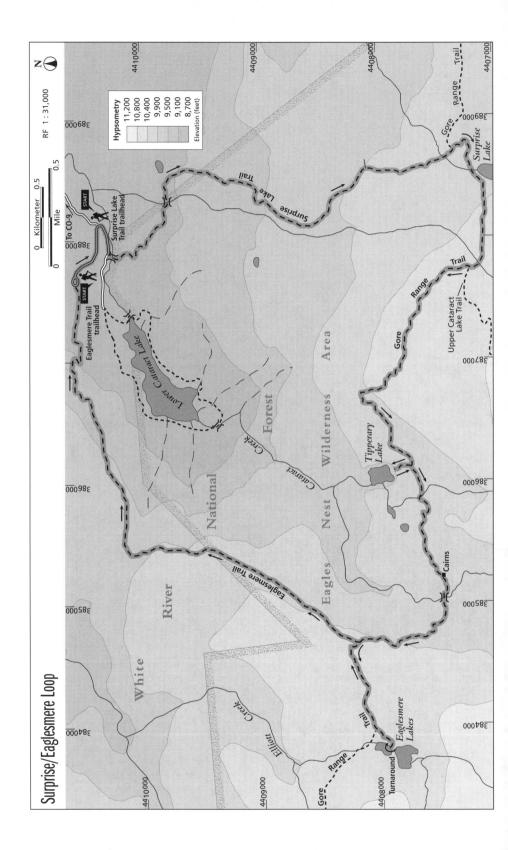

Surprise/Eaglesmere Loop

RF 1 : 31,000

Hypsometry
- 11,200
- 10,800
- 10,400
- 9,900
- 9,500
- 9,100
- 8,700

Elevation (feet)

White River National Forest

Eagles Nest Wilderness Area

Lower Cataract Lake

Cataract Creek

Elliott Creek

Eaglesmere Lakes

Tipperary Lake

Surprise Lake

Eaglesmere Trail trailhead

Surprise Lake Trail trailhead

Surprise Lake Trail

Eaglesmere Trail

Gore Range Trail

Gore Range Trail

Upper Cataract Lake Trail

Cairns

Turnaround

To CO-9

START

START

N

The Hike

The loop hike consists of a bit of dirt road, the Surprise Lake Trail, the Gore Range Trail, short side trails to Tipperary Lake and Eaglesmere Lakes, and the Eaglesmere Trail. The farther into the Eagles Nest Wilderness you travel, the more primitive the area seems. After Tipperary Lake, the trail winds around huge blocks of granite, surely a remnant of glacial times. Looking up the Cataract Creek drainage to Eagles Nest might make you feel like you're miles from civilization.

▶ **Mere means sea, lake, pool, or pond. Eaglesmere Lakes probably were named for the view of Eagles Nest from the south lake.**

Gore Canyon, Gore Pass, Gore Creek, Gore Lake, and the Gore Range are named after Sir St. George Gore, the Eighth Baronet of Manor Gore. His vast estate was located in northwest Ireland, but he lived south of London. Gore enjoyed hunting immensely, and in 1854 the 43-year-old bachelor organized a hunting trip leaving from St. Louis and heading west to New and Old Parks in Colorado and the lower Yellowstone Valley. His entourage and equipment were quite the show. England's most skilled gunsmiths had created his gun collection where every square inch of each weapon was adorned. He brought enough ammunition with him to kill the thousands of animals he did. Jim Bridger of mountain-man fame became Gore's head guide.

Gore's entourage included forty men plus two valets and a dog handler, one hundred horses, twenty yoke of oxen, fifty hunting hounds, and twenty-eight vehicles, including his fancy yellow-wheeled carriage, which Jim Bridger drove. The pack of hunting hounds consisted of eighteen purebred English foxhounds for tracking and thirty-two greyhounds trained for chasing. Each travel day, at the crack of dawn, the six heaviest wagons of the caravan lumbered slowly along the trail and headed to the next campsite. Two mess wagons carried food and cooking equipment, another hauled blacksmithing equipment, while the fourth contained carpentry, various camp provisions, and Indian trade goods. Two wagons carried the expedition's heavier supplies. Gore's carriage and lighter carts left in late morning.

Gore slept and ate in a green and white tent with a French carpet laid over a rubber pad. The tent contained a camp stove, the expedition's chests and trunks, the ornate guns in their racks, an ornamental brass bed, and a fur-lined commode. Servants brought him gourmet style meals every night. About 9:00 A.M. every morning, Gore's valet would build a fire in the stove and boil water. He cleaned the dishes from the previous evening's meal and emptied the chamber pot. When Gore awoke an hour later, he took a bath in his oval bathtub, shaved, then ate breakfast before heading out for the day's adventures.

In addition to his luxurious expedition, Gore became known and despised by Indians and whites alike for his wanton killing of wildlife. Over three years, he reportedly killed more than 2,000 buffalo, 1,600 elk and deer, and 100 bears. Most were killed for sport—some became dinner for the large party.

For all that is named after Gore in Summit and Eagle Counties, Gore did not travel south of the Grand (Colorado) River. He hunted in New (North) Park and Old (Middle) Park, including the Kremmling area.

The U.S. Forest Service built sections of the Gore Range Trail during the 1930s and early 1940s to allow access to fight fires in remote areas. Trail workers included men from local ranches and towns. The trail is approximately 54 miles long, starting at Copper Mountain in the south, crossing then traversing the east side of the Gore to Mahan Lake in the north.

Miles and Directions

You can start this hike at either the Eaglesmere Trail #61 trailhead or the Surprise Lake Trail trailhead. You can also hike in either direction because it is a loop hike.

0.0 Start at the Eaglesmere Trail trailhead. 387634mE 4410571mN Elevation 8,715 feet. Walk back down the road you drove up to the junction with the Cataract Creek Road.

0.4 Arrive at the junction of the road to Eaglesmere Trail trailhead and Cataract Creek Roads. 388133mE 4410355mN Turn right and walk up the road heading west.

0.6 Arrive at the Surprise Lake Trail #62 trailhead. 387886mE 4410270mN Turn left (south) onto the trail. Hike down, and cross the bridge over Cataract Creek.

0.8 Come to the Eagles Nest Wilderness boundary. 387953mE 4410015mN

3.3 Arrive at the trail junction with the Gore Range Trail #60. 388786mE 4407220mN Turn right (southwest) on the Gore Range Trail.

3.5 Surprise Lake is south of the trail. 388539mE 4407161mN Elevation 10,064 feet. From the lake, continue heading southwest and uphill on the Gore Range Trail.

4.0 Arrive at the trail junction with Upper Cataract Lake Trail #63. Stay on the Gore Range Trail which goes straight (northwest). 387740mE 4407206mN

5.4 Come to the trail junction with the trail to Tipperary Lake. 386106mE 4407735mN Turn right (north) and head down the trail to the lake. It's a 0.2-mile hike out and back to the lake which is at elevation 9,765 feet. Return the way you came to the Gore Range Trail and turn right (west) to continue the loop.

6.9 The trail Ys. Turn right as marked by the cairn. 385192mE 4407459mN You'll cross a creek then scramble on some boulders and through willows then cross another creek. The large rock slab is a great viewpoint of the valley and Eagles Nest (elevation 13,123 feet) to the south. On the rock slab, the trail switchbacks to the right at the cairn. Look to

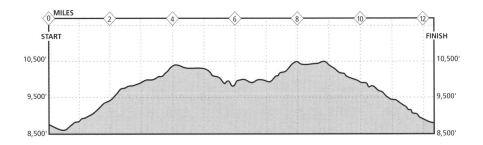

the right for the next cairn. When you reach that cairn, look to the right for a cairn by a pond. The trail switchbacks to the left at the cairn by the pond.

7.0 The trail Ys. Switchback to the left here. 385073mE 4407478mN In a few feet down the trail, cross the wooden bridge over a little chasm created by Cataract Creek.

7.5 Nice view of Green Mountain Reservoir to the east. 384720mE 4407692mN

7.8 Arrive at the trail junction with the Eaglesmere Trail. 384666mE 4408188mN Turn left (northwest) and head uphill.

8.3 Come to the trail junction where the Eaglesmere Trail and Gore Range Trail split. 383988mE 4408086mN Turn left (southwest) and hike into the two lakes.

8.5 A flat area between the two Eaglesmere Lakes. 383811mE 4407936mN Elevation 10,400 feet. Return the way you came to the first junction of the Eaglesmere and Gore Range Trails.

9.2 Trail junction with the Eaglesmere Trail (same junction as mile 7.8). 384666mE 4408188mN Turn left (north) and head downhill to your vehicle.

10.1 Eagles Nest Wilderness boundary. 385410mE 4409346mN

11.4 Open area with great views. Lower Cataract Lake is below (south). 386509mE 4410397mN

12.3 Arrive back at the Eaglesmere Trail trailhead.

Options:

1. Surprise Lake. Start at the Surprise Lake Trail trailhead (see 0.6 above) for a 5.8-mile out-and-back hike. Elevation gain 1,480 feet.

2. Tipperary Lake. Start at the Eaglesmere Trail trailhead for an 11.2-mile out-and-back hike. Elevation gain 1,565 feet plus a loss to Tipperary Lake.

3. Eaglesmere Lakes. Start at the Eaglesmere Trail trailhead for a 7.6-mile out-and-back hike. Elevation gain 1,715 feet.

Hike Information

Local Information
Kremmling Area Chamber of Commerce, Kremmling, (877) 573-4263, (970) 724-3472, www.kremmlingchamber.com

Local Events/Attractions
Krazy for Kremmling Days, (877) 573-4263, www.kremmlingchamber.com
Middle Park Fair & Rodeo, (970) 724-3436

Accommodations
The **Cataract Lake Campground** (four spaces) is just east of Lower Cataract Lake. Several **U.S. Forest Service campgrounds** exist around Green Mountain Reservoir. For more information contact White River National Forest, Dillon Ranger District, 680 Blue River Parkway, Silverthorne; (970) 468-5400; www.fs.fed.us/r2/whiteriver, www.dillonrangerdistrict.com

Restaurants
Green Mountain Inn, Heeney, (970) 724-3812
Our Family Kitchen, 104 North 6th Avenue, Kremmling; (970) 724-1107
Quarter Circle Saloon, 106 West Park Avenue, Kremmling; (970) 724-9765

Organizations
Friends of the Eagles Nest Wilderness, www.fenw.org, or call the Dillon Ranger District, (970) 468-5400, for the current contact.

6 Lower Cataract Lake

This easy and family-friendly loop trail travels through fields of colorful wildflowers, thick spruce-fir forest, and past beautiful cascades of Cataract Creek. After hiking, spend some time lounging along the shores of the lake enjoying views of Cataract Falls and Eagles Nest. The pointy peak is the second highest in the Gore Range and is the namesake for the Eagles Nest Wilderness area.

Start: At Cataract Loop Trail #57 trailhead
Distance: 2.4-mile loop
Approximate hiking time: 1.0 to 2.5 hours
Difficulty: Easy
Elevation gain: About 75 feet
Trail surface: Dirt trail and a short section of dirt road
Seasons: Best from mid-May to mid-October
Other trail users: None
Canine compatibility: Dogs must be on leash.

Land status: National forest and wilderness area
Nearest towns: Heeney and Kremmling
Fees and permits: Daily fee required in summer
Maps: USGS map: Mount Powell; National Geographic Trails Illustrated: #107 Green Mountain Reservoir, Ute Pass
Trail contact: White River National Forest, Dillon Ranger District, 680 Blue River Parkway, Silverthorne; (970) 468–5400; www.fs.fed.us/r2/whiteriver, www.dillonrangerdistrict.com

Finding the trailhead: From Interstate 70 exit 205, Silverthorne/Dillon, drive north through Silverthorne on Highway 9 16.6 miles to Heeney Road (Summit County Road 30). Turn left and drive on Heeney Road for 5.5 miles to the Cataract Creek Road sign. Turn left and follow Cataract Creek Road 2.6 miles to its end. (**Note:** At 2.2 miles the road Ys. Stay on the road to the left.) No facilities are available at the trailhead. Please pay the daily fee at the fee station near the trailhead. *DeLorme: Colorado Atlas & Gazetteer:* Page 37 B7

Special considerations: The U.S. Forest Services discourages hiking to the waterfalls because the area is hazardous due to the slippery and steep terrain. The road is closed by snow in the winter 1.3 miles from the trailhead. The Cataract Creek Road is nice for cross-country skiing, walking, or snowshoeing from the winter closure to Cataract Lake. The trail around the lake is neither marked nor maintained for winter use. Please comply with wilderness regulations.

The Hike

Cataract Lake is a gem of a lake situated below Cataract Falls. The falls were created when the land uplifted starting about five million years ago.

Locals in the late 1800s enjoyed the Cataract Lake area. Howard Hill owned Cataract Lake back in those days and also ran a fish hatchery. He stocked trout in the pretty lake. The *Summit County Journal* in July 1899 noted that "Mountain trout, from Cataract Lake, the proprietor holding a state license to market fish, [is] on sale at George E. Moon's every Friday." An article in the *Breckenridge Bulletin*, September 23, 1905, stated that Hill "has already placed 1,500,000 fish in the lake since he became its owner."

Lower Cataract Lake

Hill sold Cataract Lake and 400 surrounding acres in late 1916 to O. K. Gaymon. At $15,000, the price was considered modest in those days. Hill reportedly headed back to Maine to care for his aging mother. The article reporting the sale mentioned the attractions of the area including fishing and hunting, clubhouse, summer cottages, and high-class resort facilities. Gaymon had plans to improve the roads and trails, construct cabins, and add a motorboat to the existing primitive boats that plied that lake.

In the 1950s and 1960s, John Rockwell from Phoenix owned the lake. A nice lodge existed along with the various cabins. In the late 1960s, the U.S. Forest Service purchased the area. Photos taken in 1975 show cabins and a boat dock.

Cataract Lake had been just outside the boundary of the Gore Range–Eagles Nest Primitive Area. This special area consisting of 32,400 acres in the Arapaho National Forest was established on June 19, 1932. Another 47,250 acres in the Holy Cross National Forest was added to the primitive area in 1933. In December 1941 the primitive area was reduced by 18,425 acres for the construction of U.S. Highway 6 over Vail Pass.

Originally Cataract Lake was not included in the plans for the proposed Eagles Nest Wilderness area. In 1971, the U.S. Forest Service proposed an 87,755-acre wilderness. The boundary had been drawn west of the Gore Range Trail. Old

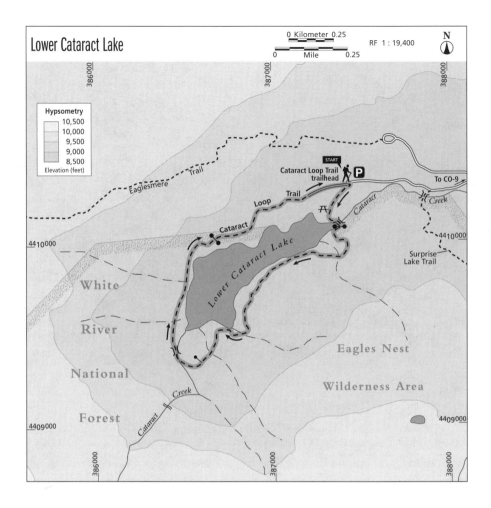

Lower Cataract Lake

Hypsometry
10,500
10,000
9,500
9,000
8,500
Elevation (feet)

0 Kilometer 0.25
0 Mile 0.25
RF 1 : 19,400
N

Cataract Loop Trail
trailhead
START
P
To CO-9
Eaglesmere
Trail
Loop
Trail
Cataract
Cataract
Creek
Surprise
Lake Trail
Lower Cataract Lake
Cataract
White
River
National
Forest
Creek
Cataract
Eagles Nest
Wilderness Area

timber cuts existed along today's Surprise Lake Trail. Other possible timber sales and cuts could be made in the area. The Denver Water Board (DWB) had plans to build the 40-mile East Gore Collection System, which would bring about 70,000 acre-feet of water from numerous branches of the Blue River back to Dillon Reservoir. Some of the tributaries included Cataract Creek and Slate Creek. The boundary for the Eagles Nest Wilderness excluded the area where the East Gore Range Canal would be built. However, the DWB only had claims to water in the area which were denied in a ruling in 1976.

After several years of negotiations, Colorado congressional representative Jim Johnson penned a bill for the Eagles Nest Wilderness that added acreage near Frisco and Maryland Creek to protect the Gore Range Trail. Main trails leading into other wilderness areas in Colorado, such as Mount Zirkel, had not been included in the designated area, and problems arose with motorized incursions into wilderness. The

Gore Range Trail provides access to about 70 percent of the Eagles Nest Wilderness and was included in the final boundaries. (See the Mesa Cortina to East Vail hike for more Eagles Nest Wilderness history.)

The Eagles Nest Wilderness, in its own bill, was officially designated on July 12, 1976, in Public Law 94-352. In November 1997, another 160 acres in the Slate Creek area were added to the Eagles Nest Wilderness in Public Law 105-75, contingent upon acquisition of the parcel by the United States, which acquisition has been completed.

Miles and Directions

0.0 Start at Cataract Loop Trail #57 trailhead at the fence at the end of the parking lot. 387453mE 4410329mN Elevation 8,650 feet. Be sure to read the trailhead bulletin board, which contains area information and regulations. Please sign the trail register. Walk down the trail which heads to the lake (not the trails to the left or right).

0.1 Arrive at a trail junction. 387315mE 4410167mN Turn left (south). The trail straight ahead goes to a picnic table and the lake.

0.2 Arrive at another trail junction. Turn right (east) and walk across the bridge over Cataract Creek. In about 200 feet pass through the wooden Z gate at the Eagles Nest Wilderness boundary. 387360mE 4410075mN At the next two trail junctions turn left as the signs indicate.

0.8 Nice view of Cataract Falls. 386871mE 4409709mN

1.2 The trail appears to Y. Turn left, which takes you to the lower cascades of Cataract Creek. 386587mE 4409356mN About 150 feet farther, come to a long bridge with handrails which crosses Cataract Creek.

1.4 Enter a meadow with views of the lake and the Williams Fork Range to the northeast. 386441mE 4409540mN

1.8 Nice view of the lake, falls, and Eagles Nest (peak). 386662mE 4410015mN In about 400 feet, pass through a wooden Z gate and exit the Eagles Nest Wilderness. Great photo spot.

2.2 Arrive at a trail junction. Turn left (east) and walk down the dirt road to the trailhead. 387170mE 4410242mN

2.4 Arrive back at the trailhead.

Option: You can walk this loop in the opposite direction.

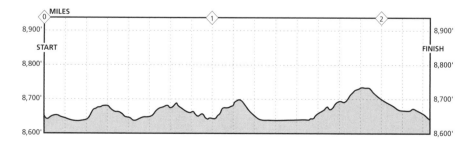

Hike Information

Local Information

Kremmling Area Chamber of Commerce, Kremmling, (877) 573-4263, (970) 724-3472, www.kremmlingchamber.com

Local Events/Attractions

Krazy for Kremmling Days, (877) 573-4263, www.kremmlingchamber.com
Middle Park Fair & Rodeo, (970) 724-3436

Accommodations

The **Cataract Lake Campground** (four spaces) is just east of Lower Cataract Lake. Several **U.S. Forest Service campgrounds** exist around Green Mountain Reservoir. For more information contact White River National Forest, Dillon Ranger District, 680 Blue River Parkway, Silverthorne; (970) 468-5400; www.fs.fed.us/r2/whiteriver, www.dillonrangerdistrict.com

Restaurants

Green Mountain Inn, Heeney, (970) 724-3812
Our Family Kitchen, 104 North 6th Avenue, Kremmling; (970) 724-1107
Quarter Circle Saloon, 106 West Park Avenue, Kremmling; (970) 724-9765

Organizations

Friends of the Eagles Nest Wilderness, www.fenw.org, or call the Dillon Ranger District, (970) 468-5400, for current contact.

7 Gore Canyon Trail

This hike meanders along the Colorado River downriver of spectacular Gore Canyon. Only boaters and train passengers can travel in the vertical-walled inner gorge. The trail passes limber pine trees, a few campsites, and finally climbs a little gully to a trail higher above the river. The first part of the hike is along a placid river. Farther upstream, the river noisily leaps through rapids where the walls of the canyon start to rise. The trail is tricky in a few spots where erosion is taking its toll. Dropping down, the visible trail ends on the river bank.

Start: At the Gore Canyon Trail trailhead.
Distance: 3.1 miles out and back
Approximate hiking time: 1.5 to 2.5 hours
Difficulty: Easy with some tricky sections
Elevation gain: Approximately 160 feet
Trail surface: Dirt trail and dirt road
Seasons: Best from April to November
Other trail users: Anglers
Canine compatibility: Dogs must be on leash.
Land status: Bureau of Land Management (BLM)
Nearest town: Kremmling
Fees and permits: Daily use fee required from

May through October (fee demonstration)
Maps: USGS maps: Sheephorn Mountain, Radium, Kremmling; National Geographic Trails Illustrated: #107 Green Mountain Reservoir, Ute Pass; #120 State Bridge, Burns; #106 Kremmling, Granby
Trail contact: Bureau of Land Management, Kremmling Field Office, Kremmling; (970) 724-3000
Other: Where the trail is about 40 to 60 feet above the river, no drinking water is readily available.

Colorado River at about mile 1.1

Finding the trailhead: From Interstate 70 exit 205, Silverthorne/Dillon, head north through Silverthorne on Highway 9 past Green Mountain Reservoir approximately 34.6 miles to Trough Road, Grand County Road (CR) 1, just past mile marker 136. Turn left (southwest) on Trough Road and drive approximately 10.8 miles to Grand CR 106, Pump House Recreation Area. Turn right (west) and stop in 1.1 miles at the fee station and pay the fee when required. In approximately 0.2 mile, the road Ys. Go right and follow the road into the parking lot in another 0.2 mile. The trailhead is in the northeast corner of the parking lot. Vault toilets are available. Potable water is available at the Pumphouse Campground (additional fee). During the rafting season please park in designated lots/spots. The BLM tries to keep boat launching areas as open as possible. These areas tend to get congested especially on the weekends. *DeLorme: Colorado Atlas & Gazetteer:* Page 37 A5.5

Special considerations: Waterfowl hunters use the trail during hunting season.

The Hike

The railroad that travels along the river opposite the hiking trail is known as the Moffat Road. At the beginning of the twentieth century, Denver found itself bypassed by transcontinental railroads that had been built on easier routes to the north in Wyoming (Union Pacific) and south near Pueblo (Rio Grande). Businesses moved from Denver to Cheyenne because freight rates to and from Denver proved costly.

Enter David Moffat, a financier, Colorado's wealthiest man. In 1885 Moffat became president of the Rio Grande Railroad. He initiated surveys to find a route from Denver to Salt Lake City through the high Rockies. Besides helping Denver grow, Moffat wanted to unlock undeveloped resources such as coal, timber, oil, iron, and wool in northwestern Colorado. The new route would be on standard gauge rails, not the narrow gauge used at the time for mountain travel. Frustrated by a lack of backing from the Rio Grande directors, Moffat started the Denver Northwestern and Pacific Railway Company.

Moffat's proposed route snaked from Denver up South Boulder Canyon, over the Continental Divide via Rollins Pass (until a tunnel could be built under it), through Fraser and Byers Canyons, then in Gore Canyon. The canyon sections were fraught with construction problems, and 3-mile-long Gore Canyon with its 3,000-foot granite cliffs prone to rockslides was the worst. Gore Pass was examined as an alternative, but the elevation gain and loss were not railroad friendly. Bids for construction on the westward route opened in December 1902.

The Moffat Road had filed for a right-of-way through Gore Canyon. In January 1903 the Denver Hydro-Electric Power Company filed for rights to build a dam in Gore Canyon. An associated hydroelectric plant would generate electricity. This action threw Moffat's plan awhirl, because the reservoir and railroad were incompatible. Some shady dealings came to light when the proposed dam's blueprints showed no connection to the power plant. The Department of Interior also decided to build a reservoir in Gore Canyon. Moffat's filings for right-of-way had

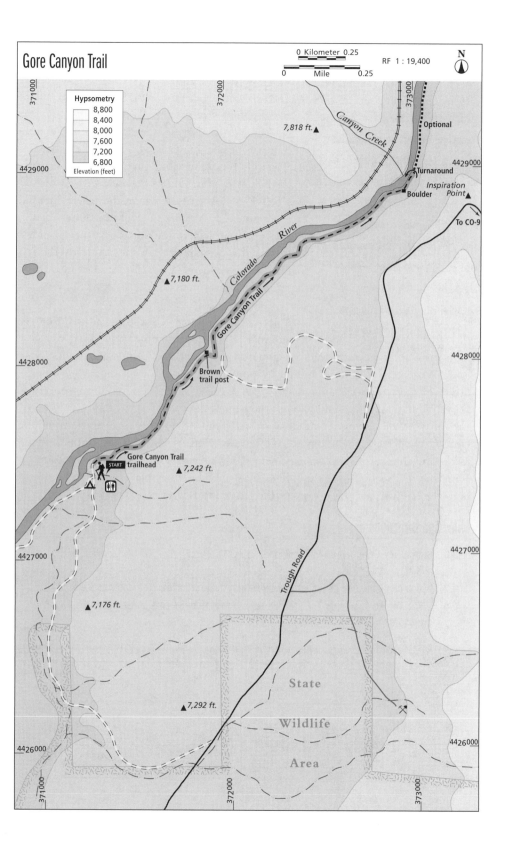

been misfiled by a clerk and not processed. President Teddy Roosevelt became involved and realized some big trusts (competing railroads) were at work behind the scenes. In the end David Moffat won the needed right-of-way through Gore Canyon.

▶ Originally the Colorado River flowed below the confluence of the Grand and the Green Rivers in Utah. The Grand originated in Colorado's Rocky Mountain National Park. In 1921, after some sneaky politics by Colorado congressman Edward Taylor, President Harding signed a bill into law that renamed the Grand River the Colorado River.

To survey the canyon for construction, men with nerves of steel built catwalks along the cliffs. A man would climb down the canyon wall and drive in 16-inch steel pins. Others floated 6- to 10-inch diameter logs downstream where they were lifted by ropes pulled by men on the cliff top. Others tied the 16-foot-long logs to the pins. Surveyors would then walk the wooden path, trying to steady their transits in high canyon winds. J. J. Argo headed up the group of hearty men known as Argo's Squirrels. Not one life was lost.

The railroad reached Kremmling in July 1906. In summer 1907, construction crews used dynamite, carts, and a steam shovel to penetrate Gore Canyon. During construction, at least 12 men died or were injured by powder explosions, rock slides, or falling drunk in the river. On September 14, 1907, the first passenger train transported David Moffat and his guests through the beautiful area.

Today boaters enjoy the thrill of class IV and V rapids in Gore Canyon. The Gore Canyon Race, including the Whitewater Cup, is held annually and permitted by the Bureau of Land Management (BLM). Anglers fish in the calmer waters along the first section of the trail. This hike provides many places to sit and enjoy both the serenity and the energy of the Colorado River.

Miles and Directions

0.0 Start at the Gore Canyon Trail trailhead. 13S 371277mE 4427502mN Elevation 6,960 feet.

0.2 Watch along the trail for limber pine trees with their distinctive five needle clusters.

0.4 Come into an open area. The trail is a little to the left between a tall stump and a downed tree. 13S 371718mE 4427871mN

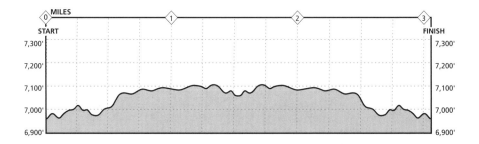

0.6 Come into another open area and dirt road. The trail Ys at a brown trail post. Turn right here and head up a little gulley where the trail switchbacks to the left and becomes a nice trail up above the Colorado River. 13S 371897mE 4428060mN

1.1 Nice view upriver. 13T 372439mE 4428666mN From here the trail gets a little narrower and slippery in spots where the erosion is slowly working on the trail.

1.5 A big boulder has slid over the trail. Make your way around the boulder. The trail drops down between bushes and heads to the river. 13T 372960mE 4428906mN

1.5+ The obvious trail ends at the Colorado River near some rusting car parts. 13T 373000mE 4428976mN Elevation 7,080 feet. Return the way you came.

3.1 Arrive back at the trailhead.

Option: You can walk another 0.8 mile upriver until the trail gets cliffed out. The trail is less obvious on this last stretch.

Hike Information

Local Information
Kremmling Area Chamber of Commerce, Kremmling, (877) 573-4263, (970) 724-3472, www.kremmlingchamber.com

Local Events/Attractions
Gore Canyon Race and Whitewater Cup, Rapidpulse LLC, (303) 989-7194, www.rapidpulse.com/events.htm

Krazy for Kremmling Days, (877) 573-4263, www.kremmlingchamber.com

Middle Park Fair & Rodeo, (970) 724-3436

Accommodations
Pumphouse Campground (fee required) is located near the Gore Canyon Trail trailhead.

For more information contact Bureau of Land Management, Kremmling Field Office, Kremmling; (970) 724-3000

Restaurants
Our Family Kitchen, 104 North 6th Avenue, Kremmling; (970) 724-1107

Quarter Circle Saloon, 106 West Park Avenue, Kremmling; (970) 724-9765

Rocky Mountain Bar and Grill, 276 Central Avenue, Kremmling; (970) 724-9219

8 Mesa Cortina to East Vail

This 14.9-mile hike traverses the Gore Range over Red–Buffalo Pass. Along the way, you can see almost everything that is special about the Eagles Nest Wilderness. Flower-filled meadows, views of craggy peaks and spires, marshes, avalanche paths, old graves, a set of waterfalls, and coniferous forests provide for a continuous change of scenery and feeling of remoteness. Most of the trail follows the route originally proposed for Interstate 70. The hike can be done as a long day hike, backpack, or separate hikes. Enjoy the beauty of the Gore Range and Eagles Nest Wilderness!

Start: At the Mesa Cortina Trail #32 trailhead (see Options for shorter hikes)
Distance: 14.9 miles point to point
Approximate hiking time: 6 to 11 hours
Difficulty: Most difficult
Elevation gain: 2,532 feet
Trail surface: Dirt trail
Seasons: Best from July to early October
Other trail users: Equestrians, joggers
Canine compatibility: Dogs must be on leash.
Land status: National forest/wilderness area
Nearest towns: Silverthorne and Vail
Fees and permits: No fees or permits required
Maps: USGS maps: Dillon, Willow Lakes, Vail East; National Geographic Trails Illustrated: #108 Vail, Frisco, Dillon

Trail contacts: Mesa Cortina and Gore Range Trail: White River National Forest, Dillon Ranger District, 680 Blue River Parkway, Silverthorne; (970) 468-5400; www.fs.fed.us/r2/whiteriver, www.dillonrangerdistrict.com
Gore Creek Trail: White River National Forest, Holy Cross Ranger District, (970) 827-5175, www.fs.fed.us/r2/whiteriver
Other: Beware of thunderstorms and possible lightning as you cross the higher elevations of this hike. The Mesa Cortina and Gore Range Trails (GRT) to South Willow Creek Falls from the east and the Gore Creek Trail to the Gore Lake Trail junction on the west are popular hikes.

Finding the trailheads: For a point-to-point hike, park one vehicle at the Mesa Cortina Trail trailhead and another at the Gore Creek Trail trailhead.

Mesa Cortina Trail trailhead: From Interstate 70 exit 205, Silverthorne/Dillon, head north on Highway 9 about 0.2 mile to Wildernest Road by the 7-11 store and across from Wendy's. Turn left (south) and follow Wildernest Road for 0.2 mile to Adams Avenue just after the bridge over the Blue River. Turn right (west) onto Adams Avenue and immediately turn left between the two car dealerships onto Buffalo Mtn Drive. Follow Buffalo Mountain Drive up a steep hill approximately 0.8 mile to Lake View Drive. Make a sharp right turn (north) and drive up Lake View Drive approximately 0.5 mile to where it curves left (south) onto Aspen Drive. Turn right in 0.1 mile into the parking lot for the Mesa Cortina Trail trailhead.

Gore Creek Trail trailhead: From I-70 exit 180, East Vail, head southeast on Big Horn Road (south side of I-70) for approximately 2.2 miles to a little parking area on the left just before Gore Creek Campground. *DeLorme: Colorado Atlas & Gazetteer:* Page 38 C1.5 to Page 37 C7

Special considerations: Hunters use this area during hunting season. Several avalanche paths cross the trail on both sides of Red-Buffalo Pass down to South Willow Creek Falls on the

Looking toward Vail down Gore Creek from Red-Buffalo Pass

east. The Mesa Cortina Trail and the GRT to the meadow with the bedsprings makes a nice ski or snowshoe tour and is usually well used. Past the meadow, avalanche chutes line the trail. The Gore Creek Trail is used by snowshoers and walkers. The road is not plowed past the last subdivision. There is avalanche danger along Gore Creek Trail the higher you go. Neither trail is marked nor maintained for winter use. Please comply with wilderness regulations.

The Hike

If the Colorado Department of Transportation's (CDOT) wish had been granted back in the mid-1960s, you would be driving along South Willow Creek and Gore Creek instead of hiking. CDOT proposed a route for I–70 that would turn at Silverthorne and head up South Willow Creek. At an elevation of about 10,700 feet, a two-lane tunnel would burrow under Red-Buffalo Pass for about 6,500 feet. On the west side, I–70 would travel down Gore Creek and then curve west past Vail.

CDOT chose the route because it would cut 11 miles off the alternate route of U.S. Highway 6 through Tenmile Canyon and over Vail Pass. Calculations estimated that the shorter route would save travelers $4 million annually over the next twenty years. Cost projections for the shorter route including the tunnel came in at $42 million plus an extra $21 million for a second tunnel. The Vail Pass route estimate was $22 million.

Not everyone agreed with CDOT about the appropriateness and cost savings of the Red-Buffalo route. CDOT held public meetings in 1966 and 1967. Some concerns mentioned included known avalanche paths along the corridor and poor sun exposure during winter because of Buffalo Mountain and other peaks along Gore Creek.

Residents of Summit County and Leadville voiced their apprehension that the Red-Buffalo route would bypass easy access to those communities. They wondered if CDOT had considered the additional cost of maintaining US 6 as well as the new I–70.

▶ **An interesting rule of thumb: For every 1,000 feet of elevation gained, the temperature drops about 5.5˚ F. So when it's 80˚ F in Denver at 5,280 feet, it may be only 58˚ F in Breckenridge at 9,300 feet.**

The proposed route cut through the Gore Range-Eagles Nest Primitive Area, which was scheduled for congressional hearings in 1968 for designation as a wilderness area. Because the route would cross national forest lands, the then secretary of agriculture, Orville Freeman, had the final say on CDOT's request. In May 1968, according to a U.S. Forest Service press release, Freeman denied the request, noting that "the public benefits of preserving this priceless wilderness area far outweigh any other considerations."

After many other battles, Congress designated the Eagles Nest Wilderness Area in 1976. (See the Lower Cataract Lake hike for more details.)

The long trail passes by some interesting places. In the meadow at about 3.6 miles, look to the left for old bedsprings and other remains of the house that once sat at its edge. The house burned down in about 1983. This meadow is a good turn-around place for a cross-country ski tour as avalanche paths cross the trail farther up.

At about mile 4.4, a side trail heads to South Willow Creek Falls. The falls are a great place for a picnic and a turnaround for a shorter hike. A nice flat rock provides a close-up view of and occasional spray from the upper falls.

The description of how to hike to the top of Red-Buffalo Pass may seem a tad confusing. Several trails exist in the area, but none connect to the trail over the pass. The description was written to use trails as much as possible to prevent trampling of the alpine meadows. If you're not sure, the pass is easily seen to the right (west) of the GRT as it curves south. The pass to the south is Eccles Pass, which takes you to Frisco, not East Vail.

Watch for the two graves at the junction of the Red-Buffalo Pass Trail and the Gore Lake Trail at about 10.5 miles. The Recen brothers had been successful miners in Tenmile Canyon.

Over its length the trail passes through waist-high flowers and thick forest, across avalanche paths, and past rushing cascades—a wonderful sampling of the beauty of the Eagles Nest Wilderness.

Mesa Cortina to East Vail

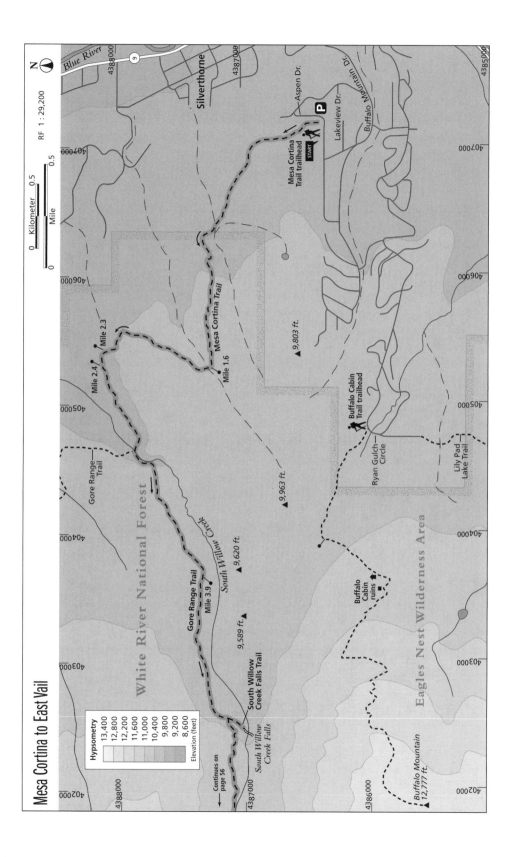

RF 1 : 29,200

Hypsometry

13,400
12,800
12,200
11,600
11,000
10,400
9,800
9,200
8,600

Elevation (feet)

N

Silverthorne

Blue River

9

Aspen Dr.

P

Mesa Cortina
Trail trailhead

START

Lakeview Dr.

Buffalo Mountain Dr.

▲ 9,803 ft.

Buffalo Cabin
Trail trailhead

Ryan Gulch
Circle

Lily Pad
Lake Trail

Mesa Cortina Trail

Mile 1.6

Mile 2.3

Mile 2.4

▲ 9,963 ft.

White River National Forest

Gore Range Trail

South Willow Creek

Mile 3.9

▲ 9,620 ft.

South Willow
Creek Falls Trail

▲ 9,589 ft.

South Willow
Creek Falls

Continues on
page 56

Gore Range Trail

Buffalo Cabin
ruins

Eagles Nest Wilderness Area

Buffalo Mountain
12,777 ft. ▲

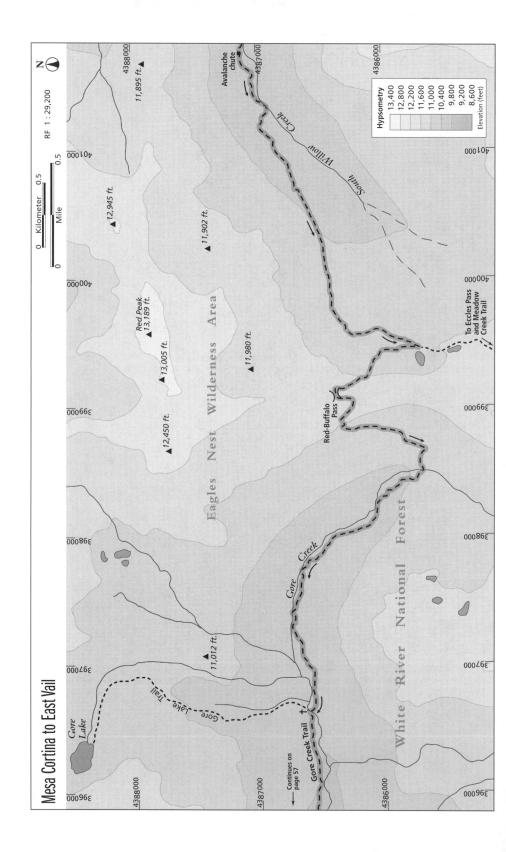

Mesa Cortina to East Vail

RF 1 : 29,200

N

0   Kilometer   0.5
0   Mile   0.5

Gore Lake

11,895 ft.

12,945 ft.

11,902 ft.

Red Peak
13,189 ft.

13,005 ft.

11,980 ft.

12,450 ft.

Eagles   Nest   Wilderness   Area

11,012 ft.

Gore Lake Trail

Continues on page 57

Gore Creek Trail

Gore Creek

White   River   National   Forest

Red-Buffalo Pass

To Eccles Pass
and Meadow
Creek Trail

South   Willow   Creek

Avalanche
chute

Hypsometry

13,400
12,800
12,200
11,600
11,000
10,400
9,800
9,200
8,600

Elevation (feet)

4388000
4387000
4386000

396000
397000
398000
399000
400000
401000

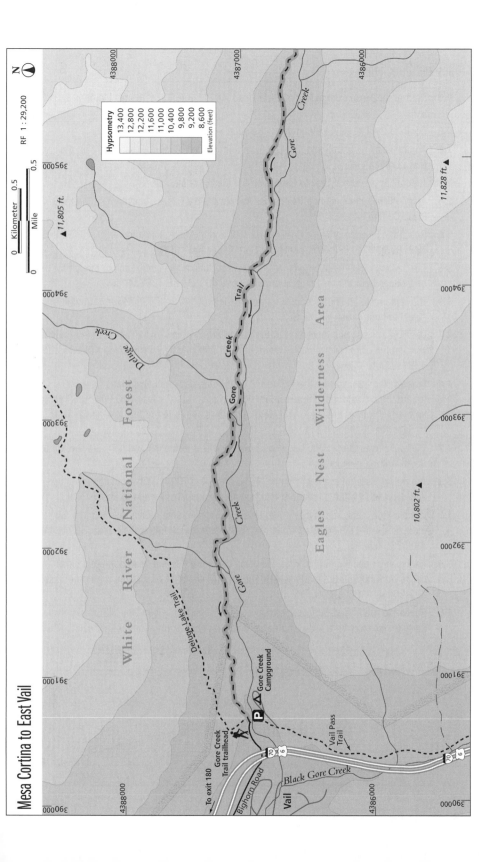

Mesa Cortina to East Vail

RF 1 : 29,200

Miles and Directions

0.0 Start at the Mesa Cortina Trail #32 trailhead. 407184mE 4386363mN Elevation 9,215 feet.

0.8 Come to the Eagles Nest Wilderness boundary. 406421mE 4387179mN

1.6 An unofficial, unmaintained trail comes in from the left. Continue to the right on the Mesa Cortina Trail.

2.3 The trail appears to Y. Stay to the left on the Mesa Cortina Trail.

2.4 An unofficial, unmaintained trail comes in from the right. Hike straight ahead on the Mesa Cortina Trail.

2.8 Reach the junction of Mesa Cortina Trail #32 and the Gore Range Trail #60. 404614mE 4387873mN Turn left (west) onto the Gore Range Trail (GRT).

3.6 The trail crosses a meadow with a good view of Buffalo Mountain. Look to the left for old bedsprings from a house that used to be here. 403636mE 4387340mN

3.9 The Buffalo Mountain Trail comes in from the left. 403278mE 4387359mN Continue straight ahead (west) on the GRT.

4.4 Come to an unsigned junction with the trail to South Willow Creek Falls. Turn left (southwest) at the cairn (pile of rocks) where the GRT makes a right switchback. 402545mE 4387115mN

4.5 To reach the falls, stay on the trail to the right of the cabin remains. Head downhill toward the creek to reach upper South Willow Creek Falls. Elevation 10,040 feet. Trails go every which way in this area. After viewing the falls, return to the GRT and go basically straight ahead and uphill at the trail junction.

4.7 The trail curves to the right, but if you walk a few feet to the left, you can view the top of South Willow Creek Falls.

5.3 The trail crosses an avalanche chute. 401635mE 4387094mN The trail continues up and curves to the left at mile 6.9 into beautiful flower-filled meadows.

7.2 Cross a little creek and in a few feet, take a sharp right onto a faint trail and in a few more feet, cross the creek again as you head north toward Red-Buffalo Pass. 399464mE 4385735 mN

7.5 As you approach a group of trees, leave the trail you're on and head northwest cross-country toward Red-Buffalo Pass until you find the trail that goes to the top of the pass. 399434mE 4386018mN

7.9 Reach the top of Red-Buffalo Pass. Elevation 11,745 feet. 399073mE 4386386mN Enjoy the scenery for a while and eat a snack. Turn left (south) and look for cairns. After

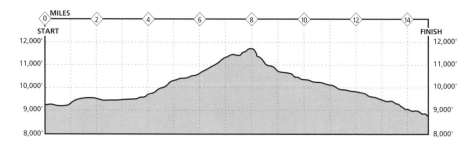

the first cairn angle a little to the right around a depression and continue on that little ridge until you see the next cairn. Two more cairns should follow.

8.0 At the fourth cairn from the top of the pass, turn right (west) and head downhill. 399046mE 4386262mN Stay in the meadow to the right of the drop-off. The cairns and trail are not always easy to see, but just keep angling downhill until you find the trail, which is well defined.

8.1 The trail makes a left switchback and becomes obvious. 398876mE 4386360mN Just beyond the switchback, the trail appears to Y. Take the right branch that heads downhill through beautiful flower-filled meadows.

8.8 Cross Gore Creek. 398488mE 4385683mN The trail heads uphill and into the forest from here.

9.1 Flower-filled meadows line Gore Creek. Look behind you to see the steep west side of Red-Buffalo Pass that you just descended. 398224mE 4386064mN

9.7 The trail traverses a slab of granite by an avalanche path. Watch for a cairn that marks the trail. 397670mE 4386666mN The trail continues across another avalanche path and moist areas with waist-high flowers that sometimes hide the trail.

10.4 The trail seems to go in various directions near a campsite here. Continue on the trail across the meadow. Look ahead to the right (northwest) to find a sign in a tree across Gore Creek. That's where the trail goes.

10.5 Cross Gore Creek and arrive at the junction with the Gore Lake Trail. 396623mE 4386620mN Check out the Recen brothers' graves before heading downhill (west) to the Gore Creek Trail trailhead.

12.0 The trail is next to a bend in the river. In about 0.2 mile, big granite boulders and rock slabs appear along the trail. Aspen start interspersing with the conifers at about 12.4 miles.

13.0 The trail crosses a braided creek. 393053mE 4387099mN Find your way across as best as possible. To the left you can use a one-log bridge if your balance is good. The trail continues from the log bridge, or if you cross higher up, stay to the left to find the trail. The trail now becomes a rocky roller coaster traversing a steep rocky slope then a jungle of thick vegetation.

13.8 Pass nice cascades in Gore Creek.

14.4 The trail climbs to the top of a little knoll. You can see I-70 through the trees. 391191mE 4387164mN

14.8 Arrive at the junction with the Deluge Lake Trail that takes off to the right (north). Continue straight and downhill. 390781mE 4387103mN The Eagles Nest Wilderness boundary is just beyond the trail junction.

14.9 Arrive at the Gore Creek Trail trailhead and your waiting vehicle. You made it! 390634mE 4387004mN Elevation 8,716 feet.

Options:

1. For a shorter hike start at the Mesa Cortina Trail trailhead and follow the directions to South Willow Creek Falls. Return the way you came for a 9-mile out-and-back hike.

2. Start at the Mesa Cortina Trail trailhead and follow the directions to the top of Red-Buffalo Pass. Return the way you came for a 15.8-mile out-and-back hike.

3. Start at the Gore Creek Trail trailhead and follow the directions in reverse to the top of Red-Buffalo Pass. Return the way you came for a 14.0-mile out-and-back hike.

4. Start at Gore Creek Trail trailhead and hike the trail in reverse. The climb uphill is steeper, but the end of the day is a more gentle hike.

Hike Information

Local Information

Summit County Chamber of Commerce, (800) 530-3099, www.summitchamber.org
Summit Visitor Information Center, Outlets at Silverthorne, 246 Rainbow Drive, Silverthorne; (970) 262-0817
Town of Silverthorne, www.silverthorne.org, (970) 262-7300
Vail Valley Chamber & Tourism Bureau, (970) 476-1000, (800) 653-4523, www.visitvail valley.com

Local Events/Attractions

Betty Ford Alpine Gardens, 183 Gore Creek Drive, Vail; (970) 476-0103; www.bettyford alpinegardens.org
Bravo! Vail Valley Music Festival, Vail and Beaver Creek, (877) 812-5700, www.vail musicfestival.org
Colorado Ski Hall of Fame, Vail and East Meadow Drives, Vail; (800) 950-7410, (970) 476-1876; www.coloradoskihalloffame.com
Vail International Dance Festival, Vail and Beaver Creek, (970) 949-1999, www.vvf.org
Blue River Festival, Town of Silverthorne, (970) 262-7390

Accommodations

Gore Creek Campground is just across Gore Creek from the Gore Creek Trail trailhead. For information, contact White River National Forest, Holy Cross Ranger District, (970)

827-5175, www.fs.fed.us/r2/whiteriver. Several campgrounds are also located along the shores of Dillon Reservoir near Frisco. For more information, contact White River National Forest, Dillon Ranger District, (970) 468-5400, www.dillonrangerdistrict.com.

Restaurants

China Gourmet, Highway 9 and Annie Road (by Target), Silverthorne; (970) 262-668
Fiesta Jalisco, Summit Place Shopping Center, Silverthorne; (970) 468-6663
MiZuppa, 2161 North Frontage Road West, Vail; (970) 476-0933
Sunshine Cafe, Summit Place Shopping Center, Silverthorne; (970) 468-9552

Hike Tours

Trail Wise Guides, (800) 261-5364 or (970) 827-5363, www.trailwiseguides.com
Vail Nature Center, Vail, (970) 479-2291, www.vailrec.com/venues_naturecenter

Organizations

Friends of the Eagles Nest Wilderness, www.fenw.org, or call Dillon Ranger District, (970) 468-5400, for the current contact.

Public Transportation (free)

Summit Stage, (970) 668-0999, www.summit stage.com
Vail Transit, (970) 479-2178, www.vailgov.com

9 Dillon Peninsula

The Dillon Reservoir Recreation Area offers easy hiking opportunities in the Dillon Nature Preserve Open Space. The mostly flat gated dirt road to the West Portal of the Roberts Tunnel is hikable year-round while the forested Meadow Loop and Ridge Trails can sometimes be obscured by snow. Various combinations of the two trails and road provide shorter or longer walks all with fantastic views of Dillon Reservoir, Dillon, the Gore Range, and the Tenmile Range. Interpretive signs created by fourth and fifth graders at Dillon Valley Elementary School add insight into the area and its inhabitants, both wild and human.

Start: At the parking lot off U.S. Highway 6 across from Cemetery Road
Distance: 5.3-mile loop and lollipop for all the trails (see Options for various hikes)
Approximate hiking time: 2 to 3.5 hours
Difficulty: Easy
Elevation gain: 225 feet
Trail surface: Paved recreational path, gated dirt road, and dirt trail
Seasons: Best from late May to late October (dirt road is year-round)
Other trail users: Bikes on paved trail

Canine compatibility: Dogs must be on leash.
Land status: Town of Dillon
Nearest town: Dillon
Fees and permits: No fees or permits required
Maps: USGS map: Frisco; National Geographic Trails Illustrated: #108 Vail, Frisco, Dillon
Trail contact: Town of Dillon, 275 Lake Dillon Drive, Dillon; (970) 468-2403; www.townof dillon.com
Other: Other than Dillon Reservoir, no water exists along these trails.

Finding the trailhead: From Interstate 70 exit 205, Silverthorne/Dillon, drive approximately 3.5 miles east on U.S. Highway 6 to Cemetery Road (on the left). Turn right (southwest) across from Cemetery Road and drive 0.1 mile to the recreation path parking lot. No facilities are available at the trailhead although a porta-potty might occasionally be there. *DeLorme: Colorado Atlas & Gazetteer:* Page 38 C2

The Hike

The Dillon Nature Preserve contains two trails but is first and foremost a nature preserve. Keep your eyes open for fox, pine squirrels, deer, red-tailed hawks, and ospreys. Being lower than many trails in central Summit County, the snow melts sooner and the flowers bloom earlier here.

This peninsula, which juts out into Dillon Reservoir along the Snake River inlet, has seen many changes over time. Bison (buffalo), deer, elk, and antelope used to feed in the lush valley now covered by water. Indians, mainly Utes, followed the game here in summer. Mountain men once rendezvoused in La Bonte's Hole where the Snake and Blue Rivers and Tenmile Creek converged. (Today the confluence lies underwater southeast of Dillon Dam.) La Bonte the man remains a mystery—perhaps a French Canadian trapper lent his name to the area.

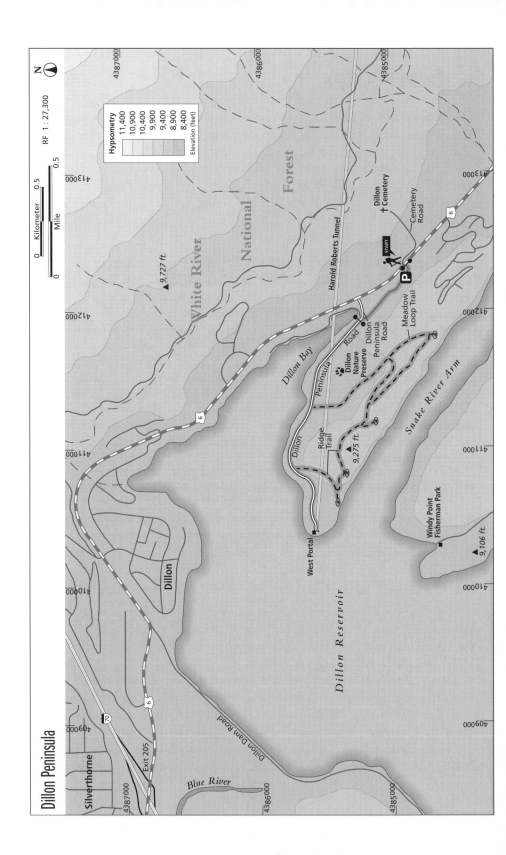

The rush for gold in the 1860s brought miners to the south and the east of La Bonte's Hole. With the Homestead Act of 1862, homesteaders claimed their 160 acres of public land by building a house and working the land. Ranchers around Dillon and down the Lower Blue Valley grew crops and raised cattle which fed the miners and other Summit County residents.

By the early 1870s, entrepreneurs built a stage stop and trading post near the confluence of the rivers in La Bonte's Hole. The growing settlement gained a post office in 1879. The Denver & Rio Grande railroad reached Dillon in 1882 and the rival Denver, South Park, and Pacific arrived in 1883. The town of Dillon incorporated on January 26, 1883, on the northeast side of the Snake River. But Dillon soon moved just south of the confluence of the three rivers to be closer to both railroads. Citizens again moved their town west of Tenmile Creek, but still close to transportation. Dillon became a hub for the ranches and farms of the area. Herds of cattle bound for Denver were driven along roads to the Dillon depot. Ore and lumber hauled by wagon to Dillon were loaded onto trains for transport.

▶ Volunteers for Outdoor Colorado (VOC) is a nonprofit organization established in 1984, which sponsors work projects throughout Colorado from April to October, partnering with various land management agencies. For more information contact VOC at (303) 715-1010 or (800) 925-2220 or log onto www.voc.org.

Dillon moved a fourth time when the Denver Water Board (DWB) started to build a reservoir to provide water for its customers. As early as 1910, plans were drawn to divert water from the Blue River drainage to the east slope for growing Denver. DWB started buying water rights on the West Slope. In 1927, alternate plans were filed showing a dam across the Blue River just below the three-river confluence. A 23.3-mile tunnel would transport the water to the South Platte River and on to Denver. When times were tough during the depression, DWB purchased many properties in and around Dillon at tax sales. In 1955, DWB met with citizens of Dillon to discuss their plans and hear concerns. Never mind the concerns, plans for the dam and tunnel progressed. Dillon would be moved to a hill to the north. Some people moved and others stayed in place. The DWB informed remaining residents that they had to evacuate Dillon by August 1, 1961. Clearing for the dam started in April 1960. The earthen dam required twelve million tons of fill dirt. Some buildings from Old Dillon moved to New Dillon and some to the Silverthorne area. Over 300 graves had to be moved from the Dillon Cemetery, established in 1885, to the new cemetery along US 6.

Workers completed the dam in July 1963, and water storage began in September of that year. Dillon Reservoir has a 24.5-mile shoreline and can store about 85.5 billion gallons of water.

Miles and Directions

These directions describe hiking all the possible trails and road at the same time. With four possible hikes here, choose your own hike.

0.0 Start at the gate at the northwest end of the parking lot. 412285mE 4384855mN Elevation 9,110 feet. Turn right (northwest) and walk on the paved recreation path heading northwest.

0.3 Arrive at the Dillon Nature Preserve Open Space sign and junction with the Dillon Peninsula Road. 411930mE 4385215mN Turn left (northwest) and walk on the gated dirt road.

0.8 Come to the junction of the dirt road and the Ridge and Meadow Loop Trails. 411282mE 4385605mN Elevation 9,050 feet. Turn left (south) here and follow the trail up the meadow. Watch for interesting interpretive signs along the way.

1.3 Arrive at the junction of Ridge and Meadow Loop Trails. 411631mE 4385021mN Turn right (southwest) here.

1.5 Come to the junction of Ridge and Meadow Loop Trails. 411333mE 4385156mN Turn left (southeast) here to hike Meadow Loop Trail.

2.0 Arrive at the junction of Meadow Loop Trail and a side trail to an overlook bench. 411799mE 4384705mN The bench is approximately 210 feet out and back.

2.25 Back at the Junction of Ridge and Meadow Loop Trails. 411631mE 4385021mN Turn left here to explore Ridge Trail. For a shorter hike, head straight down on the trail and return to the parking lot for a 3.5-mile lollipop loop hike.

2.5 Arrive at the junction of Ridge and Meadow Loop Trails. 411333mE 4385156mN Go straight here to continue on Ridge Trail.

2.6 Come to the junction with a trail to an overlook and two interpretive signs. 411151mE 4385216mN Turn left here for the overlook, approximately 425 feet out and back. Return back to this point to continue on Ridge Trail. Climb up to the high point at approximately 9,275 feet.

3.0 Come to a viewpoint on the trail and interpretive sign. 410825mE 4385351mN

3.2 Arrive at the junction with a trail to an overlook. 410691mE 4385418mN Turn left (west) to the overlook. The trail goes up a rocky stretch and ends at a Denver Water Board boundary. Approximately 0.1 mile out and back. Return the way you came to the junction. Turn left if you went to the overlook or turn right if you don't go to the overlook.

3.3 Stop and read the Town of Dillon interpretive sign.

3.5 Arrive at the junction of Ridge Trail and Dillon Peninsula Road. 410851mE 4385757mN Turn left (southwest) and walk on the dirt road to the West Portal of the Roberts Tunnel.

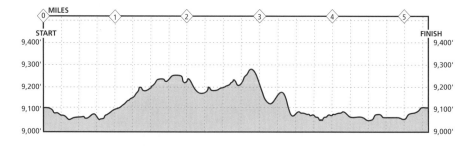

3.9 Arrive at the end of the road near the West Portal of the Roberts Tunnel. Nice views over Dillon Reservoir. Elevation 9,060 feet. 410395mE 4385576mN

4.6 The junction of the road and the Ridge and Meadow Loop Trails. 411282mE 4385605mN Continue on the dirt road.

5.0 Back to the Dillon Nature Preserve Open Space sign and junction with the gated Dillon Peninsula Road. 411930mE 4385215mN Turn right (southeast) here onto the paved recreation path.

5.3 Arrive back at the recreation path trailhead and parking lot.

Options:

1. Dillon Peninsula dirt road. Follow the directions above but stay on the dirt road for an easy, year-round 2.9-mile out-and-back hike.

2. Meadow Creek Loop. Follow the directions above but at mile 2.25, head downhill to the road and turn right to return to the parking lot. This option is an easy, 3.5-mile lollipop hike.

3. Ridge Trail. Follow the directions above but at mile 1.5 continue straight ahead on Ridge Trail until it meets the road. Turn right to return to the parking lot. This option is an easy, 3.8-mile lollipop hike.

DILLON PENINSULA BECOMES OPEN SPACE Over the years, the Denver Water Board (DWB) had purchased many acres of land for their water projects. By the 1990s, DWB decided it best not to keep land it wasn't using. DWB and the Town of Dillon entered into discussions about excess DWB land near Dillon Reservoir. DWB gave Dillon 173 acres for parks and open space but kept forty-nine acres adjacent to US 6, which the town zoned for fourteen single-family residences while allowing that density to be transferred to other DWB land on the east side of US 6. DWB also kept eighteen acres at the peninsula's tip, where the Roberts Tunnel West Portal is located.

The Town of Dillon, DWB, and Summit County reached an agreement on July 16, 1996, to protect the 173 acres of open space as a conservation easement. In 1998, Dillon's town manager asked Volunteers for Outdoor Colorado (VOC) if they would be interested in building a formal trail system the following summer. VOC enthusiastically agreed to the project.

The Town of Dillon and Dillon Valley Elementary School have had a history of partnering on community projects. The interpretive signs created by the fourth and fifth graders at the school were made possible by a grant received by the Town of Dillon from Great Outdoors Colorado (GOCO). The Town pitched in $2,475 while GOCO provided $5,775.

Partnerships created the wonderful hiking area along Dillon Reservoir.

Hike Information

Local Information

Summit County Chamber of Commerce, (800) 530-3099, www.summitchamber.org

Summit Visitor Information Center, Outlets at Silverthorne, 246 Rainbow Drive, Silverthorne; (970) 262-0817

Town of Dillon, (970) 468-2403, www.townofdillon.com

Local Events/Attractions

BBQ at the Summit, Dillon, (970) 468-2403, www.townofdillon.com

Dillon Schoolhouse Museum, 403 La Bonte Street, Dillon; (970) 468-2207; www.summit historical.org

Lake Dillon Theatre, 146 Lake Dillon Drive, Dillon; (970) 513-9386; www.townof dillon.com

Accommodations

Several campgrounds are located along the shores of Dillon Reservoir near Frisco. For more information contact White River National Forest, Dillon Ranger District, (970) 468-5400, www.fs.fed.us/r2/whiteriver, www.dillonrangerdistrict.com.

Restaurants

Arapahoe Cafe and Pub Down Under, 636 Lake Dillon Drive, Dillon; (970) 468-0873 (building moved from Old Dillon)

Dillon Dam Brewery, 754 Anemone Trail and US 6, Dillon; (970) 262-7777; www.dam brewery.com

Ristorante al Lago, 240 Lake Dillon Drive, Dillon; (970) 468-6111

Wild Bill's Pizza and Saloon, 119 LaBonte (downstairs), Dillon; (970) 468-2006; www.wildbillspizza.com

Organizations

Dillon Reservoir Recreation Area Committee, Frisco, (970) 668-4060

10 Chihuahua Lake

The hike to spectacular Chihuahua Lake (an unnamed lake on topo maps) travels first along a four-wheel-drive road through a beautiful and serene high alpine valley. Two 14,000-foot peaks, Torreys and Grays, guard the valley's eastern flank. At road's end, a single-track trail continues toward the Continental Divide and wanders above tree-line. The lake is tucked in a high bowl at 12,400 feet above a cliff band, which the trail breaks through via a steep slippery section. Wildflowers and willows line the trail, which makes umpteen creek crossings along its route.

Start: At the junction of Chihuahua Gulch Road (Forest Road 263) and Peru Creek Road (Forest Road 260)
Distance: 7.7 miles out and back
Approximate hiking time: 3 to 6 hours
Difficulty: More Difficult
Elevation gain: 1,765 feet
Trail surface: Dirt road and dirt trail
Seasons: Best from July to early October
Other trail users: Motorized users, equestrians, mountain bikers
Canine compatibility: Dogs permitted (must be under voice control)
Land status: National forest
Nearest town: Keystone

Fees and permits: No fees or permits required
Maps: USGS maps: Grays Peak, Montezuma; National Geographic Trails Illustrated: #104, Idaho Springs and Loveland Pass
Trail contact: White River National Forest, Dillon Ranger District, 680 Blue River Parkway, Silverthorne; (970) 468-5400; www.fs.fed.us/r2/whiteriver, www.dillonrangerdistrict.com
Other: A 1.5-mile section of the trail is above treeline. Keep an eye and ear open for thunderstorms and lightning and turn back if the weather turns bad. The first 2.15 miles of this hike are on a dirt four-wheel-drive road. You may encounter motorized vehicles on this section.

Finding the trailhead: From Interstate 70 exit 205, Silverthorne/Dillon, drive 7.9 miles southeast through Dillon and Keystone to the Montezuma exit. Drive on Montezuma Road past Keystone's River Run for 4.5 miles to the Peru Creek Road Trailhead. To the left you will see a big dirt parking area. Turn left into the parking area, which is the start of Forest Development Road (FDR) 260, Peru Creek Road. The dirt road is narrow and bumpy and gets rougher the farther you drive. Drive on Peru Creek Road for 2.1 miles to the junction with FDR 263, Chihuahua Gulch Road (the sign says Chihuahua Trail). Park on the right. Start hiking on FDR 263 to the left. If you have a four-wheel-drive vehicle, you may be able to drive 2.15 miles up FDR 263 to its end depending on road conditions. Most vehicles should be able to drive to the Chihuahua Gulch Road Trailhead, but if not, parking is available near the bridge over Peru Creek at 1.0 mile. No facilities are available at the trailhead. *DeLorme: Colorado Atlas & Gazetteer: Page 38 C4*

Special considerations: Hunters use this area during hunting season. The Peru Creek Road is closed by snow at the big dirt parking lot by Montezuma Road. Skiers, snowshoers, and snowmobilers enjoy the snowy road in winter. Be aware of avalanche conditions once you cross Peru Creek. The Chihuahua Gulch Road is neither marked nor maintained for winter use.

Chihuahua Lake in mid-July

The Hike

The short-lived town of Chihuahua once boasted a population of 200 people. As with other towns in the area, some confusion reigns as to the origin of its name. Some people claim it was named for the Mexican state, but others state it came from an old Indian chief called Shu-wa-wa. In September 1879 five men created the first settlement, which prospered just downstream from the trailhead. The town was incorporated in 1880. Situated in one of the richest mining districts in the state, Chihuahua became a top mining camp.

According to the June 24, 1882, issue of the *Montezuma Millrun:* "There are now fifty-four substantial buildings in town; one hotel kept by Michael Fallon; three restaurants; three saloons; two grocery stores; a butcher shop; and one large dry goods store, owned by B. Zemansky."

The *Millrun* article further claimed that "There are no physicians as their services are never required. . . . There are two lawyers, but they might as well take in their shingles, as there is nothing for them to do; the people being honest, virtuous, and happy." Town residents contended that they needed no clergy because Chihuahua had no sinners.

Some sinners did exist in the district because a story is told about a triple lynching near town. Three road agents murdered two prospectors who lived in Chihuahua.

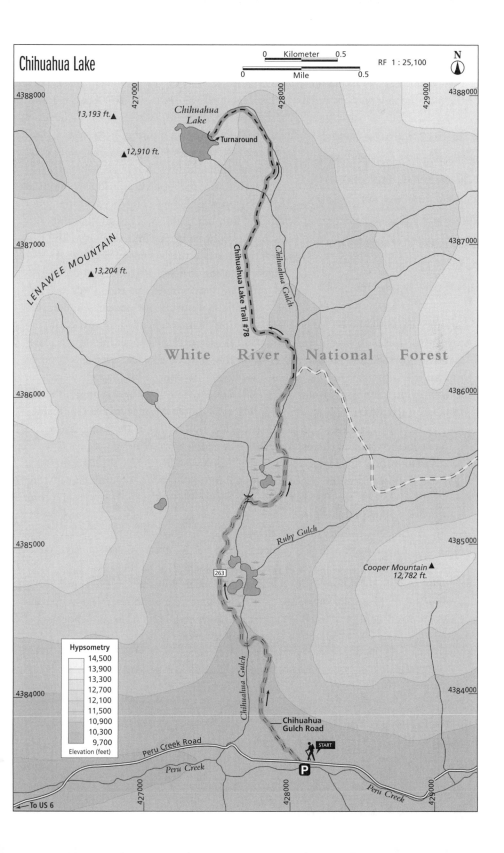

Townspeople quickly learned about the murders, and a group raced out to find the three assassins. They found the criminals near the top of Ruby Mountain and hanged them on the spot without a trial. The five dead men were buried in two separate graves.

▶ **Asa Gray, known as the father of American botany, was a close friend of Charles Darwin. Gray and John Torrey published the two volume set, *Flora of North America,* the first comprehensive books on the subject. Grays and Torreys Peaks are named after these botanists.**

In July 1882, the *Millrun* reported: "The gold strike at Chihuahua is promising better every day." The Congress Mine, located above Chihuahua, contained both gold and silver, a rare occurrence.

Chihuahua's school had twenty-four children in 1881–1882, and residents considered it the finest school in Summit County. The schoolhouse was built in the local cemetery, and while the children played, they learned the legends of the buried.

One problem that afflicted Chihuahua and its sister cities up Peru Creek was transportation. The high cost of shipping ore and supplies limited the amount that could be mined and moved. Mine owners depended on strings of burros and/or mules to haul merchandise and ores across the rugged mountain passes and trails. In 1882, the Sisapo Mill in Montezuma reportedly had over one hundred tons of ore sitting around because of inadequate transportation. Wagons were built to haul 9,000 pounds. In winter, stock pulled sleds along the snowy routes. Although the Union Pacific thought about extending a rail line to Montezuma or Chihuahua, they only laid their rails as far as Keystone. By the late 1880s the mines started to play out in the Chihuahua area. Discouraged, people started moving away.

Disaster struck the idyllic town in 1889. A forest fire swept through the area, destroying most of the town. Burning logs almost ruined the wagon road to Montezuma, and the fire threatened to spread over the mountain to that town. No one returned to rebuild Chihuahua.

As you reach treeline, look to the east. The first tall mountain is Grays Peak (14,270 feet); the one north of it is Torreys Peak (14,267 feet). Straight ahead is Grizzly Peak (13,427 feet). Lenawee Mountain (13,204 feet) is to the west.

The trail climbs through the rock band up a steep slope of slippery gravel. Once on top, the trail basically disappears. Just head uphill to a pond—the lake is actually downhill from here in a bowl. Head left to a little saddle then down a short slope, which may be snow-filled, to the large, beautiful lake.

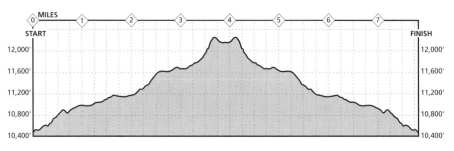

Miles and Directions

0.0 Start at the junction of Peru Creek Road (FDR 260) and Chihuahua Gulch Road (FDR 263). 428093mE 4383542mN Elevation 10,480 feet.

0.6 When you reach the top of a little hill, head left down to the creek crossing.

0.7 Cross Chihuahua Creek. You can head either left or right around the big willow to cross depending on water height. 427728mE 4384351mN

0.9 Water may cover the road. You can hike in either direction around the huge boulder. 427632mE 4384525mN

1.5 Cross Chihuahua Creek again on a plank bridge. 427743mE 4385314mN

1.8 The road Ys. Hike to the left (northwest) on FDR 263. 427975mE 4385626mN

2.2 Arrive at the end of the four-wheel-drive road. Chihuahua Lake Trail #78 starts to the left (north). Several rocks are available to sit on for a break. 427997mE 4386034mN

2.4 The trail goes up steeply here and Ys in two places. Either direction works.

2.5 The trail becomes flatter as it traverses a high alpine meadow and crosses many tiny creeks. 427843mE 4386438mN

3.6 The trail starts to climb steeply through the rock band on your left. The trail has many "ball-bearing" rocks.

3.75 Pond in the high alpine meadow. 427584mE 4387869mN Elevation 12,245 feet. Go to the left side of the pond and head toward the little saddle. Hike down the slope, which may have snow in it. Stay to the right near the big rocks to find a trail if you don't want to walk down the snowfield.

3.9 Chihuahua Lake. 427503mE 4387744mN Elevation 12,195 feet. Return the way you came.

7.7 Arrive back at the trailhead.

Hike Information

Local Information

Keystone Resort, (800) 354–4FUN, (970) 496-2316, www.keystoneresort.com
Summit County Chamber of Commerce, (800) 530-3099, www.summitchamber.org
Summit Visitor Information Center, Outlets at Silverthorne, 246 Rainbow Drive, Silverthorne; (970) 262-0817

Local Events/Attractions

Annual Wine, Jazz & Art Festival, Keystone, (800) 354–4FUN, (970) 496–2316, www .keystoneresort.com
National Repertory Orchestra, (800) 354–4FUN, (970) 496-2316, www.keystoneresort.com
Taste of Keystone, (800) 354–4FUN, (970) 496-2316, www.keystoneresort.com

Restaurants

Dos Locos, 22869 U.S. Highway 6, Keystone; (970) 262-9185

Hiking Tours

Colorado Bike & Ski Tours, P.O. Box 1041, Silverthorne 80498; (970) 668-8900; www.coloradobikeandski.com
At **Keystone Resort,** the Adventure Center offers hiking tours at the ski area during the summer. (800) 354–4FUN, (970) 496-2316, www.keystoneresort.com

Organizations

Friends of Dillon Ranger District, www.fdrd.org, or call Dillon Ranger District, (970) 468-5400, for the current contact.

11 Buffalo Mountain

The huge granite dome called Buffalo Mountain towers above Dillon Reservoir and the towns of Silverthorne, Dillon, and Frisco. Such an imposing mountain attracts climbers and over the years people scrambled up, creating "climbers' trails" to the summit. Buffalo Mountain now boasts a new summit trail that, while still difficult, is much more hiker and environmentally friendly. "Still difficult" means a 23 percent grade for 0.6 mile through a boulder field. The climb is well worth the effort for the views, beautiful tundra flowers, and a chance to see the mountain goat family that grazes on the high slopes.

Start: At the Buffalo Cabin Trail #31 trailhead

Distance: 6.0 miles out and back

Approximate hiking time: 3 to 7 hours

Difficulty: Strenuous

Elevation gain: 3,017 feet

Trail surface: Dirt and boulders

Seasons: Best from July to late September

Other trail users: Hikers, equestrians on lower part of trail

Canine compatibility: Dogs must be on leash.

Land status: National forest/wilderness area

Nearest town: Silverthorne

Fees and permits: No fees or permits required

Maps: USGS maps: Vail Pass, Frisco; National Geographic Trails Illustrated: #108 Vail, Frisco, Dillon

Trail contact: White River National Forest, Dillon Ranger District, 680 Blue River Parkway, Silverthorne; (970) 468–5400; www.fs.fed.us/r2/whiteriver, www.dillonrangerdistrict.com

Other: Very little water can be found along this trail and none above Buffalo Cabin. Make sure to bring plenty. Lightning from thunderstorms can be deadly on the upper 1.1 miles of the trail. Make sure to start early and be down below treeline before thunderstorms develop.

Finding the trailhead: From Interstate 70 exit 205, Silverthorne/Dillon, head north on Highway 9 about 0.1 mile to Wildernest Road by the 7-11 store and across from Wendy's. Turn left and follow Wildernest Road (which becomes Ryan Gulch Road) for 3.5 miles. The parking lot for the Buffalo Cabin Trail trailhead is on the left (east) as the road curves. No facilities are available at the trailhead. *DeLorme: Colorado Atlas & Gazetteer:* Page 37 C1.5

Special considerations: Hunters use this area. Avalanches have left two big scars on the east face of Buffalo. Weather can change quickly and unexpectedly, including snow in the middle of July. The trail to Buffalo Cabin is a nice ski or snowshoe tour in winter. Beyond the cabin, the trail is neither marked nor maintained for winter use. Wilderness regulations apply.

The Hike

Buffalo Mountain has long been a landmark in Summit County. Called Buffalo by early settlers who thought it looked like a buffalo's back, the peak towered over La Bonte's Hole below, at the intersection of the Blue River, Snake River, and Tenmile

View from Buffalo Mountain summit toward Mount of the Holy Cross

Creek. Buffalo (bison) grazed in the lush valley during the summer, retreating over Hoosier Pass to South Park for the long winters. Ute Indians summered in the valleys, hunting the plentiful game.

The east face of Buffalo sports a cirque created by glaciers, not a crater formed by volcanic action. The dome shape is the result of its granite eroding off like layers of an onion, not from glaciation. The two avalanche paths show the destructive force of Mother Nature. Trees are growing again in the smaller path. An avalanche in 1986 created the larger path, knocking down hundreds of trees as the white death roared off the tundra after a major snowstorm. Trees still standing at the bottom had other trees skewered in their tops like spears. A second avalanche in 2003 widened and lengthened the path after another period of heavy snow.

The Buffalo Cabin Trail starts innocently enough, passing wetlands and traveling through lodgepole pine forest. When you reach the four-way trail junction and head left (west), make sure to look back to remember what the junction looks like. People have a knack of missing the turnoff on their return and find themselves miles from their car.

The cabins were probably used by miners—locals call the highest cabin ruins Buffalo Cabin. From here, a new trail built by the U.S. Forest Service (USFS) trail

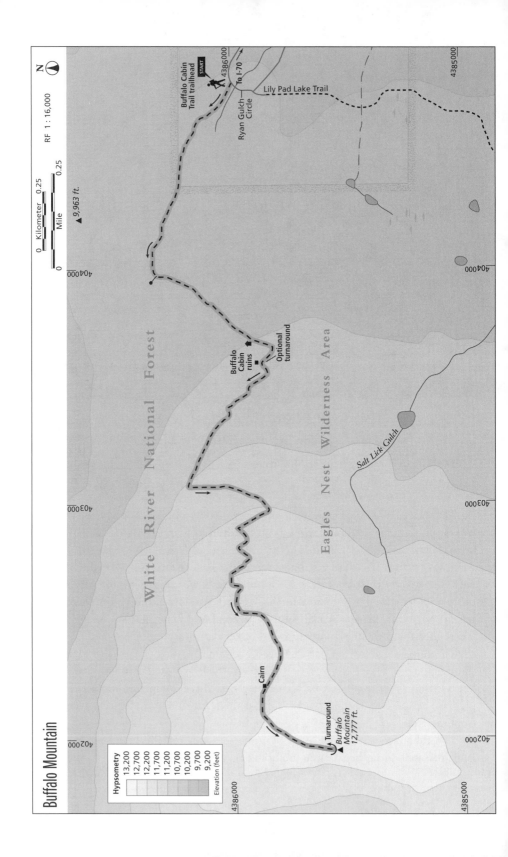

Buffalo Mountain

Hypsometry

Elevation (feet)

- 13,200
- 12,700
- 12,200
- 11,700
- 11,200
- 10,700
- 10,200
- 9,700
- 9,200

RF 1 : 16,000

N

0   Kilometer   0.25

0   Mile   0.25

▲ 9,963 ft.

White River National Forest

Eagles Nest Wilderness Area

Salt Lick Gulch

Buffalo Cabin Trail trailhead

START

Ryan Gulch Circle

To I-70

Lily Pad Lake Trail

Buffalo Cabin ruins

Optional turnaround

Cairn

Turnaround

Buffalo Mountain 12,777 ft.
▲

crew and the Rocky Mountain Youth Corps (RMYC) in summer 2004 switchbacks and climbs steadily through the forest then up through the boulder field. Friends of the Eagles Nest Wilderness (FENW) received a grant from State Parks/Trails to hire RMYC for four weeks of strenuous work. Various community businesses and The Summit Foundation donated matching funds for the grant. The USFS crew worked mainly in the boulder field and above for four weeks, destroying pairs of work gloves in eight days. After the crews completed the new trail, FENW volunteers spent two days building cairns to mark the trail through the boulder field. Volunteers for Outdoor Colorado spent two days revegetating the old braided trail system that had been created over time by hikers.

The trail through the boulder field is steep, but a great improvement over the old trail that was even steeper and consisted of slippery ball-bearing soil. Wildflowers grow between boulders in places and trees struggle to gain a toe hold in soil between the rocks. A sub-peak blocks the view of any incoming weather, and any sound of thunder should advise a quick retreat.

Once above the boulder field, keep an eye open for the family of mountain goats that calls the summit home. They may cooperate and stand still for pictures, while keeping a watchful eye and comfortable distance. Please make sure dogs are on leashes and respect the goats so others may enjoy seeing them.

People have argued over the years whether mountain goats are indigenous to Colorado. The Colorado Division of Wildlife once reported that mountain goats were first introduced into Colorado in 1947 to provide trophy-hunting opportunities. However, after two years of historical research that found documentation that mountain goats roamed Colorado in the 1880s, the Colorado Wildlife Commission declared them a native species.

Buffalo Mountain provides great views of much of Summit County and the Vail area. The scenery, wildlife, and wildflowers reward a successful climb!

Miles and Directions

0.0   Start at the Buffalo Cabin Trail trailhead. 404792mE 385985mN Elevation 9,760 feet.

0.35   Reach the Eagles Nest Wilderness boundary. 404348mE 4386240mN The trail is fairly flat for the next 0.2 mile.

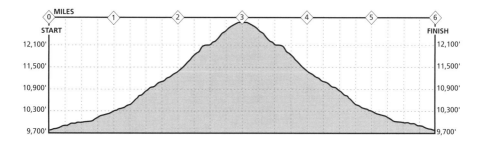

0.6 Reach a four-way junction. 403991mE 4386350mN Turn left and head uphill.

0.9 Come to the first cabin ruins by a little creek, which is the last water along the trail—if the creek is running. 403723mE 4385966mN

1.1 Reach Buffalo Cabin ruins. 403606mE 4385867mN Optional turnaround for a 2.1-mile out-and-back. This is a good rest place—the trail climbs steeply from here.

1.9 The trail enters a boulder field. Look for cairns that mark the rocky trail. 402923mE 4385936mN

2.5 The trail exits the boulder field and crosses the alpine tundra. 4025714mE 4385993mN

2.8 Come to a cairn with a post that marks the final summit climb. Follow the ridgeline. 402201mE 4385882mN

3.0 Reach the summit. Elevation 12,777 feet. Two rock windbreaks about 200 feet apart provide some shelter and great views. 401954mE 4385627mN Return the way you came.

6.0 Arrive back at the trailhead.

Option: Hike to Buffalo Cabin ruins for an easy 2.1-mile out-and-back hike with a 600-foot elevation gain.

FRIENDS OF THE EAGLES NEST WILDERNESS When local journalist M. John Fayhee tagged along on a three-day backpack in the Eagles Nest Wilderness one summer with two U.S. Forest Service wilderness rangers, he was appalled by their lack of resources. He wrote a column about their financial plight in the Summit Daily News that spurred the formation of Friends of the Eagles Nest Wilderness (FENW) in May 1994. The group began to help the Dillon Ranger District of the White River National Forest maintain and preserve the Summit County portions of the Eagles Nest and Ptarmigan Peak Wildernesses. Only three wilderness portal signs existed in the two wildernesses in those days. About 25 percent of Summit County is congressionally designated wilderness. Since 1994 the group has received grants and raised funds to install portal signs and bulletin boards with interpretive posters and to host three trail maintenance projects each year. In 2005, FENW started a noxious weed treatment program and Volunteer Wilderness Steward program, which includes volunteer rangers. Starting in summer 2006, FENW is expanding its programs and volunteer opportunities to help the Holy Cross Ranger District to maintain and preserve the Eagle County portions of the Eagles Nest and Holy Cross Wildernesses. To help FENW with their efforts or for more information about how a grassroots group can make a difference, log onto www.fenw.org or contact the Dillon Ranger District, (970) 468-5400, for the current contact. Citizen support may be what protects and maintains the Eagles Nest, Holy Cross, and Ptarmigan Peak Wilderness areas throughout time.

Hike Information

Local Information
Summit County Chamber of Commerce, (800) 530-3099, www.summitchamber.org
Summit Visitor Information Center, Outlets at Silverthorne, 246 Rainbow Drive, Silverthorne; (970) 262-0817
Town of Silverthorne, www.silverthorne.org, (970) 262-7300

Local Events/Attractions
Blue River Festival, Town of Silverthorne, (970) 262-7390

Accommodations
Several campgrounds are located along the shores of Dillon Reservoir near Frisco. For more information, contact White River National Forest, Dillon Ranger District, (970)

468-5400, www.fs.fed.us/r2/whiteriver, www.dillonrangerdistrict.com.

Restaurants
China Gourmet, Highway 9 and Annie Road (by Target), Silverthorne; (970) 262-6688
Fiesta Jalisco, Summit Place Shopping Center, Silverthorne; (970) 468-6663
Sunshine Café, Summit Place Shopping Center, Silverthorne; (970) 468-9552

Organizations
Friends of the Eagles Nest Wilderness, www.fenw.org, or call the Dillon Ranger District, (970) 468-5400, for the current contact.

Public Transportation (free)
Summit Stage, (970) 668-0999, www.summit stage.com

12 Lily Pad Lake

Lily Pad Lake is a very popular destination especially from the Lily Pad Lake Trail #50 trailhead (see Option 2). Hiking the complete trail from Frisco to Ryan Gulch provides the most diverse scenery and wildflowers. The Summit Stage bus provides a nice shuttle opportunity with just one vehicle. Lily Pad Lake is actually two lakes, with Buffalo Mountain towering above. Good views of the Frisco area can be seen along the trail from the Meadow Creek trailhead. This trail section also contains the best variety of wildflowers. The hike from Ryan Gulch is easy and popular year-round.

Start: At either the Meadow Creek Trail #33 trailhead near Frisco or the Lily Pad Lake Trail #50 trailhead (Ryan Gulch) near Silverthorne (see Options for various possibilities)
Distance: 3.3 miles point to point
Approximate hiking time: 1.5 to 2.5 hours
Difficulty: Moderate (easy for one option)
Elevation gain: 795 feet (160 feet for one option)
Trail surface: Dirt trail
Seasons: Year-round from Ryan Gulch
Other trail users: Equestrians

Canine compatibility: Dogs must be on leash.
Land status: National forest/wilderness area
Nearest towns: Silverthorne and Frisco
Fees and permits: No fees or permits required
Map: USGS map: Frisco; National Geographic Trails Illustrated: #108 Vail, Frisco, Dillon
Trail contact: White River National Forest, Dillon Ranger District, 680 Blue River Parkway, Silverthorne; (970) 468-5400; www.fs.fed.us/r2/whiteriver, www.dillonrangerdistrict.com
Other: Water is sparse along parts of the trail.

Finding the trailheads: To reach the Meadow Creek Trail trailhead near Frisco: From Interstate 70 exit 203, Frisco/Breckenridge, as you drive around the elk roundabout, turn right (southwest) onto the dirt frontage road (not the one that says private drive). The dirt road dead-ends at the trailhead in 0.6 mile. No facilities are available at the trailhead. The Frisco Transfer Station for the Summit Stage is located behind Safeway on the south side of I–70, about a 1.0-mile walk from the trailhead.

To reach the Lily Pad Lake Trail trailhead (Ryan Gulch) near Silverthorne: From I–70 exit 205, Silverthorne/Dillon, drive north on Highway 9 about 0.1 mile to Wildernest Road by the 7-11 store and across from Wendy's. Turn left (southwest) and follow Wildernest Road (which becomes Ryan Gulch Road) for 3.5 miles. The parking lot for the Lily Pad Lake Trail trailhead is on the left (southeast) as the road curves. No facilities are available at the trailhead. To reach the trailhead, walk south on the road to where a road takes off on the right. You'll see the trailhead sign. (**Note:** This parking area also serves the Buffalo Cabin Trail so be sure to find the correct trailhead.) The Summit Stage has a bus stop near the parking area. *DeLorme: Colorado Atlas & Gazetteer:* Page 37 C1.5

Special considerations: The best winter hike is from the Lily Pad Lake Trail trailhead in Ryan Gulch. Please comply with wilderness regulations.

The Hike

When you arrive at Lily Pad Lake, the bigger of the two lakes, you might wonder why it has no lily pads on it. The lake used to be smaller, but beavers built a dam and enlarged it. The yellow pondlilies did not like the enlarged lake, perhaps because of the change in depth or water flow. The smaller lake is probably a kettle pond left over from glacial times, and sports a large quantity of yellow pondlilies. Watch closely for duck families that enjoy swimming among the lilies. The little ducklings appear to be walking on water as they waddle across the green pads.

If you hike up Meadow Creek Trail to the west end of the Lily Pad Lake Trail and then on to Lily Pad Lake, a few viewpoints offer you vistas of Frisco and Dillon Reservoir. Much of the land under water and the area along I–70 used to be ranch land. To the south and east of Lily Pad Lake, the Giberson family once owned 720 acres where they raised beef cattle, ten to twelve milk cows, and ten to twelve horses. The ranch started small at 160 acres in 1909. In 1916 through provisions of the Homestead Act of 1862, they added 160 acres to their spread. They used all the land behind the ranch for grazing, including the lake the family called Pond Lily (today's Lily Pad Lake). Even back in those days the U.S. government charged a fee of about 50 cents a head to graze cattle on national forest lands. The family didn't own a tractor at first, and planting and harvesting hay was done manually with the help of a team of horses. The annual cattle sale brought cash to the family. The Gibersons also sold dairy products to people in the area and shipped cream via train to creameries in Denver. The family leased then purchased an additional 400 acres. Today only 189 acres remain of the Giberson Ranch. Of those, 179 acres are a conservation easement called the Giberson Pre-

Lily Pad Lake and Buffalo Mountain

serve held by the Continental Divide Land Trust. The preserve is private (no public access), protecting elk habitat, meadows, wetlands, the forest, and the view corridor from Frisco.

Before the Meadow Creek Trail intersects with the Lily Pad Lake Trail, you'll pass the ore chute for the Foremost Mine on the left (south). The mine is farther up the flank of Chief Mountain to the west and produced lead ore into the early 1900s.

Hiking in from Ryan Gulch Road, the Lily Pad Trail intersects with Salt Lick Trail. Salt Lick Gulch once contained a hydraulic mining operation. Over 1.5 miles of wooden pipe carried water from North Tenmile Creek to the gulch. Parts of the wooden flume still hang on the east side of Chief Mountain, easily seen from I–70. The water pipes/flume brought water at 150 pounds per square inch to the cone-shaped pit in Salt Lick Gulch. Hydraulic guns loosened gravel on the walls of the pit. The water then moved the gravel through a hydraulic elevator and deposited it in a sluice with riffles to separate the gold from the gravel. The effects of hydraulic mining can be seen from I–70 driving up Silverthorne Hill just past the Wildernest subdivision.

Hiking in from Ryan Gulch Road, a little boulder field to the right (north) at about 0.7 mile seems to be a favorite with younger hikers. This very family-friendly

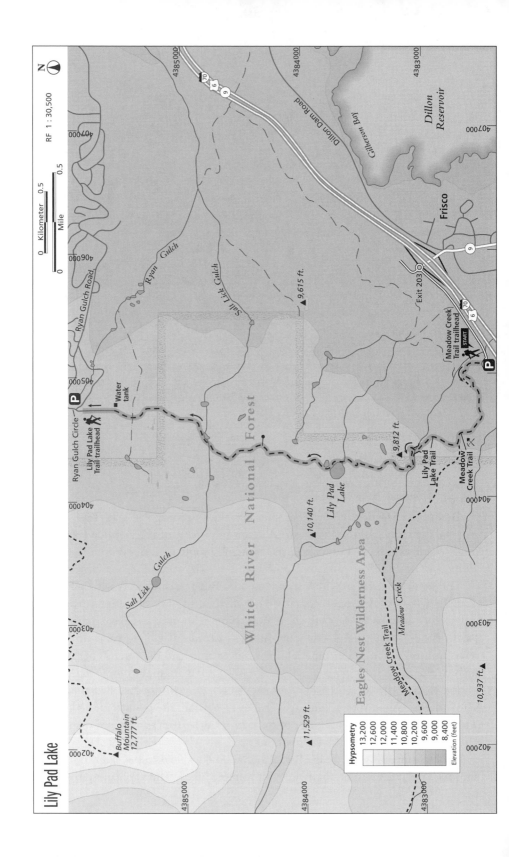

Lily Pad Lake

RF 1 : 30,500

trail is 3.2 miles out and back with just a 160-foot elevation gain. The trail travels mainly through lodgepole pine forest but passes several beaver ponds and wetter areas where the vegetation change is quite obvious.

Miles and Directions

These instructions are for the 3.3-mile point-to-point hike from the Meadow Creek Trail trailhead to the Lily Pad Lake Trail trailhead.

0.0 Start at the Meadow Creek Trail trailhead. 405076mE 4382521mN Elevation: 9,155 feet.

0.5 Look for the old mine relics to your left. 404508mE 4382704mN

0.6 Arrive at the junction of Meadow Creek and Lily Pad Lake Trails. Turn right (northeast) onto Lily Pad Lake Trail. 404451mE 4382719mN

0.8 Cross Meadow Creek on a nice bridge and in a few feet find the Eagles Nest Wilderness portal sign. 404386mE 4383041mN

1.2 Stop to enjoy the nice view of Grays and Torreys Peaks, Dillon Reservoir, Tenderfoot Mountain, and the Keystone Ski Area runs. 404298mE 4383324mN

1.4 The trail appears to Y. Stay on the main trail to the left. 404300mE 4383576mN

1.6 Nice view of Lily Pad Lake and Buffalo Mountain. A little farther up the trail on the right is a little pond with lily pads in it.

1.7 Trail to Ryan Gulch end of the Lily Pad Lake Trail goes to the right (northeast) here. 404241mE 4383801mN Elevation 9,915 feet.

2.1 Come to the junction of Lily Pad Lake and Salt Lick Trails. Continue on the left (northwest) on Lily Pad Lake Trail. High point of the hike. Elevation 9,951 feet. 404448mE 4384356mN

2.5 The trail Ys in two places. Stay on the main trail which is to the right then the left in either direction you are walking. 404513mE 4384850mN

3.0 Cross the Eagles Nest Wilderness boundary. 404657mE 4385408mN

3.2 The trail becomes a dirt road with a big water tank on the right.

3.3 Arrive at the Lily Pad Lake Trail trailhead on Ryan Gulch Road. Elevation 9,789 feet. 404738mE 4385878mN Walk to your waiting vehicle, or the Summit Stage bus stop is just to your left.

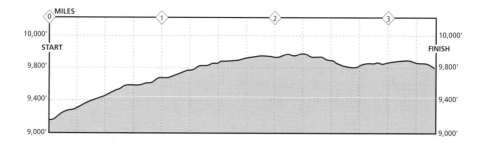

Options:

1. A moderate 3.3-mile out-and-back from the Meadow Creek Trail trailhead to Lily Pad Lake and back.

2. An easy 3.2-mile out-and-back from the Lily Pad Lake Trail trailhead to Lily Pad Lake and back.

3. A moderate 6.5-mile out-and-back hike from the Meadow Creek Trail trailhead to the Lily Pad Lake Trail trailhead on Ryan Gulch road and then return to Meadow Creek (or vice versa).

WINTER HIKING
When winter brings a blanket of snow to Colorado's mountains, don't hibernate! Cross-country skis and snowshoes open a new world to summer hikers. Many trails are still used in the winter, and ski trails are often marked with blue diamonds (but not in wilderness areas). Orange diamonds denote snowmobile routes. Unmarked trails may be extremely hard to find as a snow-blanketed forest looks very different. Also be aware of and avoid avalanche danger.

The type of equipment you buy depends on how you are going to use it. Lightweight, small snowshoes are great on packed trails, but sink in deep, off-trail snow where larger snowshoes work better. Snowshoeing is like walking with wide and long feet. Hiking or ski poles can help with balance.

For backcountry skiing, wider skis than those made for groomed Nordic Center trails are typically used. For novices or spring skiing, waxless skis are the way to go. As you gain skill, Colorado's snow is great for waxed skis. Waxes grip the snow so you don't slide backwards while going uphill but let you slide downhill. Waxless skis work the same but are usually less efficient. Skins placed on the bottom of your skis can help you climb interestingly steep or hard-packed hills (remember avalanche danger though). Backcountry skiers use free-heel bindings which are great for both touring and for telemarking (a downhill turn).

Colorado has fantastic backcountry hut systems. Traveling to these huts requires good winter backcountry and route-finding skills and equipment. Trails may not be obvious and many a skier has camped overnight outdoors without finding the hut.

Summer hiking trails may or may not be the best winter ski trails. Check with the local land management agency for recommended winter trails.

Then have a great winter "hike" on your snowshoes or skis!

Hike Information

Local Information

Frisco Chamber of Commerce, 300 Main Street, Frisco; (970) 668-5547; www.friscocolorado.org
Town of Silverthorne, www.silverthorne.org, (970) 262-7300
Summit County Chamber of Commerce, (800) 530-3099, www.summitchamber.org
Summit Visitor Information Center, Outlets at Silverthorne, 246 Rainbow Drive, Silverthorne; (970) 262-0817

Local Events/Attractions

Blue River Festival, Silverthorne, (970) 262-7390
Coors Colorado Barbecue Challenge, Frisco, www.townoffrisco.com/bbq.html

Accommodations

Several campgrounds are located along the shores of Dillon Reservoir near Frisco. For more information, contact White River National Forest, Dillon Ranger District, (970) 468-5400, www.fs.fed.us/r2/whiteriver, www.dillonrangerdistrict.com.

Restaurants

The Boatyard Pizzeria and Grill, 304 Main Street, Frisco; (970) 668-4728
The Butterhorn Bakery, 408 Main Street, Frisco; (970) 668-3997
China Gourmet, Highway 9 and Annie Road (by Target), Silverthorne; (970) 262-6688
Fiesta Jalisco, Summit Place Shopping Center, Silverthorne; (970) 468-6663
MiZuppa, 842 North Summit Boulevard, Frisco; (970) 668-8138
Q4U, 857 North Summit Boulevard, Frisco; (970) 668-1775
Sunshine Cafe, Summit Place Shopping Center, Silverthorne; (970) 468-9552

Organizations

Friends of the Eagles Nest Wilderness, www.fenw.org, or call the Dillon Ranger District, (970) 468-5400, for the current contact.

Public Transportation (free)

Summit Stage, (970) 668-0999, www.summitstage.com

In Addition

Mountain Pine Beetles

The lodgepole pine forests of Summit County are turning red in many places. No, the U.S. Forest Service is not growing red trees for Christmas. During the mining years of the late 1800s and early 1900s, loggers deforested much of Summit County, harvesting wood for mines, railroads, buildings, smelting, and heating. Fire suppression became the law of the land, but the lodgepole-pine forest ecosystem depends on fire to stay healthy.

Lodgepole pine is typically called the tree of fire. Most trees produce serotinous cones that are sealed shut by resin until a very hot fire opens them and releases the seed. Some lodgepole have nonserotinous cones, so they can also regenerate without fire. An interesting statistic from studies after the 1988 Yellowstone fire: From 50,000 to 970,000 seeds per acre covered burned areas. Lodgepole stands may have lower-intensity fires that clear undergrowth and fuel build-up (interval 25 to 50 years) or high-intensity crown stand-replacement fires (interval perhaps 300 years). As lodgepole age, they become more susceptible to fires and pine beetles, nature's method of making way for new tree life.

Summit County's forests today contain many same-age lodgepole pines that are more than one hundred years old. Colorado recently experienced several years of drought, which stressed high-country forests. Temperatures have also been slightly warmer than average. Mix all the ingredients together and the time is ripe for a mountain pine beetle epidemic. The little insects have been around for thousands of years helping to recycle forests. Usually outbreaks occur in unhealthy and over-mature stands of pines.

Mountain pine beetles have a one-year life cycle. Adults leave their birth tree in late summer to find a home for the next generation. They bore into a live tree under the bark. If the tree cannot repel them with its sap, the beetles mate and the female lays about seventy-five eggs in a vertical tunnel. When the eggs hatch, the larvae tunnel through the tree, feeding as they go, until they become pupae in June and July. The insects transmit bluestain fungi, which help kill the tree by preventing the necessary flow of sap. As adults, the beetles fly from the dead tree to a live tree in late July to start the cycle again. They may number enough to attack two or three trees. The needles of dead trees turn red and eventually fall off. The dead tree dries out and becomes fuel for any fire that comes along.

If the forest is left alone, the natural cycle could take a couple of different paths. Fire might destroy the dead trees, while the heat opens lodgepole cones and releases the seeds. A new lodgepole pine forest would start the cycle again as in Yellowstone National Park. Depending on the fire and location, aspen trees might be the first tree species to appear, sprouting from underground root suckers. If an extremely intense and hot fire occurs, the soil may be sterilized. The area may remain open, colonized in time by grasses and forbs. Eventually the soil will recover enough nutrients to support tree growth.

In some areas, lodgepole pine would naturally be replaced by spruce-fir forest. If spruce and fir seedlings are growing in a lodgepole pine forest infested with mountain pine beetles and no fire occurs, the young seedlings will continue to grow amidst the dead lodgepole. Spruce and fir both need the shade and shelter provided by the dead trees to grow and thrive. In this case, the lodgepole pine ecosystem would be replaced by the spruce-fir ecosystem.

The beetles have been at work in the Vail area for several years already. They started attacking trees in Summit County in earnest in about 2003, and the number of red dead trees has been increasing each year.

The U.S. Forest Service and Congress have been trying to figure out how best to deal with this recent pine beetle problem. As more people move to the high country and build homes in the forest, using fire to keep the lodgepole ecosystem healthy is unpopular and dangerous. Homeowners are learning to use fire mitigation techniques around their homes, and many are treating their private forests for mountain pine beetle with advice from the Colorado State Forest Service. The U.S. Forest Service is thinning some forests, but does not have ample funding to treat everywhere. If trees can be cut and treated before the beetles fly, the number of newly infected trees can be minimized. In wilderness areas, nature is typically allowed to take its course.

In Summit County, residents have formed the Summit County Pine Beetle Task Force to serve as a resource for people to learn more about the insect epidemic facing the community. The group works with local governments and the U.S. Forest Service. For more information on this task force, check out www.summitpine beetle.org, a service of Our Future Summit, (970) 468–7875.

Until the mountain pine beetle epidemic subsides due to whatever reason(s), expect to see more red trees in Summit County and surrounding counties in the future.

For more information, see these resources:

mountain pine beetle: www.ext.colostate.edu/pubs/insect/05528.html

mountain pine beetle life cycle: www.for.gov.bc.ca/hfp/publications/00133/cycle.htm

lodgepole pine fire ecology: www.fs.fed.us/database/feis/plants/tree/pinconl/fire_ecology.html

13 Masontown / Mount Royal

The trail to Masontown is a pleasant family hike. A side trip to the east of town can provide fun exploring the area for mining relics. The hike from Masontown to Mount Royal and farther up to the ridge of Mount Victoria is strenuous but passes more mine and cabin ruins. The upward grunt is worth the climb for the views, especially the straight-down, birds-eye view of Interstate 70 in Tenmile Canyon. Limber pine, which grow in harsh conditions, live on the ridges. Four different hikes along these trails make the area well worth exploring during several visits.

Start: At the west Frisco Tenmile Canyon National Recreation Trail trailhead parking lot
Distance: Masontown 2.2 miles out and back; Mount Royal 3.8 miles out and back
Approximate hiking time: Masontown: 1 to 2 hours; Mount Royal: 2 to 4 hours
Difficulty: Masontown: moderate; Mount Royal from Masontown: strenuous because of 19 percent grade
Elevation gain: Masontown: 490 feet; Mount Royal: 1,300 feet
Trail surface: Paved recreational path and dirt trail
Seasons: Best from June to October
Other trail users: Mountain bikers, equestrians

Canine compatibility: Dogs permitted (must be under voice control); on paved recreation path dogs must be leashed.
Land status: National forest
Nearest town: Frisco
Fees and permits: No fees or permits required
Maps: USGS map: Frisco; National Geographic Trails Illustrated: #108 Vail, Frisco, Dillon
Trail contact: White River National Forest, Dillon Ranger District, 680 Blue River Parkway, Silverthorne; (970) 468-5400; www.fs.fed.us/r2/whiteriver, www.dillonrangerdistrict.com
Other: Bring water because the area is very dry.

Finding the trailhead: From I-70 exit 201, Frisco Main Street, drive east approximately 0.1 mile toward town to a parking lot on your right (south). Turn right into the parking lot and park. Porta-potties are usually available at the trailhead in the summer. Summit Stage bus stops are located close to the trailhead. *DeLorme: Colorado Atlas & Gazetteer:* Page 38 D2

Special considerations: Hunters may use this area during hunting season. Be aware of avalanche danger near and above Masontown in winter. These trails are neither marked nor maintained for winter use.

The Hike

While walking along the paved recreational path toward the Mount Royal Trail,
▶ The official name of the peak near Frisco is Royal Mountain, but locals call it Mount Royal.
imagine the sounds of the old trains which steamed along here. Two railroads served Frisco. The first, the Denver & Rio Grande (D&RG), came from Leadville down Tenmile Canyon, arriving in town in summer 1882. The Denver, South Park & Pacific, later called

A twisted limber pine ghost guards Mount Royal with Buffalo Mountain in the background.

the Colorado & Southern (C&S), chooed and chugged down the recreational path from Breckenridge arriving in Frisco in July 1883. At mile 0.3 the depot for the C&S once stood. Across the field you can see the tailings from the Frisco Tunnel, which operated into the 1930s. The D&RG ended service in 1911, while the C&S ran until 1937.

In 1866, General Buford discovered gold and copper leads above Rainbow Lake on the side of Royal Mountain. He built a road from the lake to the site—the old path still exists today. Buford built a mill and a little town started to grow. In 1880, the Victoria mine produced about $10,000 in gold. Lack of affordable transportation created problems. The nearest railroad stopped in Georgetown, and ore had to be shipped via mule or wagons over Argentine or Loveland passes.

From here the story varies depending on what one reads. Several history books indicate that the Masontown Mining and Milling (M&M) Company planned to build a reduction works in 1872, and that the company leased the Victoria mine. The *Summit County Journal* reported in its September 26, 1903, issue that Lars Matsson sold the 115-acre Victoria-Eureka property to Masontown M&M Company. J. V. Hoover of Masontown, Pennsylvania, was president of the well-capitalized company. The article also reported that about 2,000 feet of work had been done in

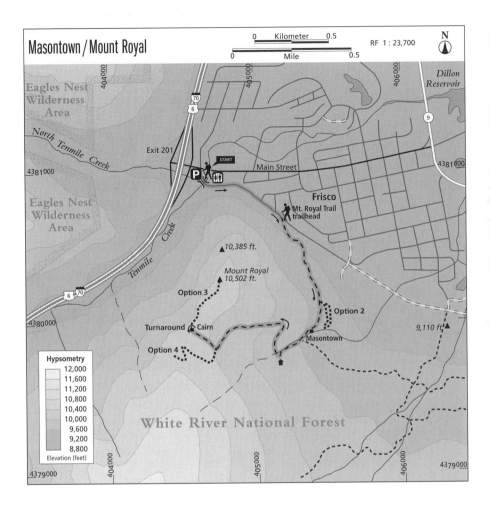

Masontown / Mount Royal

Kilometer
0   0.5
Mile
0   0.5

RF 1 : 23,700

N

Hypsometry

12,000
11,600
11,200
10,800
10,400
10,000
9,600
9,200
8,800
Elevation (feet)

the mine, exposing a large body of low-grade gold, and that the new owners were building a mill.

The *Summit County Journal*'s June 4, 1904, issue reported that the Masontown mill was fully operational with electric lighting and "runs with the accuracy of a watch." A tram brought ore from the mine to the mill. The ore then passed through a Blake crusher to automatic feeders which sent it to four battery boxes containing twenty stamps, a double discharge, and amalgamating plates. The pulp then passed to four concentrating tables which extracted the sulphides and heavy minerals. The remaining pulp flowed into cyanide tanks, where the solution percolated for some appropriate amount of time. That solution ran into a tank and then into zinc boxes. The precipitates were treated in a room with an acid tank, filter box, vacuum pump, centrifugal pump, and drying and melting furnaces. The process produced gold amalgam, cyanide precipitates, and auriferous sulphides. The first two became gold bars and the concentrates were shipped to smelters. The paper further reported the ore's value at $5.00 to $20.00 per ton in gold, while the costs of mining and milling ran about $3.00 per ton. The June 11, 1904, *Breckenridge Bulletin* stated the sulphide ore containing gold and silver was assaying at $12 to $80 per ton.

Disagreements among the company's owners closed the operation for about a year according to articles in July 1905 in both the *Breckenridge Bulletin* and the *Summit County Journal*. By December 1905 the *Breckenridge Bulletin* reported Masontown M&M Company as "preparing for aggressive work."

Frisco mining played out about 1910. Some legends say that while Masontown's residents partied in Frisco on New Year's Eve in 1912, a snow slide roared down Mount Victoria taking Masontown's buildings with it. Other accounts relate the snow slide that wiped out Masontown occurred in 1926, leaving only a few cabins on the north side (see the option at mile 1.2 below).

Miles and Directions

0.0 Start at the recreation path bulletin board. 404629mE 4380953mN Elevation 9,120 feet. Cross Tenmile Creek on the wooden bridge. In approximately 250 feet, turn left (east) on the paved recreational path. Stay on the paved path heading southeast, ignoring any paths on the left.

0.3 To the right (southwest) of the trail is an open area across which you can see the tailings from the Frisco Tunnel. 405009mE 4380835mN

0.4 Mount Royal Trail trailhead is on the right (southwest). A sign explains some of the history of Masontown. 405184mE 4380691mN Turn right and hike up the dirt single-track trail.

0.8 The trail Ys. Continue uphill (south) on the right branch. 405135mE 4380133mN (See Option 2 for information on the left branch.)

1.0 Arrive in the remains of Masontown. Take some time to wander around and see old bricks, twisted metal, and other artifacts. 405332mE 4379914mN When the trail appears to split in three directions, continue straight ahead (mostly west).

1.1 The avalanche path comes through here. 405225mE 4379850mN Elevation 9,610 feet. The trail climbs steeply from here. For a shorter and easier hike, return the way you came to the trailhead for a 2.2 mile out-and-back hike. (See Option 1.)

1.2 A faint trail takes off to the left (southeast) as the main trail curves to the right. 405131mE 4379796mN An optional 0.1-mile out-and-back on the faint trail takes you

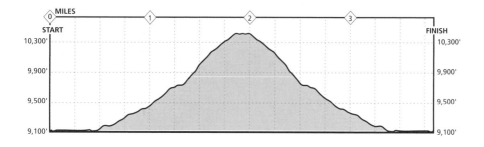

to the remains of the cabin that escaped the avalanche that wiped out Masontown. The trail continues to climb steeply.

1.7 The trail Ys. 404717mE 4379825mN Turn right (northwest) and head uphill. (See Option 4 for information on the left branch.)

1.9 Arrive at the big cairn in a saddle that most people consider Mount Royal. Enjoy the views. 404541mE 4379970mN Elevation 10,421 feet. (See Option 3 for a hike to a higher point on Mount Royal.) Return the way you came.

3.8 Arrive back at the trailhead.

Options:

1. The hike to Masontown is a 2.2-mile out-and-back moderate hike.

2. Hike to some old mine tunnels and other relics east of Masontown. A 2.0-mile out-and-back depending on where you explore. Easy. Turn left (south) at mile 0.8 in the above directions and follow the rightmost trail to some obvious old shafts. Walk beyond these tunnels to find the old smokestacks from the mill. Do not enter any tunnels—they are dangerous.

3. Hike from the Mount Royal saddle to the "top" of Mount Royal, a 0.4-mile out-and-back, by following the trail to the northeast. Nothing marks the summit. Moderate from the saddle.

4. Instead of turning right to go to Mount Royal, continue southwest up the steep trail which switchbacks another quarter mile to a ridge full of limber pine trees with views to the ridge at elevation 10,625 feet. You'll pass several mine and cabin remains along the way. From here, an unofficial unmaintained ridgeline route continues steeply up Mount Victoria (unofficial name) to 11,785 feet.

FRIENDS OF DILLON RANGER DISTRICT
In early 2004, Friends of the Dillon Ranger District (FDRD) formed to help "bridge the gap caused by increased visitation and costs and declining congressionally appropriated budgets." FDRD's mission is to promote stewardship of the White River National Forest in Summit County through partnerships, volunteer service, education, and support. FDRD is focused on addressing the following natural resource issues: community-based forestry, recreation, invasive species, and fire mitigation through fuel reduction. Over 75 percent of Summit County is part of the White River National Forest. To help FDRD with their efforts, log onto www.fdrd.org or contact the Dillon Ranger District, (970) 468-5400, for the current contact.

Hike Information

Local Information

Frisco Chamber of Commerce, 300 Main Street, (970) 668-5547; Frisco; www.friscocolorado.org
Summit County Chamber of Commerce, (800) 530-3099, www.summitchamber.org
Summit Visitor Information Center, Outlets at Silverthorne, 246 Rainbow Drive, Silverthorne; (970) 262-0817

Local Events/Attractions

Coors Colorado Barbecue Challenge, Frisco, www.townoffrisco.com/bbq.html

Accommodations

Several campgrounds are located along the shores of Dillon Reservoir near Frisco. For more information, contact White River National Forest, Dillon Ranger District, (970) 468-5400, www.fs.fed.us/r2/whiteriver, www.dillonrangerdistrict.com.

Restaurants

The Boatyard Pizzeria and Grill, 304 Main Street, Frisco; (970) 668-4728
The Butterhorn Bakery, 408 Main Street, Frisco; (970) 668-3997
MiZuppa, 842 North Summit Boulevard, Frisco; (970) 668-8138
Q4U, 857 North Summit Boulevard, Frisco; (970) 668-1775

Organizations

Friends of Dillon Ranger District, www.fdrd.org, or contact Dillon Ranger District, (970) 468-5400, for the current contact.

Public Transportation (free)

Summit Stage, (970) 668-0999, www.summit stage.com

14 Iowa Hill

The Iowa Hill Hydraulic Placer Mine is explored along this historic interpretive trail. The hikes takes you back 145 years in history to the days when miners panned for gold then developed techniques using water cannons, called hydraulic giants, to wash the sides of gulches into sluice boxes to capture gold particles. *Mining History News* rates this trail as "one of the best hydraulic mining exhibits in the world." A restored two-story log Miners' Boarding House on the trail can be toured by appointment.

Start: At the Iowa Hill Trail trailhead sign
Distance: 1.2-mile lollipop including three side spurs
Approximate hiking time: 1 to 2 hours
Difficulty: Moderate
Elevation gain: 310 feet
Trail surface: Dirt trail
Seasons: Best from late May to late October
Other trail users: Hikers only
Canine compatibility: Dogs must be on leash.
Land status: Town of Breckenridge

Nearest town: Breckenridge
Fees and permits: No fees or permits required
Maps: USGS map: Frisco; National Geographic Trails Illustrated: #108 Vail, Frisco, Dillon
Trail contact: Town of Breckenridge, 150 Ski Hill Road, Breckenridge; (970) 547-3155; www.townofbreckenridge.com (click on Leisure)
Other: No water is available along the trail.

Finding the trailhead: From Interstate 70 exit 203, Frisco/Breckenridge, drive south on Highway 9 9.3 miles to Valley Brook Road. Turn right (west) and travel 0.2 mile to Airport Road. Turn right (north) on Airport Road, then turn left in 0.3 mile, then immediately right onto the dirt road by the Iowa Hill Trail trailhead sign. Drive north 0.1 mile to the parking lot. No facilities are available at the trailhead. A Breckenridge Free Ride bus stop is located 0.2 mile south of the trailhead. *DeLorme: Colorado Atlas & Gazetteer:* Page 38 D2

Special considerations: If the trail is muddy, please walk through the mud puddles and not on the vegetation around the trail. Trampled vegetation results in bigger mud puddles! The trail is neither marked nor maintained for winter use. Please stay on the trail to avoid trespassing on nearby private properties.

The Hike

The Iowa Hill interpretive displays were created by following old pictures and knowledge of how the miners first panned for gold in streams and then evolved hydraulic techniques to remove gold from the hills.

The interpretive signs begin with explanations of gold panning and use of a rocker box and Long Tom for greater efficiency. A sluice box exhibit comes complete with a resident pine squirrel, chattering at hikers. Other exhibits contain an old derrick, hydraulic giant, ore car, and examples of flumes. At the top of the hike is an old diversion dam, which captured water that was released into the flume. This particular dam sent water into either of two gulches. A flume was reconstructed in summer 2005, and the remains of the original wood can still be seen in the area.

A real gem on this hike is the restored and furnished Miners' Boarding House. Presently tours are only available by appointment. Once inside, you're transported back 125 years. The tour explains how the miners returned from a hard day of work and lived their lives. If you ever wondered what hobnailed boots looked like, a pair survives in the house. The docent explained that they think eight men lived in the boardinghouse. Bunks in the cabin were re-created from pictures. Sample boxes of herbs used to cure ills line a shelf near the old wood cookstove. The boardinghouse dates back to at least 1876. One picture on the wall shows snow up to the eaves of a cabin.

Hiking up the trail through dry forest begs the question of where did the miners get the water for the hydraulic giants. At the turn of the century, the Banner Placer Company owned the mine and built a reservoir to provide water. According to the

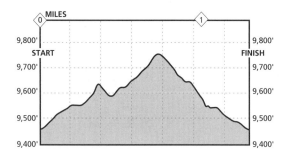

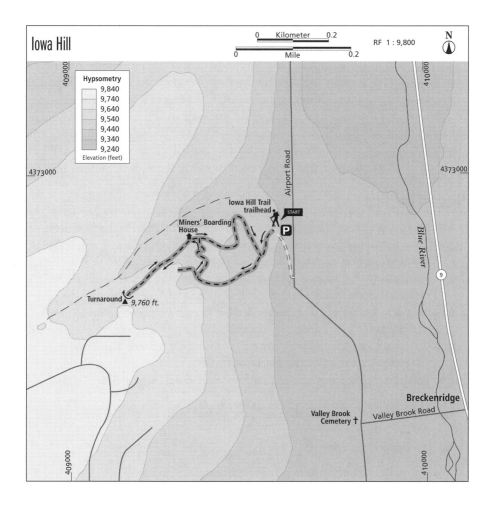

Hypsometry

9,840
9,740
9,640
9,540
9,440
9,340
9,240
Elevation (feet)

RF 1 : 9,800

N

Iowa Hill Trail trailhead

START

Miners' Boarding House

P

Turnaround ▲ 9,760 ft.

Airport Road

Blue River

9

Breckenridge

Valley Brook Cemetery †

Valley Brook Road

October 15, 1904, *Breckenridge Bulletin*, the Banner Placer Mining Company, managed by Colonel L. Kingsbury, was preparing to operate the well-known Iowa placer on Iowa Hill in 1905. "A storage reservoir is being built on a portion of the Boom placer (ten acres of which were purchased for that purpose) to hold water for supplying a couple of 'giants' under a head of pressure of over 200 feet." Another report stated the reservoir was located between the head of the north fork of Cucumber Creek and South Barton Creek. The company built a road to the storage reservoirs and dug miles of ditches to make the hydraulic placer operation a success. The water dropped over 200 feet in elevation through a 3,200-foot-long, 22-inch steel pipe to the Iowa placers. Kingsbury picked a series of sites for little reservoirs, like the diversion dam, so when one filled, the overflow would fill the others. Headgates were placed in two of the lakes. The headgate now on display was once used in another mining operation in Illinois Gulch south of town. Pressure generated was estimated at 260 pounds per square inch. Lateral pipes ran three 6-inch nozzles which played on the 18- to

40-foot-high gravel banks. The gravel passed through a 4-foot-wide sluice with riffles that caught the gold. Two Acme concentrating tables made a product of the heavy black sand, which in the past had been hard to reclaim. A dynamo run by water generated power for the tables and lights for night work. The December 30, 1905, issue of the *Summit County Journal* reported that Banner gold had a value of $19 per ounce.

The newspapers reported that Kingsbury exhibited several beautiful gold nuggets from Iowa Hill, one of which resembled a bear's foot. Gold nuggets from Iowa Hill were also exhibited at the 1893 Chicago World's Fair.

Hike back into time and learn about some of the mining history of Breckenridge.

Miles and Directions

0.0 Start at the Iowa Hill Trail trailhead sign. 409570mE 4372840mN Elevation 9,450 feet.

322 ft The trail Ys. Turn left (south) and follow the trail which leads you to many interpretive signs. Take time to explore the side trails to several signs and displays.

0.3 The trail Ys. Turn left (west) to two interpretive signs then return to the junction and the derrick interpretive sign. Head uphill from here. 409365mE 4372732mN

0.6 The trail Ys. Turn left and head uphill (southwest) for more interpretive signs. 409336mE 4372816mN

0.75 Arrive at the diversion dam and top of the trail. Elevation 9,765 feet. 409161mE 4372680mN Return back to the last junction.

0.9 Back at the junction, turn left and head down to the Miners' Boarding House. Continue on the downhill trail.

1.0 The trail crosses an old road. Continue straight ahead (east) and downhill. 409410mE 4372821mN

1.2 Arrive back at the trailhead.

Hike Information

Local Information

Breckenridge Resort Chamber, Daniels Cabin Information Center, 309 North Main Street, Breckenridge; (877) 864-0868; www.go breck.com
Summit County Chamber of Commerce, (800) 530-3099, www.summitchamber.org
Summit Visitor Information Center, Outlets at Silverthorne, 246 Rainbow Drive, Silverthorne; (970) 262-0817
Town of Breckenridge, 150 Ski Hill Road, Breckenridge; (970) 547-3155; www.townof breckenridge.com

Local Events/Attractions

Backstage Theatre, 121 South Ridge Street, Breckenridge; (970) 453-0199; www.back stagetheatre.com
Barney Ford House Museum, Main and Washington, Breckenridge; (970) 453-5761
Breckenridge Music Festival, (970) 453-9142 (all summer), www.breckenridge musicfestival.com
Country Boy Mine, 0542 French Gulch Road, Breckenridge; (970) 453-4405, www.country boymine.com
Edwin Carter Museum, 111 North Ridge Street, Breckenridge; (970) 453-9022

Restaurants

Breckenridge Brewery, 600 South Main Street, Breckenridge; (970) 453-1550; www.breckenridgebrewery.com

Cool River Coffee House & Bakery, 325 South Main Street, Breckenridge; (970) 453-1716

Crown Coffee House & Tavern, 215 South Main Street, Breckenridge; (970) 453-6022

Mi Casa Mexican Restaurant & Cantina, 600 South Park Avenue, Breckenridge; (970) 453-2071; www.stormrestaurants.com/micasa/

Hike Tours

Miners' Boarding House tours, Dillon: Summit Historical Society, (970) 453-9022, www.summithistorical.org

Organizations

Town of Breckenridge Open Space and Trails Division, (970) 547-3155

Public Transportation (free)

Breckenridge Free Ride, Town of Breckenridge, (970) 547-3141, www.townofbreckenridge.com (click on Visitor then Transportation)

Summit Stage, (970) 668-0999, www.summit stage.com

15 Cucumber Gulch

This easy hike along the edges of Cucumber Gulch provides not only great views of the Tenmile Range, but also glimpses of a fen wetland that is considered prime habitat for the endangered boreal toad. Hike in the early morning or evening when the wild inhabitants come out. Moose, bears, beavers, foxes, coyotes, ospreys, bald eagles, and various duck species might be seen. The Town of Breckenridge has designated Cucumber Gulch a wildlife preserve because of its sensitive natural resources. Trails do not enter the fragile gulch, but travel its edges. The town plans to install interpretive signs in the future.

Start: At the Breckenridge Nordic Center, in the parking lot in front of the little lodge

Distance: 2.2-mile T hike

Approximate hiking time: 1 to 2 hours

Difficulty: Easy

Elevation gain: 150 feet

Trail surface: Dirt trail

Seasons: Best from end of May to October

Other trail users: Mountain bikers

Canine compatibility: Dogs are not permitted in the center of the Cucumber Gulch Preserve.

Land status: Town of Breckenridge

Nearest town: Breckenridge

Fees and permits: No fees or permits required

Maps: USGS map: Breckenridge; National Geographic Trails Illustrated: #109 Breckenridge, Tennessee Pass

Trail contact: Town of Breckenridge, 150 Ski Hill Road, Breckenridge; (970) 547-3155; www.townofbreckenridge.com (click on Leisure)

Other: Water is not readily available on most of the hike. Dogs are not permitted in the center of the Cucumber Gulch Preserve in order to protect the endangered boreal toad and other wildlife species.

Finding the trailhead: From Interstate 70 exit 203, Frisco/Breckenridge, drive south on Highway 9 approximately 9.6 miles to where Highway 9 turns onto North Park Avenue. Turn right (west) onto North Park and follow it 0.7 mile to Ski Hill Road. Turn right (west) on Ski Hill Road

Cucumber Gulch and Breckenridge Ski Area from the overlook

and follow it uphill 0.9 mile to the Breckenridge Nordic Center. Turn right (north) into the Nordic Center parking lot and park. No facilities are available at the trailhead in the summer. *DeLorme: Colorado Atlas & Gazetteer:* Page 48 A2

Special considerations: During the winter, this area is part of the Breckenridge Nordic Center. The summer and winter trails differ in some places. Cross-country skiing or snowshoeing during the winter months is allowed on the various trails by purchasing a trail pass. For winter information, visit www.breckenridgenordic.com, or call (970) 453-6855.

The Hike

To experience Cucumber Gulch, hike first to the overlook near Shock Hill, which provides a great view of the whole gulch and its various ponds nestled in the forest. The Tenmile Range and Breckenridge Ski Area tower above the gulch. Look closely below to see if you can see a coyote or family of ducks.

The Town of Breckenridge recognized the importance of this very special wetland and went to great lengths to preserve Cucumber Gulch. The town has spent over $5 million to purchase valuable habitat in the gulch and now owns the majority of the wetlands area. The town has also worked with Vail Resorts (owner of Breckenridge Ski Area) and other developers to modify their development and construction plans in order to protect the wildlife and habitat in the gulch. The

Environmental Protection Agency lists Cucumber Gulch as an aquatic resource of national importance. Most of Cucumber Gulch is in a protective management area (PMA) which restricts the activities allowed.

The town started doing environmental studies in Cucumber Gulch in 1998. These studies provide baseline information that can be compared over the years to track changes and provide mitigation for any problems that arise. Vegetative surveys use one-meter-square plots, some of which have contained over thirty-five different plant species.

The boreal toad is the main focus of Cucumber Gulch, listed as prime habitat for the little amphibian. Boreal toads are Colorado's only alpine toad species and are on the state's endangered species list. The females measure 11 centimeters while males are about 9 centimeters. They live in ponds and marshy areas in spruce-fir forests and alpine meadows between 7,000 and 12,000 feet. Boreal toads eat various grasshoppers and insects, while they in turn become a tasty toad treat for foxes and raccoons. Since 1970, the boreal toad population has declined across the state, with the deadly Chytrid fungus a possible culprit.

▶ Gold was first discovered in the Blue River near present-day Breckenridge in 1859. One of the early miners went by the name of "Cucumber." Cucumber Creek and Cucumber Gulch are probably named for him.

Male boreal toads chirp for their lovers rather than calling loudly like other toad species. Females lay between 3,000 and 8,000 eggs in the beaver ponds in Cucumber Gulch. The tadpoles hatch and develop there. After laying their eggs, females migrate up to 2 miles toward the ski area. The males hang around the pond to protect their breeding territory, but don't provide any fatherly oversight of the eggs.

Living in high altitude poses challenges, including dry air, for any species. Boreal toads spend a lot of time under logs and under ground where it's moist to prevent their skin from drying out.

Local citizens reported a large population of boreal toads in Cucumber Gulch over the years. In 2005, the survey found only two. One of those was found dead along the Toad Alley Trail with toothmarks in it. Biologists believe that the teeth may have belonged to a small dog or a fox. The town hopes that boreal toads can be reintroduced into Cucumber Gulch from another area with a more substantial population.

Beavers are an important species in Cucumber Gulch, creating the various ponds in the area. Old beaver dams create grassy lines across the wetlands. The nocturnal critters are hard to spot. They keep their lodges neat and free of grasses, constantly maintaining them by adding sticks and mud on top. According to the gulch's research biologist, the beaver population has recently been in decline. Researchers count the number of inactive, grassy lodges versus the neat active lodges. One possible explanation for the disappearing beaver is lack of aspen in the area. The beaver cut down what aspen grew along the gulch. One neighboring landowner is helping to stabilize the beaver population downstream by providing a supply of cut aspen.

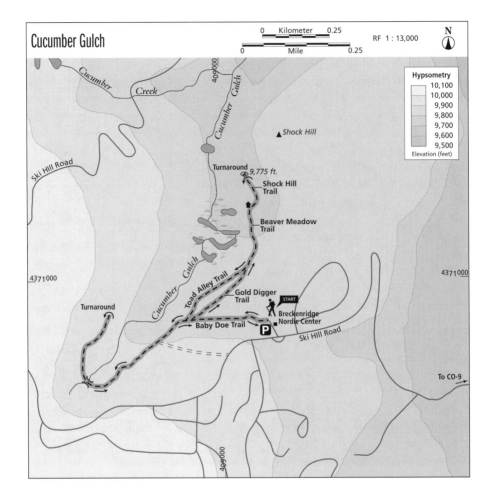

Cucumber Gulch is a fen wetland, meaning the water coming up and being dammed by the beavers is groundwater fed. The pools provide habitat for all types of wildlife, including the boreal toad. The fen also contains peat, an anaerobic soil that contains microbes that don't need oxygen. The peat is created over about 1,000 years and takes a long time to recover if it's disturbed.

The trails edging Cucumber Gulch are still a work in progress as this book goes to print.

Miles and Directions

0.0 Start in the parking lot at the fence opening in front of the Nordic Center building. 409168mE 4370850mN Walk to the left (west) down the parking lot and turn right through the next fence opening in about 112 feet. In another 42 feet turn left onto a trail in the trees.

0.2 Come to the junction of Baby Doe and Gold Digger Trails. 408912mE 4370872mN Turn right (northeast) onto Gold Digger Trail.

0.3 Arrive at the junction of Gold Digger and Beaver Meadow Trails. Turn left (north) onto Beaver Meadow Trail and continue straight on Beaver Meadow past the intersection with Toad Alley Trail.

0.4 Pass an old restored cabin. This cabin may only be open during the winter. 409096mE 4371222mN In about 100 feet, turn right (northeast) onto Shock Hill Trail and follow it uphill to the overlook.

0.6 Arrive at the overlook of Cucumber Gulch by a huge boulder. 409094mE 4371362mN Elevation 9,775 feet. Return the way you came.

0.8 Arrive back at the junction of Beaver Meadow and Toad Alley Trails. 409088mE 4371032mN Turn right (southwest) onto Toad Alley Trail.

0.9 Enjoy the great views of beaver ponds just past the Toad Alley Trail sign. 408908mE 4370938mN

1.0 The trail Ts. Turn right (southwest) here to continue along Cucumber Gulch.

1.1 The trail Ts. Turn right here to continue along Cucumber Gulch. 408747mE 4370764mN

1.2 The trail Ys by a big cut stump. Turn right (west) here to continue along Cucumber Gulch. 408556mE 4370613mN

1.3 The trail Ys. Turn right (north) here to continue along Cucumber Gulch. About 200 feet farther, cross a little creek on a nice bridge. 408475mE 4370707mN Follow the trail as it curves to the right.

1.5 The trail ends where it starts to head uphill to the left. An observation interpretive overlook may be built near here. 408581mE 4370873mN and Return the way you came to the 1.0 mile junction above, which is a just a few feet from mile 2.0. Turn right and walk to mile 2.0.

2.0 Arrive at the junction of Toad Alley and Gold Digger Trails. Turn left (northeast) and walk to the junction of Gold Digger and Baby Doe Trails. Turn right (east) on Baby Doe Trail.

2.2 Arrive back at the parking lot.

Options:

1. Hike to the overlook and back for a 1.2-mile out-and-back hike.

2. Skip the hike to the overlook and follow the directions backward for a 1.4-mile out-and-back hike.

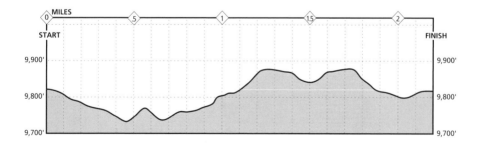

Hike Information

Local Information

Breckenridge Resort Chamber, Daniels Cabin Information Center, 309 North Main Street, Breckenridge; (877) 864-0868; www.go breck.com

Summit Visitor Information Center, Outlets at Silverthorne, 246 Rainbow Drive, Silverthorne; (970) 262-0817

Town of Breckenridge, 150 Ski Hill Road, Breckenridge; (970) 547-3155; www.townof breckenridge.com

Local Events/Attractions

Backstage Theatre, 121 South Ridge Street, Breckenridge; (970) 453-0199; www.back stagetheatre.com

Barney Ford House Museum, Main and Washington, Breckenridge; (970) 453-5761

Breckenridge Music Festival, (970) 453-9142 (all summer), www.breckenridgemusic festival.com

Country Boy Mine, 0542 French Gulch Road, Breckenridge; (970) 453-4405; www.country boymine.com

Edwin Carter Museum, 111 North Ridge Street, Breckenridge; (970) 453-9022

Hike Tours

Town of Breckenridge Open Space and Trails Division, (970) 547-3155, www.townof breckenridge.com (click on Leisure)

Restaurants

Breckenridge Brewery, 600 South Main Street, Breckenridge; (970) 453-1550; www.breckenridgebrewery.com

Cool River Coffee House & Bakery, 325 South Main Street, Breckenridge; (970) 453-1716

Crown Coffee House & Tavern, 215 South Main Street, Breckenridge; (970) 453-6022

Mi Casa Mexican Restaurant & Cantina, 600 South Park Avenue Breckenridge; (970) 453-2071; www.stormrestaurants.com/micasa/

Organizations

Town of Breckenridge Open Space and Trails Division, (970) 547-3155

Public Transportation (free)

Breckenridge Free Ride, Town of Breckenridge, (970) 547-3141, www.townofbreckenridge.com (click on Visitor then Transportation)

16 Barney Ford Trail

This hike actually follows three trails: Carter Park, Moonstone, and Barney Ford. The majority of the hike is on the Barney Ford Trail, which was built along old mining trails and ditches past mine ruins and plenty of glory holes. Except for the first grunt uphill on the Carter Park Trail, the hike through coniferous forest is fairly gentle. You can hike this trail as an out-and-back, point-to-point, or bus shuttle. The Barney Ford story is a fascinating account of a slave who believed he would become free and rich. His dreams turned to reality as he became a prominent Colorado citizen.

Start: At the Carter Park Trail trailhead. See Options for other possibilities.
Distance: 4.8 miles out and back
Approximate hiking time: 2 to 3 hours
Difficulty: Moderate
Elevation gain: 780 feet
Trail surface: Dirt trail with one paved road crossing
Seasons: Best from June to October
Other trail users: Mountain bikers
Canine compatibility: Dogs must be on leash within town limits and under voice control within the county.
Land status: Multiple jurisdictions
Nearest town: Breckenridge

Fees and permits: No fees or permits required
Maps: USGS map: Breckenridge; National Geographic Trails Illustrated: #109 Breckenridge, Tennessee Pass
Trail contact: Town of Breckenridge, 150 Ski Hill Road, Breckenridge; (970) 547-3155; www.townofbreckenridge.com (click on Leisure)
Other: No water is available along the trail, so be sure to bring a supply. Much of the Barney Ford Trail is built on easements across seven private properties. Please stay on the trail and respect the private property owners' rights. The Barney Ford Trail is also a very popular mountain bike trail, so heads up!

Finding the trailheads: Carter Park Trail trailhead: From Interstate 70 exit 203, Frisco/Breckenridge, drive south through Frisco on Highway 9 approximately 10.4 miles to Ski Hill Road in Breckenridge. Turn left on Ski Hill Road and continue across Main Street where Ski Hill Road becomes Lincoln. Continue up Lincoln to High, which is 0.4 mile from Highway 9 (North Park Avenue). Turn right on High and drive a quarter mile to the Carter Park parking lot. The trailhead is at the end of the left (east) side of the parking lot. Restrooms and water are available in the Carter Park pavilion. If you would like to do this hike as a point-to-point and leave another vehicle at the upper trailhead (which has limited parking), leave one car at Carter Park. Drive back on High 0.1 mile to Adams and turn left. Drive 0.1 mile to Ridge Street and turn left. In 0.3 mile turn left on Main Street. In another 0.1 mile turn left onto Boreas Pass Road. Follow the directions below starting with "Follow Boreas Pass Road . . ."

　　Sallie Barber Road trailhead: From I-70 exit 203, Frisco/Breckenridge, drive south through Frisco on Highway 9 approximately 11.1 miles to Boreas Pass Road (across from the gas station). Turn left onto Boreas Pass Road. Follow Boreas Pass Road as it twists and climbs for 2.1 miles to Baldy Road. Turn left onto Baldy Road and drive 0.9 mile to Sallie Barber Road on the left. Turn left onto Sallie Barber Road and drive 0.2 mile to the upper trailhead parking area. No facilities are available at the upper trailhead. A Summit Stage bus stop is also available

0.1 mile up Baldy Road from the intersection of Baldy Road and Sallie Barber Road. DeLorme: Colorado Atlas & Gazetteer: Page 48 A2

Special considerations: The Barney Ford Trail is marked by blue diamonds for cross-country skiing.

The Hike

Barney Ford was born into slavery in 1822, his mother a slave and his father the plantation owner. Barney had blue-hazel eyes, olive skin, and wavy chestnut hair. He learned to read and write, skills most slaves could not acquire. As a teenager, his owner hired him out on steamboats on the Mississippi River. Several years later, Barney escaped from a steamboat and made his way to Chicago via the Underground Railroad. He married Julia Lyoni in 1849. Barney had no last name and Julia helped him choose the names Lancelot Ford after a steam engine locomotive. In 1851 they headed for riches in the California gold rush, traveling by boat from New York to Nicaragua.

Sidetracked in Nicaragua, the Fords opened a hotel where Barney hosted many United States dignitaries. His hotel was destroyed during a political dispute with Great Britain. After opening a second hotel, the prohibition against slavery in Nicaragua was lifted. The Fords returned to Chicago with $5,000. Barney built a livery stable which became part of the Underground Railroad.

Barney's gold fever awakened again in 1860 during the Pikes Peak gold rush, and he headed to Denver. Before moving to Breckenridge he consulted a white Denver lawyer about owning a claim. The Dred Scott decision had denied blacks the right to own land. The lawyer suggested that Barney file the claim in his name, and in turn he would send Barney a legal agreement that he could keep 80 percent of the findings. Barney arrived in Breckenridge crowded with hopeful miners and their claims. Barney worked his way up a gulch south of French Gulch, finally finding some gold, and filed the claim in the lawyer's name. He and his black helpers built a log cabin and kept filling a bottle with gold flakes. One day the sheriff arrived with a twenty-four-hour eviction notice from the lawyer, who assumed Barney had struck it rich. That night a group of whites on horseback thundered up the gulch. Barney grabbed the bottle of gold and scrambled up the hill above the claim with his workers. The whites found no gold and rumors grew that Barney had cached his riches on the mountainside. Locals called the area Nigger Gulch and Nigger Hill. In 1964 the names were changed to Ford Gulch and Barney Ford Hill.

Returning to Denver, Barney opened a barbershop and Ford's People's Restaurant. He prided himself on serving the finest and freshest food and the best liquor and cigars. Over the years, Ford prospered in the barbershop, hotel, and restaurant

◀ *Carter Park, Breckenridge, ski area, and Tenmile Range from Carter Park Trail*

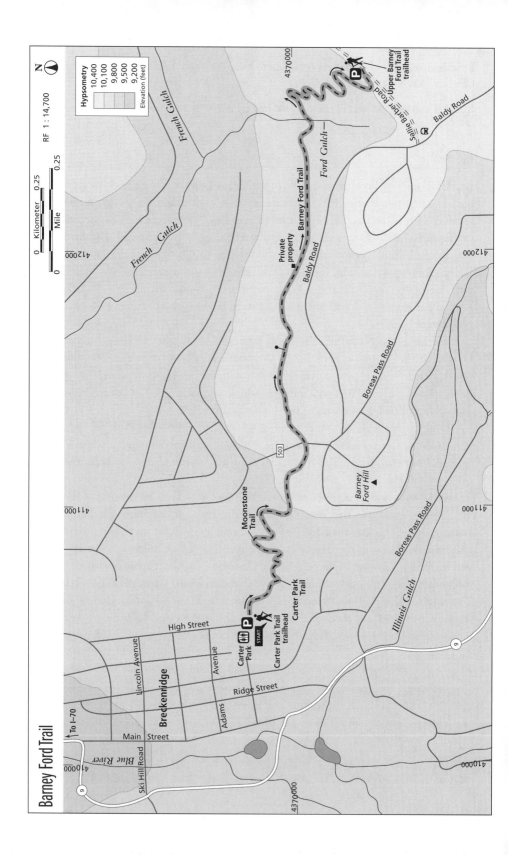

Barney Ford Trail

Hypsometry

	10,400
	10,100
	9,800
	9,500
	9,200

Elevation (feet)

RF 1 : 14,700

N

0   0.25
Kilometer

0   0.25
Mile

French Gulch

French Gulch

Ford Gulch

Barney Ford Trail

Private property

Baldy Road

Sallie Barber Road

Upper Barney Ford Trail trailhead

Baldy Road

503

Moonstone Trail

Barney Ford Hill

Boreas Pass Road

Boreas Pass Road

Illinois Gulch

Carter Park Trail

Carter Park Trail trailhead

Carter Park

High Street

START

Lincoln Avenue

Avenue

Ridge Street

Adams

Main Street

Breckenridge

Blue River

Ski Hill Road

To I-70

9

9

4370000

412000

412000

411000

411000

410000

4370000

410000

business. He built the luxurious Inter-Ocean Hotels in Cheyenne and Denver, where he hosted noted guests such as President Ulysses S. Grant. By the 1870s, Barney's dream of being rich had come true. At one time he was listed as the fourteenth wealthiest man in Colorado.

Barney had a burning desire to assure that black men could vote and own property when Colorado became a state. After the Civil War ended, Ford influenced congressmen to deny Colorado its bid for statehood until the state constitution gave blacks their rights as free citizens. He finally succeeded, and when Colorado became a state in 1876, the constitution included the right for blacks to vote.

In 1879, Barney opened Ford's Chop Stand in Breckenridge. Three years later he hired Elias Nashold to build him a fine house, which today is a museum. He retired to Denver in 1890.

This trail provides an opportunity to enjoy the forest and mining history surrounding Breckenridge without having to drive out of town.

Miles and Directions

0.0 Start at the Carter Park Trail trailhead. 410596mE 4370185mN In about 285 feet, there's a trail junction. Go left and uphill on the Carter Park Trail.

0.15 The trail Ts. Walk right. Immediately the trail forks. Take the left fork and keep switchbacking uphill.

0.3 Reach the junction of Carter Park and Hermit Placer Trails. 410828mE 4370129mN Turn left and walk about 50 feet to the next trail junction sign and turn right onto Moonstone Trail.

0.8 The Moonstone Trail ends at County Road 503. 411228mE 4369951mN The Barney Ford Trail starts across the road and a little to the left.

1.1 Come to a four-way trail junction. Go straight ahead on the Barney Ford Trail. In less than 0.1 mile, there's a T intersection. Turn left and follow the trail marked by the blue diamond (cross-country ski trail marker).

1.3 An old shaft lies just off the trail to the left. Do not enter and respect the private property owner's rights. 411935mE 4369983mN

1.6 The trail turns left at a "hitching post" with a long arrow pointing left.

1.7 Arrive at Ford Gulch and the remains of a mine and two cabins. 412487mE 4369921mN

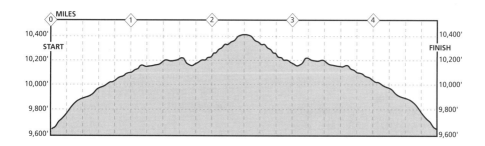

1.8 The trail makes a right switchback onto an old dirt road.

1.9 The trail makes a left switchback off the old dirt road onto a single track. 412583mE 4369928mN The trail switchbacks up the hill from here.

2.3 The trail turns left onto an old dirt road.

2.4 Arrive at the upper Barney Ford Trail trailhead on Sallie Barber Road. 412685mE 4369717mN Elevation 10,424 feet. Return the way you came or arrive at a waiting vehicle or hike another 0.3 mile to the Summit Stage bus stop (see Option 1).

4.8 Arrive back at Carter Park if you chose the out-and-back option.

Options:

1. For a 2.4-mile point-to-point hike, you can start at either trailhead and leave a car at the other end. Or the Summit Stage bus stop is only 0.3 mile from the upper trailhead. Turn right and head down Sallie Barber Road to Baldy Road. Turn left (uphill) on Baldy Road and walk about 0.1 mile to the bus stop on the left side of the road. Be sure to check the bus schedule before starting your hike.

2. For a 3.2-mile out–and–back on just the Barney Ford Trail, start at the upper Barney Ford Trail trailhead on Sallie Barber Road.

Hike Information

Local Information

Breckenridge Resort Chamber, Daniels Cabin Information Center, 309 North Main Street, Breckenridge; (877) 864-0868; www.go breck.com

Summit County Chamber of Commerce, (800) 530-3099, www.summitchamber.org

Summit Visitor Information Center, Outlets at Silverthorne, 246 Rainbow Drive, Silverthorne; (970) 262-0817

Town of Breckenridge, 150 Ski Hill Road, Breckenridge; (970) 547-3155; www.townof breckenridge.com

Local Events/Attractions

Backstage Theatre, 121 South Ridge Street, Breckenridge; (970) 453-0199; www.back stagetheatre.com

Barney Ford House Museum, Main and Washington, Breckenridge; (970) 453-5761

Breckenridge Music Festival, (970) 453-9142 (all summer), www.breckenridge musicfestival.com

Country Boy Mine, 0542 French Gulch Road, Breckenridge; (970) 453-4405; www.country boymine.com

Edwin Carter Museum, 111 North Ridge Street, Breckenridge; (970) 453-9022

Restaurants

Breckenridge Brewery, 600 South Main Street, Breckenridge; (970) 453-1550; www.breckenridgebrewery.com

Cool River Coffee House & Bakery, 325 South Main Street, Breckenridge; (970) 453-1716

Crown Coffee House & Tavern, 215 South Main Street, Breckenridge; (970) 453-6022

Mi Casa Mexican Restaurant & Cantina, 600 South Park Avenue Breckenridge; (970) 453-2071; www.stormrestaurants.com/micasa/

Organizations

Town of Breckenridge Open Space and Trails Division, (970) 547-3155

Public Transportation (free)

Breckenridge Free Ride, (970) 547-3141, Town of Breckenridge, www.townofbreckenridge .com (click on Visitor then Transportation)

Summit Stage, (970) 668-0999, www.summit stage.com

BUILDING THE BARNEY FORD TRAIL
The Open Space Departments of the Town of Breckenridge and Summit County dedicated the Barney Ford Trail on September 26, 2003. The ceremony celebrated not only the trail, but also all the community support and cooperation involved. The trail crosses jointly owned county/town open space, portions of the White River National Forest, and seven private parcels. The seven landowners granted trail easements across their parcels for the trail. The Barney Ford Trail enables people to hike or mountain bike from town out to the backcountry trails east of town without having to get on a paved road or trespassing.

The trail was mostly built by the race/event promotion company Maverick Sports and a teenage crew from the Rocky Mountain Youth Corps. The people of Summit County love their trails, and local trail groups such as Friends of Breckenridge Trails and Summit Fat Tire Society put volunteers on the ground to finish different sections.

17 Mohawk Lakes

The Spruce Creek trails gently climbs through thick forest for 1.5 miles. After the junction with the Wheeler National Recreation Trail, various open areas provide glimpses of the silver ribbon of Continental Falls. After passing the remains of a mill and two old cabins, the trail switchbacks up a steep hill south of the falls through rock gardens of beautiful flowers with views to distant peaks. Passing the top of an old tram, the trail snakes uphill then pops out on a bench containing crystal clear Lower Mohawk Lake with its backdrop of craggy peaks, waterfalls, and mining relics.

Start: At Spruce Creek Trail #58 trailhead
Distance: 6 miles out and back to Lower Mohawk Lake
Approximate hiking time: 2.5 to 5 hours
Difficulty: More Difficult
Elevation gain: 1,480 feet to Lower Mohawk Lake
Trail surface: Dirt trail and boulders
Seasons: Best from late June to early October
Other trail users: Mountain bikers
Canine compatibility: Dogs permitted (must be under voice control)

Land status: National forest
Nearest town: Breckenridge
Fees and permits: No fees or permits required
Maps: USGS map: Breckenridge National Geographic Trails Illustrated: #109 Breckenridge, Tennessee Pass
Trail contact: White River National Forest, Dillon Ranger District, 680 Blue River Parkway, Silverthorne; (970) 468–5400; www.fs.fed.us/r2/whiteriver, www.dillonrangerdistrict.com

Finding the trailhead: From Interstate 70 exit 203, Frisco/Breckenridge, drive south through Frisco and Breckenridge on Highway 9 for 13.1 miles to Spruce Creek Road (The Crown subdivision). Turn right (west) onto Spruce Creek Road. At the first junction, stay to the right. At the second

Lower Mohawk Lake from trail to Mohawk Lake

junction turn left (southwest). The road is well marked with Spruce Creek Road signs at different intersections. Drive on Spruce Creek Road for about 1.3 miles to the trailhead parking area. The trail starts on the south side of the parking lot. No facilities are available at the trailhead. *DeLorme Colorado Atlas & Gazetteer:* Page 48 A2

Special considerations: The lower part of the trail is nice for cross-country skiing in winter. Be aware of avalanche danger higher up. Hunters may use this area during hunting season.

The Hike

Colorful wildflowers, ribbons of waterfalls, and spectacular peaks coupled with a close-up look at remains of the mining era make this trail a very popular hike. The first 1.5 miles of the trail are quite gentle and enjoyed by both hikers and mountain bikers. The Summit Fat Tire Society worked on this section of trail in the 1990s as evidenced by the nice bridges along the way. When you reach the Wheeler National Recreation Trail, take a quick walk to the right then left to a little viewpoint. Some logs provide seats to enjoy the view of Continental Falls and the peaks above Mohawk Lakes.

The trail intersects and joins an old road after about 2 miles. Follow the road staying left of a huge boulder and find the trail again to the right below the diversion

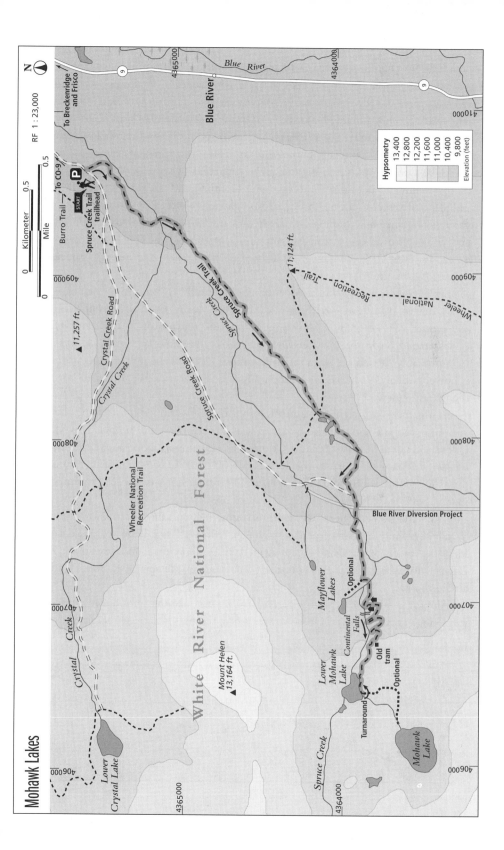

Mohawk Lakes

RF 1 : 23,000

Hypsometry

13,400
12,800
12,200
11,600
11,000
10,400
9,800

Elevation (feet)

N

To Breckenridge
and Frisco

Blue River

Blue River

Burro Trail

To CO-9

START

P

Spruce Creek Trail
trailhead

▲ 11,257 ft.

Crystal Creek Road

Crystal Creek

Spruce Creek

Spruce Creek Trail

Spruce Creek Road

Wheeler National
Recreation Trail

Wheeler National
Recreation Trail

▲ 11,124 ft.

White River National Forest

Blue River Diversion Project

Mayflower Lakes

Optional

Lower
Mohawk Lake

Continental Falls

Old tram

Optional

Mount Helen
▲ 13,164 ft.

Crystal Creek

Lower
Crystal Lake

Turnaround

Spruce Creek

Mohawk
Lake

0   Kilometer   0.5

0   Mile   0.5

dam. The trail climbs steeply from here then levels out with more views of Continental Falls. If you have time, take the side trip to little Mayflower Lake and the remains of the old town. Back on the trail to the lakes, pass several more cabin ruins. The trail becomes a braided confusion of trails, which the U.S. Forest Service plans to remedy in September 2006. The trail suddenly comes upon the remains of an old mill. The Mohawk Company built a mill in 1888.

Make sure to look up to the left at the mill ruins to see a cabin. The trail passes by that cabin and does not climb up along Continental Falls. After passing the cabins, the trail switchbacks up through some glorious fields of wildflowers. The rock gardens contain blue chiming bells, rosy and scarlet paintbrush, yellow sunflowers, and white bistort. Blue Colorado columbines bloom nearby. This hike is known as a "century" or "100 wildflower" trail because more than one hundred species of flowers can be found in the area.

Little side trips take you to overlooks of the falls. Across the forest below are views east to Baldy and Red Peak and north to Mount Helen. The trail occasionally crosses slabs of granite. Above one slab is the remains of an old tram, its two cables draped across the trail. The flywheel looks like those on today's ski lifts. This tram probably carried ore from the mines above down to the mill. A little farther up is Lower Mohawk Lake, where a little trail to the right leads to a rock shelf to enjoy the fantastic view.

Across the lake are the remains of an old building and behind it along the cliff are mine tailings. Look to the north to see another old mine tunnel. The Mount Gilead and Glen-Mohawk Mining Companies dug tunnels above treeline at the base of Pacific Peak at the turn of the century (1900). The 13,950-foot peak culminates the ridge to the south of Mohawk Lake. The tunnels bored into the mountain as much as 900 feet into veins of gold and silver ore.

Trout swim in the clear lake, fed from snowmelt and the waterfalls to the west. Watch for white-crowned sparrows flying overhead. These large sparrows can be identified by their black-and-white-striped heads. They mate and nest in areas like Lower Mohawk Lake, at the boundary (ecotone) of the spruce-fir forest and the alpine tundra.

Along the edge of the lake, riparian-area flowers like the pink queen's crown or ruby king's crown flourish. Other flowers along the trail include white globeflowers,

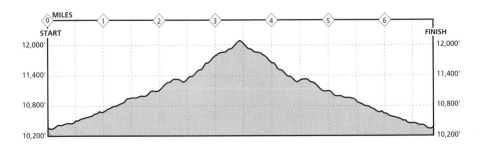

yellow paintbrush, clover, daisies, pink Parry's primrose, lavender Jacob's ladder, and bright yellow alpine avens. Pink alpine lousewort hides under the plentiful willows.

If you have time, hike up to Mohawk Lake on the willow-lined trail with views of the lower lake, Breckenridge area, and Grays and Torreys Peaks.

Miles and Directions

0.0 Start at the Spruce Creek Trail #58 trailhead bulletin board. 409636mE 4365593mN Elevation 10,370 feet. The trail Ys not far from the trailhead; go straight and uphill.

1.5 Arrive at the junction with the Wheeler National Recreatioin Trail. Continue straight ahead on Spruce Creek Trail. 408155mE 4364132mN

2.0 Come to a dirt road. Walk left on the road to a huge boulder and stay on the road to the left of the boulder. Near the diversion dam, turn right onto the trail by the trail sign. 407511mE 4363893mN

2.3 The trail Ys. 407149mE 4363851mN Take an optional 0.25-mile out-and-back hike to Mayflower Lake and the remains of several cabins. Return the way you came. The trail to Mohawk Lake is to the left at the Y. After crossing the creek the trail becomes many trails. Stay more to the right as you head uphill. (**Note:** The U.S. Forest Service plans to remedy the braided trail system and improve signage and drainage in September 2006.)

2.4 Come to the remains of an old mill. Follow the trail to the right of the mill, then by a lone tree stump and boulder where the trail Ys, go left. At the next Y take the left trail to the two old cabins. (This route may change after trail work is completed.)

2.5 The trail passes between two cabins by the sign. 406982mE 4363824mN Elevation 11,385 feet. The trail switchbacks up a steep headwall with some rock slabs in the trail.

2.6 Side trail to the right for an optional view of Continental Falls. About 0.1-mile out-and-back.

2.7 Side trail to the right for an optional view of Continental Falls. About 0.05-mile out-and-back.

2.8 Look up to see the remains of an old tram. 406779mE 4363781mN Cross the two cables. Either head to the tram or follow the trail to the right. Past the tram, the trail Ys. Hike up the trail to the left up a boulder.

3.0 Trail Ys. 406554mE 4363878mN. The right branch goes to a big rock slab with views of Lower Mohawk Lake, old mining remnants, and a cascade. Elevation 11,850 feet. The left branch continues around the lower lake and heads to Mohawk Lake (optional hike). Return the way you came if you don't want to hike to Mohawk Lake.

3.1 Trail Ys. The right branch leads to the creek and the other side of Lower Mohawk Lake. See Options for the hike to Mohawk Lake.

6.0 Arrive back at the trailhead and parking lot.

Options:

1. At mile 2.3 a trail leads north past the remains of Mayflower town to Mayflower Lake. The hike is an easy 0.25-mile out-and-back.

2. Mohawk Lake at 12,095 feet is about 0.3 mile from the Lower Mohawk Lake. Continue around the lower lake on the trail. At 3.1 miles (from the trailhead),

the trail Ys. 406444mE 4363845mN The trail to Mohawk Lake clambers up the boulder before you and climbs up through some scratchy willows. At 3.4 miles you'll arrive at Mohawk Lake. 406252mE 4363640mN Elevation 12,095 feet. Enjoy the lake and great scenery. Return the way you came for a 6.8-mile out-and-back hike. Total elevation gain from the trailhead is 1,725 feet. Mohawk Lake is above treeline, so be aware of thunderstorms and lightning. Snow lingers here into July.

Hike Information

Local Information

Breckenridge Resort Chamber, Daniels Cabin Information Center, 309 North Main Street, Breckenridge; (877) 864-0868; www.go breck.com

Summit County Chamber of Commerce, (800) 530-3099, www.summitchamber.org

Summit Visitor Information Center, Outlets at Silverthorne, 246 Rainbow Drive, Silverthorne; (970) 262-0817

Local Events/Attractions

Backstage Theatre, 121 South Ridge Street, Breckenridge; (970) 453-0199; www.back stagetheatre.com

Barney Ford House Museum, Main and Washington, Breckenridge; (970) 453-5761

Breckenridge Music Festival, (970) 453-9142 (all summer), www.breckenridgemusic festival.com

Country Boy Mine, 0542 French Gulch Road, Breckenridge; (970) 453-4405; www.country boymine.com

Edwin Carter Museum, 111 North Ridge Street, Breckenridge; (970) 453-9022

Hike Tours

Colorado Bike & Ski Tours, P.O. Box 1041, Silverthorne, 80498; (970) 668-8900; www.coloradobikeandski.com

Restaurants

Breckenridge Brewery, 600 South Main Street, Breckenridge; (970) 453-1550; www.breckenridgebrewery.com

Cool River Coffee House & Bakery, 325 South Main Street, Breckenridge; (970) 453-1716

Crown Coffee House & Tavern, 215 South Main Street, Breckenridge; (970) 453-6022

Mi Casa Mexican Restaurant & Cantina, 600 South Park Avenue Breckenridge; (970) 453-2071; www.stormrestaurants.com/micasa/

Organizations

Friends of Dillon Ranger District, www.fdrd.org or call the Dillon Ranger District, (970) 468-5400, for current contact.

In Addition

Leave No Trace

Leaving no trace in the backcountry is a true backcountry skill. How good are your skills?

As the number of people visiting our public lands increases, impacts are also on the rise. Conflicts between visitors, dogs harassing wildlife and other visitors, trash, messy campsites, degraded trails, undesignated trails (user created), and improper waste disposal are a few obvious problems. You may be only one hiker, but there are hundreds of thousands of us now. Think of 200,000 feet (or more) instead of just two!

If each of us takes a little time to learn about the environments which we love to explore, we can minimize many impacts. The concept of Leave No Trace was developed to help us make informed decisions about our behavior and habits in the backcountry and also on public lands closer to home (frontcountry).

The principles of Leave No Trace are

1. Plan Ahead and Prepare.
2. Travel and Camp on Durable Surfaces.
3. Dispose of Waste Properly.
4. Leave What You Find.
5. Minimize Campfire Impacts.
6. Respect Wildlife.
7. Be Considerate of Other Visitors.

1. **Plan Ahead and Prepare.** Prior planning prevents poor performance. The basic tenet is to know where you're going, what the environment is like, and come prepared for current conditions. By planning ahead, you can avoid most problems that typically result in leaving a trace. Prior planning includes weather forecast, area regulations, fire restrictions, difficulty of the trail versus your group's abilities, availability of water, etc. Knowing these items will help you decide what to pack, how far you can travel per day, etc. Wet trails imply waterproof boots, not running shoes. Good backcountry skills include map and compass reading and perhaps Global Positioning System (GPS) use. Repackaging the needed amount of food into nonbreakable containers minimizes trash amounts. A good mountain-oriented first-aid course helps prepare you for various emergencies. Remember, cell phones don't always work in mountains, canyons, or away from main highways and towns. Your brain is your most important resource.

2. **Travel and Camp on Durable Surfaces.** Durable surfaces do not easily sustain damage. Dry grass is less susceptible to damage than wet areas and woody plants. Special care is needed in fragile environments such as alpine tundra. What is appropriate for one is not appropriate for the other. Until trails dry out, either avoid muddy ones or get muddy! Walking around mud holes kills the veggie and widens the bog. To protect riparian areas on which most wildlife depend and to minimize being seen by others, camp 200 feet away—about seventy adult male steps—from streams, lakes, and trails. Use an existing campsite that's an appropriate distance whenever possible.

3. **Dispose of Waste Properly.** Who wants to see trash when they're hiking? Pack out everything you bring in. Food scraps, apple cores, and orange peels do harm animals. They become used to human food or get sick. Animals dig up buried food and tampons. For human feces, walk at least 200 feet (about seventy adult male steps) away from campsites, water sources, and trails, dig a cathole 6 to 8 inches deep, then cover it. Pack out or bury dog feces too. If you're above treeline, pack out feces because holes damage the tundra. Likewise, to wash yourself or dishes, carry water 200 feet away and use and dispose of it there. Use only biodegradable soap away from water sources. Contaminated water affects all of us!

4. **Leave What You Find.** Indian artifacts, petroglyphs and pictographs, old cabins and equipment are protected by law. Even antlers or cool rocks belong where they are. Enjoy them where you find them and leave them for others to enjoy. Wildflowers die quickly after being picked. If you find berries, pick only one out of ten. Animals depend on the rest. Leave the area cleaner than you found it, taking some time to restore pine needles and twigs to hide your traces. Besides leaving no trace, leave no weeds! Noxious weeds are becoming a major problem in our wild places. Clean your boots and other equipment between trips to avoid transporting non-native weed seed.

5. **Minimize Campfire Impacts.** Campfires are really an indulgence and not a necessity. Lightweight stoves are easier to cook on and don't leaves scars. Candles propped in aluminum foil create a nice cozy atmosphere. Enjoy the stars! Fires can leave scars for years. Many areas are picked clean of dead and downed wood. If you do build a fire, learn to build a mound fire or use an existing fire ring. Gather no bigger than wrist-sized dead and downed wood from dispersed places. Make sure your fire has burned completely, and when the ashes are thoroughly cooled, scatter them.

6. **Respect Wildlife.** With development encroaching farther into the backcountry and more people recreating, wildlife is under more stress than ever. Never let your dog chase wildlife, even squirrels. It's illegal under Colorado state law to harass wildlife anyway. Make sure to hang your food and trash or use bear-proof containers. Mice, chipmunks, and pine martens rip into packs too! Feeding

wildlife can be very harmful to them and possibly to you. Watch wildlife from a distance—they need personal space like we do.

7. **Be Considerate of Other Visitors.** Remember you are not alone in the backcountry very often. Others come to enjoy peace and quiet. Avoid talking loudly or bringing boom boxes for noise. Barking dogs can ruin a peaceful setting. Camp and take breaks off the trail to allow others a sense of solitude. "Natural quiet" is becoming a precious resource these days. Please help preserve it. Horses have the right of way. Backcountry users are typically friendly and thoughtful. Let's keep the tradition going!

Leaving no trace in the backcountry is a true backcountry skill. Accept the challenge to Leave No Trace!

For further information contact the Leave No Trace Center for Outdoor Ethics at (800) 332–4100, (303) 442–8222, or www.LNT.org.

Leave No Weeds

On January 16, 2004, U.S. Forest Service chief Dale Bosworth talked about the four threats to our nation's forests and grasslands. One threat is the spread of invasive species. The chief said: "These are species that evolved in one place and wound up in another, where the ecological controls they evolved with are missing. They take advantage of their new surroundings to crowd out or kill off native species, destroying habitat for native wildlife."

Even if you do your best to Leave No Trace, did you Leave No Weeds? Weed seed can cling to anything. After a hike, you might unknowingly transport these seeds to a new location and start a new infestation. Here are some ideas of how to prevent spreading weed seed from one area to another.

1. **Be Aware and Prepare.** Learn to identify noxious weeds. Rid camping gear and clothes of mud and weed seed before each trip and at each campsite. Brush animals before and after hiking trips to remove weed seed.

2. **Camp and Travel in Weed Free Areas.** Wash your vehicle, boots, hiking poles, tents, and clothes before and after each outing. Stay on established roads and trails. Avoid camping in or hiking through weed infested areas. Avoid soil disturbing activities and practices.

3. **Report It.** Report weed infestations to your local U.S. Forest Service or Bureau of Land Management office.

For more information on noxious weeds, contact the Colorado Weed Management Association at (970) 887–1228 or www.cwma.org.

18 Wheeler Lake

Wheeler Lake is a gem of an alpine lake, tucked in an elbow turn of the Continental Divide. A hillside covered with white cascades pours into the lake from snow melting under the crystal blue Colorado sky. The hike follows an extreme four-wheel drive road under part of the old Magnolia Mill and past various relics of mining days. Hikers should expect to see vehicles on this multiple-use road. Mount Lincoln at 14,286 feet watches over the broad valley of the Middle Fork of the South Platte River, above which lies Wheeler Lake.

Start: At the three-way road split below the Magnolia Mill
Distance: 6.8 miles out and back
Approximate hiking time: 2.8 to 4.5 hours
Difficulty: More difficult
Elevation gain: 1,220 feet
Trail surface: Dirt road and boulders
Seasons: Best from July to early October
Other trail users: Multiple use
Canine compatibility: Dogs permitted (must be under voice control)
Land status: National forest
Nearest towns: Alma and Fairplay

Fees and permits: No fees or permits required
Maps: USGS maps: Alma, Climax; National Geographic Trails Illustrated: #109 Breckenridge, Tennessee Pass
Trail contact: Pike National Forest, South Park Ranger District, 320 U.S. Highway 285, Fairplay; (719) 836-2031; www.fs.fed.us/r2/psicc
Other: Some water is found along the trail. About 2.2 miles (one way) of the hike is above treeline. Keep an eye and ear open for thunderstorms and lightning and turn around if the weather turns bad.

Finding the trailhead: From Interstate 70 exit 203, Frisco/Breckenridge, head south on Highway 9 through Frisco and Breckenridge about 20.7 miles to the top of Hoosier Pass. About 0.9 mile below the top of the pass on the south side, make a sharp right turn onto Park County Road (CR) 4. At the next intersection take the right fork past the NO WINTER MAINTENANCE sign. At the following junction Park CR 4 switchbacks to the left. Continue to the right onto Forest Development Road (FDR) 408, which takes you past Montgomery Reservoir. The unofficial trailhead is up a steep, rocky road that some vehicles may not be able to negotiate. Parking is available near the Blue River Diversion Project tunnel about 0.4 mile from the unofficial trailhead. Beyond the tunnel, parking is available for only a few cars at small pullouts. Do NOT block the road. If you have a vehicle that can make the steep, rocky hill, drive up it and park where you can without blocking the road. The road dead-ends near the creek in a parking area in which you can turn around. The four-wheel-drive road up to Wheeler Lake is rated extreme. No facilities are available at the unofficial trailhead. *DeLorme: Colorado Atlas & Gazetteer:* Page 48 B2

Special considerations: The road is closed at the NO WINTER MAINTENANCE sign about 1.2 miles from the trailhead. Be aware of avalanche danger in this entire area.

Snowmelt cascades into Wheeler Lake in mid-July. ▶

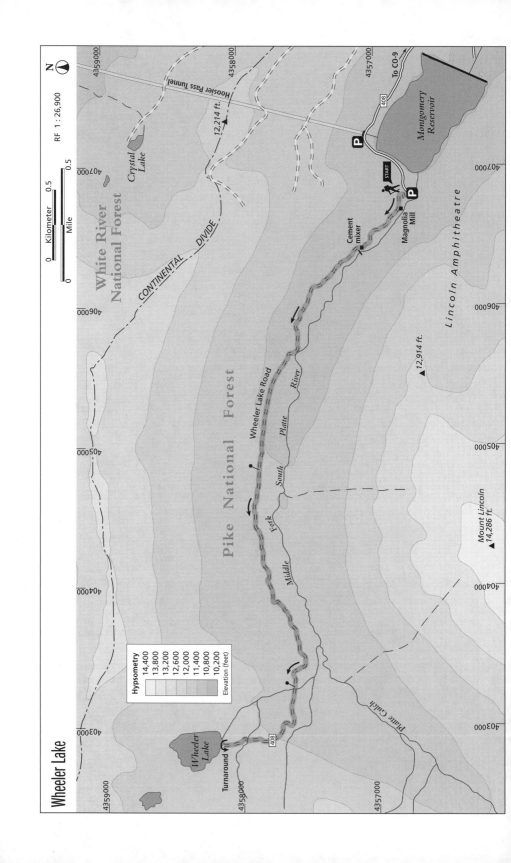

Wheeler Lake

RF 1 : 26,900

N

0   Kilometer   0.5

0   Mile   0.5

Hypsometry

14,400
13,800
13,200
12,600
12,000
11,400
10,800
10,200

Elevation (feet)

White River
National Forest

Pike National Forest

CONTINENTAL DIVIDE

Crystal
Lake

Hoosier Pass Tunnel

12,214 ft.

Wheeler Lake

Turnaround

408

Middle Fork

South Platte River

Wheeler Lake Road

Platte Gulch

START

Magnolia
Mill

Cement
mixer

408

P

P

Montgomery Reservoir

To CO-9

12,914 ft.

Lincoln Amphitheatre

Mount Lincoln
14,286 ft.

4359000
4358000
4357000

403000
404000
405000
406000
407000
4358000
4359000

The Hike

Below the waters of Montgomery Reservoir lie the remains of the town of Montgomery. The little town started in 1859 after gold was discovered on nearby mountains. Within two years the town had two hotels, seventy cabins, and two sawmills. In one two-week period, miners found between fifteen and twenty rich strikes. Citizens decided to name the towering peak to the west, which they believed to be the highest in Colorado, after President Lincoln. They even sent him a bar of gold from one of the mines located on his namesake. The following year 1,000 people called Montgomery home. A drugstore, mercantile, dry goods store, and various saloons served their needs. Six gold mills worked the ore from the area's mines, with the Magnolia, Montgomery, and Pendleton being top producers. As many as 2,000 people may have lived in town at one time. They even proposed Montgomery as the state capital!

Montgomery produced $500,000 in gold, but after a few years the surface ores played out. The little town faded away and was mostly deserted by 1868. In the 1870s, Montgomery enjoyed a little resurgence due to silver mines in the area, especially the Moose Mine on the slopes of Mount Bross. In 1883 W. E. Traver and several others petitioned to establish a public road from Montgomery to Wheeler Lake along the Platte. By 1898 a third breath of life came to Montgomery, and the *Fairplay Flume* reported that all the Montgomery mines were very active. One person believed the area would be the second Klondike. The Magnolia Mine was still producing in 1914, its shipments returning about $40 per ton. By the 1950s, Colorado Springs had purchased the land where Montgomery once thrived, and built a dam to store water diverted from the Blue River south of Breckenridge. The old town site drowned under water bound for the growing east slope city.

The hike along the jeep road makes one wonder how any four-wheeled vehicle can climb over some of the slabs of rock in the road. Most of the hike is actually gentle along the willow-lined road. A few mud puddles challenge the hiker and some calf-deep pools are avoided by finding trails hidden in the willows. The Continental Divide at the end of the broad valley produces beautiful views as does Mount Lincoln to the south. Between mile 0.5 and 2.5, look for old mine buildings high on the flank of North Star Mountain to the north.

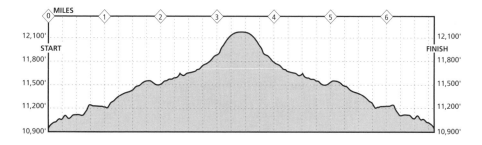

The valley is riddled with private mining claims and old prospect holes. To avoid trespassing, please stay on the road and away from the old mines. Some old prospect holes have been covered by wood, then by eroded soil posing danger if one breaks through the rotted covering. The tops of Mounts Lincoln and Bross are privately owned mining claims, many patented back in the 1800s. Some people are not respecting private property, destroying gates, breaking into the mines and historic buildings, and pilfering. Owners are concerned about litigation if anyone gets hurt by falling into mining tunnels and shafts. Climbing these peaks has become a hot topic. The 1994 version of the Alma and Climax USGS topo maps show the private mining claims interspersed in public lands.

Just before you arrive at the lake, mine tailings cover an area to the left of the road. When you reach the end of the road, head down toward the lake. A huge slab of rock provides a great lunch spot with views all around the lake. The remains of an old mine can be seen on the west side. The lakeshore is quite marshy and walking on wet vegetation can easily damage it. Multiple cascades pouring down and the bountiful colorful alpine wildflowers make Wheeler Lake a very special place.

Miles and Directions

0.0 Start at the three-way road junction with FDR 408 near the creek below the Magnolia Mill. Start hiking on the middle road, which switchbacks around and heads to the old mill. 406792mE 4356776mN Elevation 10,955 feet.

0.1 Walk beneath part of the Magnolia Mill.

0.4 Check out the old cement mixer and dam to the left. 406407mE 4357090mN

1.6 An unimproved road comes in from the right (north). 404774mE 4357865mN Continue straight ahead. Look to the right for mine tailings.

2.8 The road crosses a creek from Wheeler Lake. 403275mE 4357630mN If the creek is flowing down the road, walk in the creek if the current isn't too strong, or there's a trail to the right that goes through some willows and crosses the braided creek up higher.

2.9 The road Ys. Stay to the right (west) and head uphill.

3.4 Arrive at Wheeler Lake. 402864mE 4358129mN Elevation on rock slab above the lake is 12,175 feet. Return the way you came.

6.8 Arrive back at the trailhead.

Hike Information

Local Information
South Park Chamber of Commerce, Fairplay, (719) 386-3410, www.parkchamberof commerce.org
South Park Historical Foundation, Inc., (719) 836-2387, www.southparkcity.org

Local Events/Attractions
South Park City, Fairplay, (719) 836-2387, www.southparkcity.org,
Alma Fest, Town of Alma, (719) 836-2712.
Annual Como Mountain Man Rendezvous, Como, (719) 836-2698

Burro Days, Fairplay, (719) 836-2597, www.burrodays.com

Restaurants
Beary Beary Tastee Bakery, Fairplay, (719) 836-3212
Dinky Dairy, Fairplay, (719) 836-3465

Front Street Cafe, Fairplay, (719) 836-7031
Patti's, Fairplay, (719) 836-9500

Organizations
South Park 4X4 Club has adopted the Wheeler Trail. Contact the South Park Ranger District, (719) 836-2031, for the current contact.

19 Wheeler Trail

This trail to the top of Wheeler Pass (unofficial name) is the Wheeler National Recreation Trail. The Colorado Trail and the Continental Divide National Scenic Trail follow part of the same route. It climbs steadily at about a 15 percent grade through spruce-fir and lodgepole forest on the west slope of the Tenmile Range. The tundra flowers bloom brilliantly in July. From the ridge of the Tenmile Range, you can view the upper Blue River valley, the town of Breckenridge, the Breckenridge Ski Area, and the scars of mining days. Views of the Gore Range, Copper Mountain, and the Front Range are fabulous!

Start: At the Wheeler Flats Trailhead
Distance: 8.8 miles out and back
Approximate hiking time: 3.9 to 7 hours
Difficulty: Most Difficult
Elevation gain: 2,710 feet
Trail surface: Dirt trail
Seasons: Best from July to early October
Other trail users: Mountain bikers, equestrians
Canine compatibility: Dogs permitted (must be under voice control)
Land status: National forest
Nearest town: Copper Mountain and Frisco
Fees and permits: No fees or permits required

Maps: USGS maps: Vail Pass, Copper Mountain, Breckenridge; National Geographic Trails Illustrated: #108 Vail, Frisco, Dillon; #109 Breckenridge, Tennessee Pass
Trail contact: White River National Forest, Dillon Ranger District, 680 Blue River Parkway, Silverthorne; (970) 468-5400; www.fs.fed.us/r2/whiteriver, www.dillonrangerdistrict.com
Other: This hike ends on a ridge above treeline, so be sure to get an early start to avoid thunderstorms and accompanying lightning. Only a few tiny streams cross the trail, so bring plenty of water with you.

Finding the trailhead: From Interstate 70 exit 195, Copper Mountain/Leadville, drive southwest less than 1 mile on Highway 91 to the traffic light at the entrance to Copper Mountain Resort. Turn left at the traffic light and drive past the Copper Mountain Retail Center about 0.3 mile to the Wheeler Flats Trailhead parking lot. No facilities are available at the trailhead. The Summit Stage (free bus) stops at the entrance to Copper Mountain on the north, west of Highway 91. *DeLorme: Colorado Atlas & Gazetteer:* Page 38 D1.5 and Page 48 A1.5

Special considerations: The trail crosses several avalanche paths. Hunters may use this area during hunting season. The trail is neither marked nor maintained for winter use.

Wheeler National Recreation Trail with Copper Mountain ski runs and Gore Range

The Hike

In 1879, Judge John S. Wheeler purchased 320 acres, now part of Copper Mountain Resort, and started a hay ranch. The next year silver miners arrived, and the ranch became a town known by various names: Wheeler's Ranch, Wheeler Station, Wheeler's, Wheeler, and Wheeler Junction. Wheeler Junction prospered with a hotel, saloons, a post office, and several sawmills. In 1884 the Colorado & Southern Railroad finished laying tracks to Wheeler Junction on the east side of Tenmile Creek. Their railroad station at Wheeler was named Solitude Station. On the other side of the creek, the Denver & Rio Grande railroad had their line with a station called Wheeler's.

The trail is mostly flat the first mile while it follows part of the old Colorado & Southern Railroad route, now covering a gas pipeline. In one place the trail seems lower than the creek! This section used to be part of the Colorado Trail, but a trail reroute was completed in 2002 to avoid walking through Copper Mountain Resort. (See the Colorado Trail to Guller Creek hike for a hike along the new section of the Colorado Trail.)

After 1 mile, reach the junction with the Colorado Trail. Turn left up the trail to access Wheeler Pass. Judge Wheeler used this trail to take his stock from Wheeler Junction to his ranch in South Park. The trail, designated a national recreation trail in 1979, now ends near McCullough Gulch south of Breckenridge.

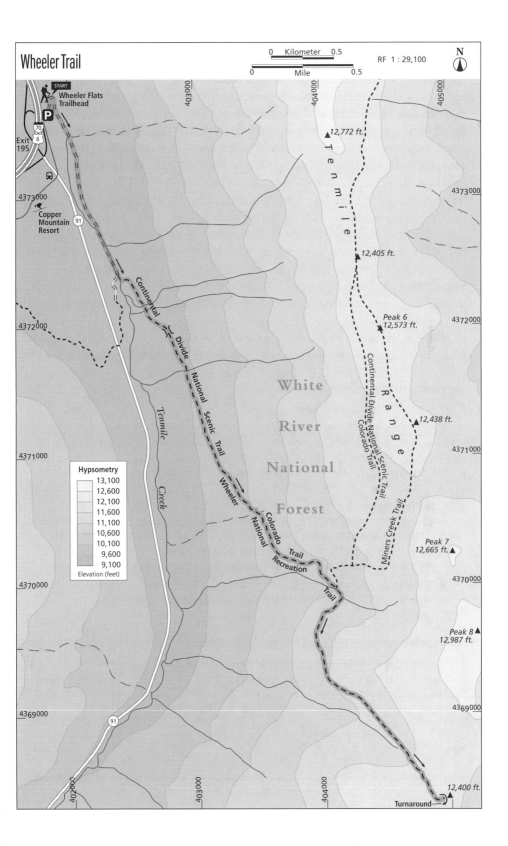

Wheeler Trail

Kilometer 0.5 / Mile 0.5

RF 1 : 29,100

N

START
Wheeler Flats
Trailhead

P

70
6
Exit
195

4373000

Copper
Mountain
Resort

91

Continental

Divide

National

Scenic

Trail

Wheeler

Colorado

National

Recreation

Trail

Tenmile

Creek

Hypsometry

Elevation (feet)
13,100
12,600
12,100
11,600
11,100
10,600
10,100
9,600
9,100

White

River

National

Forest

Tenmile

Range

▲12,772 ft.

▲12,405 ft.

Peak 6
12,573 ft. ▲

Continental Divide National Scenic Trail
Colorado Trail

▲12,438 ft.

Miners Creek Trail

Peak 7
12,665 ft. ▲

Peak 8 ▲
12,987 ft.

▲12,400 ft.

Turnaround

4373000

4372000

4371000

4370000

4369000

4373000

4372000

4371000

4370000

4369000

402000

403000

404000

405000

At about 3.6 miles, the trail exits the forest for a view south to Climax Molybdenum Mine's settling ponds. Several prosperous mining towns, including Robinson and Kokomo of Wheeler Junction's era, are buried there. Watch and listen for marmots. As you contour left into another drainage, you can see the ridge of the Tenmile Range and cairns marking the trail. From here the trail winds in and out of forest, meadow, and willows. Colorful wildflowers line the trail. Trees become twisted krummholz near treeline and finally give up. The trail is sometimes smothered by willows, but is passable. Three cairns made of good-sized logs mark the trail; however, the second one isn't even on the trail! Finally when your breath is short from elevation and steep trail, you see the summit cairn. That is, until you reach it and realize that the trail continues up. Notice the vegetation along the trail. Willows and little red elephants grow in little depressions that hold snow and water. The drier areas contain sedges and grasses, old-man-of-the-mountains, paintbrush, American bistort, chickweed, and alpine avens. The tundra is fragile, so if you go off the trail, step on rocks when you can. Spread your party out to prevent trampling the delicate tundra plants.

The sign at the top of Wheeler Pass reports an elevation of 12,460 feet, but the topo map clearly indicates just under 12,400 feet. Be sure to hike to the little rocky knob on the left (12,408 feet) for the best views east. Breckenridge, French Gulch, and part of the Breckenridge ski area are on the east side; Copper Mountain and the Gore Range lie to the northwest.

Today both Breckenridge and Copper Mountain Resort boast of their popular ski areas. You can see lifts at each area from various points along the trail. Skiing, other forms of recreation, and vacation homes have replaced mining in a new "gold rush" to the Rockies.

Miles and Directions

0.0 Start at Wheeler Flats Trailhead. 401850mE 4376702mN Elevation 9,690 feet. Walk across the wooden bridge and turn right on the paved recreation path. In 360 feet, turn right across another bridge and walk down the dirt trail under which lies a gas pipeline.

1.0 Arrive at the junction with the Colorado Trail and Continental Divide National Scenic Trail. 402411mE 4372381mN Turn left here and start the long climb to the top of the Tenmile Range.

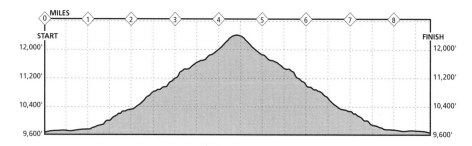

1.4 Bridge over a creek in an avalanche chute. 402785mE 4371983mN

3.1 Come to the junction with Miners Creek Trail (also the Colorado Trail and Continental Divide National Scenic Trail). 404111mE 4369943mN Continue onward and upward on the trail to the right.

3.6 The trail curves into a drainage that goes to the top of the Tenmile Range and the hike's destination. Great views to the southwest of Highway 91 and the tailings ponds from the Climax Molybdenum Mine. 404006mE 4369291mN

4.4 Reach the top of Wheeler Pass (unofficial name) and the Tenmile Range. 404882mE 4368321mN Elevation 12,400 feet. To the left of the pass is a little hump of rocks, which makes a great spot for lunch and view of Breckenridge and the Blue River drainage. Return the way you came.

8.8 Arrive back at the trailhead.

Hike Information

Local Information

Copper Mountain Resort, (866) 841-2481, www.coppercolorado.com

Copper Mountain Resort Chamber, (970) 968-6477, www.copperchamber.com

Frisco Chamber of Commerce, 300 Main Street, (970) 668-5547; Frisco; www.friscocolorado.org

Summit County Chamber of Commerce, (800) 530-3099, www.summitchamber.org

Local Events/Attractions

Coors Colorado Barbecue Challenge, Frisco, www.townoffrisco.com/bbq.html

Copper Mountain Resort hosts various events throughout the year, (866) 841-2481, www.coppercolorado.com

Accommodations

Several campgrounds are located along the shores of Dillon Reservoir near Frisco. For more information, contact White River National Forest, Dillon Ranger District, (970) 468-5400, www.fs.fed.us/r2/whiteriver, www.dillonrangerdistrict.com.

Restaurants

Imperial Palace, Village at Copper, (970) 968-6688

MiZuppa, 842 North Summit Boulevard, Frisco; (970) 668-8138

Q4U, 857 North Summit Boulevard, Frisco; (970) 668-1775

Salsa Mountain Cantina, Village at Copper, (970) 968-6300

Organizations

Friends of Dillon Ranger District, www.fdrd.org, or call the Dillon Ranger District, (970) 468-5400, for the current contact.

Public Transportation (free)

Summit Stage, (970) 668-0999, www.summitstage.com

SKY AVALANCHE CHUTES ON THE TENMILE
On the first mile and a half of the Wheeler Trail, several little creeks fall steeply down gullies devoid of tall trees. These gullies are winter avalanche chutes. When seen from eastbound I-70 between Vail Pass and Copper, several chutes in this area (with a little imagination) spell the word "SKY."

20 Colorado Trail from Wheeler Flats to Guller Creek

In summer 2002, volunteer crews from the Colorado Trail Foundation completed a reroute of the Colorado Trail where it traverses above Copper Mountain Resort. The new trail crosses several ski runs, travels under chairlifts, drops near the Village at Copper, then winds down to meet the older part of the Colorado Trail near the confluence of Jacque Creek and Guller Creek. Various wildflowers and remnants of the old days of mining and logging mix with today's white gold (snow riding) along this trail.

Start: At the Wheeler Flats Trailhead (see Options for shorter possibilities)

Distance: 12.4 miles out and back

Approximate hiking time: 5 to 8.5 hours

Difficulty: More Difficult

Elevation gain: 890 feet

Trail surface: Dirt trail and dirt road

Seasons: Best from late June to early October (whenever Copper Mountain starts snowmaking)

Other trail users: Equestrians, mountain bikes

Canine compatibility: Dogs permitted (must be under voice control)

Land status: National forest

Nearest towns: Copper Mountain and Frisco

Fees and permits: No fees or permits required in summer

Maps: USGS maps: Copper Mountain, Vail Pass; National Geographic Trails Illustrated: #108 Vail, Frisco, Dillon; #109 Breckenridge, Tennessee Pass

Trail contacts: White River National Forest, Dillon Ranger District, 680 Blue River Parkway, Silverthorne; (970) 468-5400; www.fs.fed.us/r2/whiteriver, www.dillonrangerdistrict.com Colorado Trail Foundation, (303) 384-3729, www.coloradotrail.org

Other: This trail is popular with mountain bikers. Copper Stables uses some sections of the trail for guided horseback rides.

Finding the trailhead: From Interstate 70 exit 195, Copper Mountain/Leadville, drive southwest less than 1 mile on Highway 91 to the traffic light at the entrance to Copper Mountain Resort. Turn left at the traffic light and drive past the Copper Mountain Retail Center about 0.3 mile to the Wheeler Flats Trailhead parking lot. No facilities are available at the trailhead. The Summit Stage (free bus) stops at the entrance to Copper Mountain. *DeLorme: Colorado Atlas & Gazetteer:* Page 38 D1.5 to Page 48 A1

Special considerations: The Guller Creek valley is popular with hunters during hunting season. The trail between mile 1.5 (Highway 91) and mile 5.8 (ski-area boundary) is closed in fall and winter whenever Copper starts making snow. Winter access to Guller Creek is via Copper Mountain chair lifts (fee charged) or ski runs. For more winter usage information, log onto www.huts.org and click on Huts and Routes then Janet's Cabin. In winter, the Guller Creek area is a day-fee area. No day use, no summer use, and no dogs at Janet's Cabin.

An old cabin lies in ruins near Guller Creek.

The Hike

For Colorado Trail aficionados, hikers on the old section walked on the road from Wheeler Flats trailhead through Copper Mountain then along the paved recreational path to a bridge over Tenmile Creek. From there the trail followed Guller Creek to its headwaters and east to Searle Pass. To provide a better backcountry experience, part of this segment was rerouted during the summers of 2000, 2001, and 2002. The Colorado Trail Foundation and Copper Mountain Resort worked together to plan the new route and the U.S. Forest Service (USFS) approved the plan. Over three years, thirteen weeklong trail crews averaging eighteen people each worked creating new tread. The USFS and Volunteers for Outdoor Colorado (VOC) then revegetated the old trail from Jacque Creek down (east) to the paved recreational path. This hike follows the new section of the Colorado Trail to Guller Creek.

The official trailhead starts at Wheeler Flats Trailhead although the first mile of trail, which follows the old railbed of the Colorado & Southern Railroad, is no longer part of the Colorado Trail.

Silver was discovered in Tenmile Canyon in 1878 between Copper Mountain and the top of Fremont Pass. The mines and buildings needed lumber, and Judge

John S. Wheeler built the first sawmill in Tenmile Canyon in 1878. He and seven legislators purchased numerous mining claims in Tenmile Canyon, operating as the Federal Silver Mining Company of Colorado.

In 1879, Judge Wheeler purchased 320 acres, now part of Copper Mountain Resort, and started a hay ranch. The next year silver miners arrived, finding silver on Copper Mountain's slopes. Wheeler's ranch became a town known by various names: Wheeler's Ranch, Wheeler Station, Wheeler's, Wheeler, and Wheeler Junction. Wheeler prospered with a hotel, saloons, a post office, and several sawmills. By 1881, the town had 225 residents. The Denver & Rio Grande Railroad reached the town from Leadville in fall 1881 and opened Wheeler's Station. The railroad ceased service in 1911.

▶ Copper Mountain's skiing potential was first realized by the U.S. Forest Service in 1952. In 1962 investors started inquiring about building a ski area. Formal applications to develop Copper were submitted in 1969, and the resort opened on December 5, 1972, with five ski lifts, twenty-six miles of trails, and six new buildings.

Despite its status as a mining town, Wheeler became a logging center. Silver-ore smelters in the area ran on charcoal fuel. Loggers often set fire to the forest because dry timber proved best for making charcoal. By 1899 loggers had basically stripped the mountains of trees and the charcoal industry put itself out of business.

Wheeler also attracted tourists who came for the beautiful scenery and excellent fishing. In 1884 the Colorado & Southern (C&S) Railroad finished laying tracks to Wheeler on the east side of Tenmile Creek. Their trains arrived over Boreas Pass to Breckenridge and on to Frisco. The C&S railroad called their Wheeler station Solitude Station. Rail service ended around 1937.

At mile 1, the old railbed intersects with the Colorado Trail and the Continental Divide National Scenic Trail. Here begins the new segment. When you reach mile 2.7 near the snowmaking pump house, the ski run coming down from your left is called Skid Road. In winter loggers often slid their newly cut logs downhill on snow on trails such as Skid Road. From here the trail wanders near buildings and crosses above the Village. If you need a snack or restroom, it's time to sneak off the trail into civilization. The trail travels on a dirt ski-area road for about 0.4 mile. About mile 4.3 tall stumps provide evidence of winter logging. At the bridge over Guller Creek, the new and old segments of the Colorado Trail intersect. Off to the right (north), the remains of an old cabin make a great place to enjoy lunch and the scenery.

Miles and Directions

0.0 Start at Wheeler Flats Trailhead. 401850mE 4373702mN Elevation 9,690 feet. Walk across the wooden bridge and turn right (northeast) on the paved recreation path. In approximately 360 feet, turn right (south) across another bridge and walk down the dirt trail under which lies a gas pipeline.

Colorado Trail from Wheeler Flats to Guller Creek

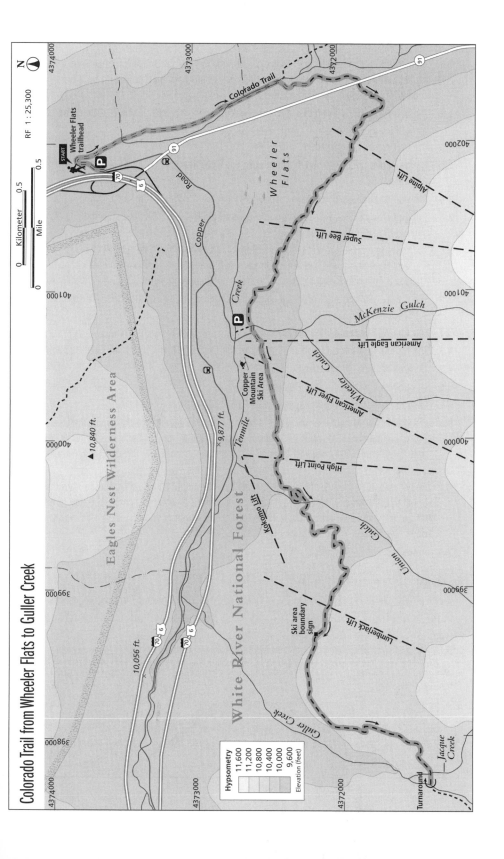

1.0 Arrive at the junction with the Colorado Trail and Continental Divide National Scenic Trail. 402411mE 4372381mN Turn right (west) and walk across the bridge and up a small knoll. Turn left (south) at the trail sign.

1.2 The trail Ys. Take the left (closest to the creek) branch. 402390mE 4372205mN The trail becomes a singletrack and follows power poles.

1.5 The trail crosses Highway 91. 402379mE 4371849mN

2.0 The trail goes under Alpine Lift and across the Triple Treat ski run. 401994mE 4371900mN

2.5 The trail goes under Super Bee Lift. 401441mE 4372296mN

2.7 The trail crosses Skid Road ski run and goes to the left (south) of the snowmaking pump house. 401129mE 4372426mN

3.1 The trail turns off to the left (uphill). Watch for a rock with the Colorado Trail logo on it. The trail traverses above the American Eagle Lift base. The trail becomes a road and crosses a little creek above Copper Mountain's Village area. 400782mE 4372627mN

3.5 The trail Ys. Walk straight onto the single-track trail where the road curves. 400068mE 4372438mN

3.7 The trail Ys. Turn left on the Colorado Trail.

4.2 The trail Ys. Turn left and continue uphill on the Colorado Trail. 399513mE 4372283mN

4.3 The trail Ys. Turn right on the Colorado Trail.

4.6 The trail Ys. Turn right on the Colorado Trail.

5.1 Pass the ski-area boundary sign. 398697mE 4372148mN

5.8 The trail is above cabin remains to the right. Take a few minutes to check out the interesting construction. In about 260 feet, is a trail junction with Elk Track, the winter access trail. 398019mE 4371696mN Continue straight ahead on the Colorado Trail. Elevation 10,545 feet.

6.2 Arrive at Guller Creek. 397659mE 4371392mN Elevation 10,485 feet. The cabin ruins uphill to the right (north) is a great lunch spot. Return the way you came. You can jump off the trail above American Eagle Lift base for refreshments and rest stop on the way back. See Option 1 for more information.

12.4 Arrive back at the trailhead.

Options:

1. The official USFS trailhead for this section of the Colorado Trail is at Wheeler Flats Trailhead. Both the Colorado Trail Foundation and Copper Mountain

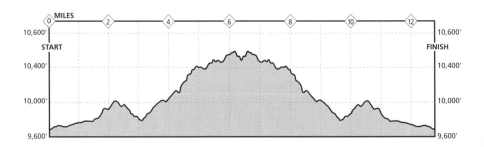

Resort stated that people can access the trail from the Village at Copper just west of the waypoint at mile 3.1 of the featured hike. Per Copper Mountain Resort, access to the Colorado Trail will be from the east side of Burning Stones Plaza to the east of the minigolf course, which is near American Eagle Lift (summer chairlift rides). The hike to Guller Creek from here is about 6.2 miles out and back, elevation gain 760 feet, difficulty moderate. Parking is available in/on the parking structure at the Ten Mile Circle cul-de-sac. You can also take the Summit Stage from the Frisco Transfer Center to Copper and get off at the Passage Point bus stop in Copper. Walk through the Village to Burning Stones Plaza to access the Colorado Trail.

2. If you would like to use the bus and hike the entire trail section as described, depart the Summit Stage at the entrance to Copper Mountain Resort, walk east across Highway 91 and down the access road to the Wheeler Flats Trailhead.

3. From where the trail crosses Guller Creek, you can continue farther up the valley toward Searle Pass, approximately an additional 4.7 miles one way. The Guller Creek valley is very beautiful and quiet. More cabin remains can be seen farther up the trail.

THE COLORADO TRAIL AND ITS FOUNDATION

In 1973, Merrill Hastings, in *Colorado Magazine,* suggested a trail that would take hikers from Denver to Durango. Bill Lucas, the U. S. Forest Service's Rocky Mountain regional forester at the time, became the advocate of this idea to be called the Colorado Trail. The trail would provide more hiking opportunities and relieve pressure on existing trails in the state. In November 1973 various forest user groups met with Lucas to discuss the possibility of the long trail. The 470-mile route would use existing trails where possible and build new trails in certain areas. After various starts and stops, Gudy Gaskill from the Colorado Mountain Club and Governor Richard Lamm helped create a two-year plan to finish the long trail. Gaskill created the nonprofit Colorado Trail Foundation (CTF) in 1986 to organize the volunteer crews that would complete the work and to take responsibility for the trail in partnership with the U.S. Forest Service. In two summers, about 1,400 volunteers in sixty-six trail crews completed the trail. Work to reroute some segments and trail maintenance on all sections continues in 2006.

The CTF sponsors trail crews each summer to keep the Colorado Trail an experience to enjoy and remember. For more information on the CTF or to volunteer, log onto www.coloradotrail.org or call (303) 384-3729.

Hike Information

Local Information

Copper Mountain Resort, (866) 841-2481, www.coppercolorado.com

Copper Mountain Resort Chamber, (970) 968-6477, www.copperchamber.com

Frisco Chamber of Commerce, 300 Main Street, (970) 668-5547; Frisco; www.friscocolorado.org

Summit Visitor Information Center, Outlets at Silverthorne, 246 Rainbow Drive, Silverthorne; (970) 262-0817

Local Events/Attractions

Coors Colorado Barbecue Challenge, Frisco, www.townoffrisco.com/bbq.html

Copper Mountain Resort hosts various events throughout the year, (866) 841-2481, www.coppercolorado.com

Accommodations

Several campgrounds are located along the shores of Dillon Reservoir near Frisco. For more information contact White River National Forest, Dillon Ranger District, (970) 468-5400, www.fs.fed.us/r2/whiteriver, www.dillonrangerdistrict.com.

Restaurants

Boatyard Pizzeria and Grill, 304 Main Street, Frisco; (970) 668-4728

Imperial Palace, Village at Copper, (970) 968-6688

Q4U, 857 North Summit Boulevard, Frisco; (970) 668-1775

Salsa Mountain Cantina, Village at Copper, (970) 968-6300

Hike Tours

Copper Mountain Resort offers naturalist-guided hikes at the ski area July 1 to Labor Day, (866) 841-2481, www.coppercolorado.com

Organizations

Colorado Trail Foundation, www.colorado trail.org, (303) 384-3729

Friends of Dillon Ranger District, www.fdrd.org, or call the Dillon Ranger District, (970) 468-5400, for the current contact.

Summit Huts Association, www.summithuts.org, (970) 453-8583

Public Transportation (free)

Summit Stage, (970) 668-0999, www.summit stage.com

21 Shrine Mountain

Shrine Mountain is a very popular family hike. The wildflowers in July are fabulous, a colorful masterpiece painted across the meadows and hills. Views from Shrine Mountain and Wingle Ridge are equally fabulous, with the Tenmile Range to the south, Gore Range to the north and east, and Mount of the Holy Cross and the Sawatch Range to the southwest. Hikers often enjoy snowball fights in July before snowbanks below the ridge finally melt.

Start: At the Shrine Ridge parking lot at the top of Shrine Pass by the bulletin board
Distance: 4.5 miles out and back
Approximate hiking time: 1.8 to 3 hours
Difficulty: Moderate
Elevation gain: 855 feet
Trail surface: Dirt road and dirt trail
Seasons: Best from July to early October
Other trail users: Equestrians
Canine compatibility: Dogs permitted (must be under voice control)
Land status: National forest
Nearest towns: Copper Mountain and Frisco

Fees and permits: No fees or permits required in summer. Daily fee required in winter.
Maps: USGS maps: Vail Pass, Red Cliff; National Geographic Trails Illustrated: #108 Vail, Frisco, Dillon
Trail contact: White River National Forest, Holy Cross Ranger District, 24747 U.S. Highway 24, Minturn; (970) 827-5715; www.fs.fed.us/r2/whiteriver
Other: Water is not plentiful along this trail. Please walk through any muddy spots and avoid trampling trailside vegetation. Staying on the trail also avoids spread of noxious weeds and prevents the trail from widening.

Finding the trailhead: From Interstate 70 exit 190, Vail Pass Rest Area, turn left, drive over the bridge and basically straight ahead onto the sometimes rough dirt road marked Shrine Pass and Red Cliff, Forest Development Road 709. Drive approximately 3.9 miles to the top of Shrine Pass. Park in the parking lot on the south side of the road. Vault toilets are available at the top of Shrine Pass. Restrooms and water are available at the rest area if it is open. *DeLorme: Colorado Atlas & Gazetteer:* Page 38 D1 to Page 37 D7

Special considerations: Hunters use this area in the fall. In winter, the Shrine Pass area is a favorite with both snowmobilers and backcountry skiers/snowboarders. The winter trailhead is the Vail Pass Rest Area and a daily fee is charged. A separate ski trail takes off from the first switchback on Shrine Pass Road. For more information on winter travel, log onto www.huts.org (huts and routes, Shrine Mountain Inn) and call (970) 827-5715, or visit www.fs.fed.us/r2/whiteriver.

The Hike

The trail to Shrine Mountain and Wingle Ridge once was known to a few people and sheepherders. Word of the colorful wildflowers and beautiful vistas made the rounds, and soon more and more people wandered along the trail. Part of the trail

crosses fragile alpine wetlands and willows. Unfortunately, people trampled the area, widening the bogs, and the little single-track trail became a muddy mess. In September 2002 a weekend crew of about 175 volunteers with Volunteers for Outdoor Colorado worked on 2 miles of trail, building erosion controls to prevent further damage.

Long before modern humans wandered the area, the Frontrangia part of the Ancestral Rockies rose about 300 million years ago a little west of where today's Front Range lies. Colorado was situated near the equator in a tropical climate. As Frontrangia eroded, gray to red sediments came to rest in the shallow seas that surrounded the mountain range. By the time the current Rockies rose, the shallow sea sediments had been metamorphosed into sandstone, shale, conglomerate, and marine limestone called the Minturn formation. Above it sits the reddish conglomerate and sandstone of the Maroon Formation, which can be seen along the hike to Shrine Mountain.

▶ Shrine Ridge was officially named Wingle Ridge in November 2003 in memory of Pete Wingle. Pete, a long-time U.S. Forest Service employee, administered recreation on national forest lands and assisted in the development of Copper Mountain Ski Resort. He served on the boards of 10th Mountain Division Hut Association and Summit Huts Association.

Many moons ago, Native Americans traveled across Vail Pass following game that summered in the Blue River valley (in today's Summit County). The Utes called the area "Nah-oon-kara," meaning "where the river of the blue rises." When excavation started for the I–70 rest area in 1974, evidence was uncovered of use by native peoples over 7,000 years. Campfire remains, butchered animal bones, scrapers, and projectile points led archaeologists to believe at least seven different waves of native occupation occurred there, probably as a summer hunting camp. About 200 years ago, evidence of occupation stopped, probably because with horses, the Utes no longer camped on the pass.

The trail to Shrine Mountain leaves from the road going to the Shrine Mountain Inn. The privately owned facility consists of three cabins, all with hot and cold running potable water and flush toilets. Reservations can be made through 10th Mountain Division Hut Association. The Inn is open year-round and is located on private property. Please do not visit unless you have reservations.

Today's hiker can enjoy subalpine wildflowers in all their glory. Varieties of daisies, bistort, willows, Jacob's ladder, monkshood, chiming bells, and little red elephants bloom along the first part of the trail. After crossing a little creek, the trail starts to climb through forest with blackened stumps and tall stumps, probably a reminder of the large fire and logging activity in the late 1800s. Meadows painted in hues of yellow, red, and purple dazzle the eye. The little creek at about 1 mile is

◀ *View of the Gore Range across meadows along the Shrine Ridge Trail*

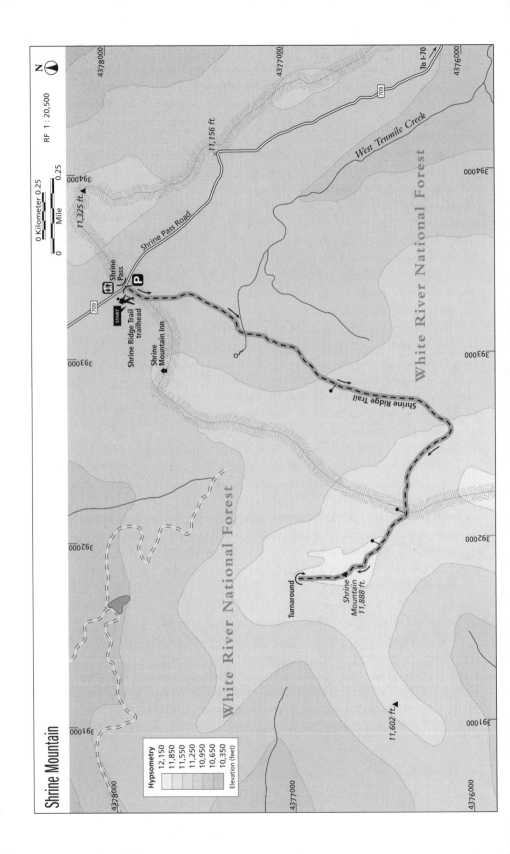

Shrine Mountain

Hypsometry

12,150
11,850
11,550
11,250
10,950
10,650
10,350

Elevation (feet)

RF 1 : 20,500

0 Kilometer 0.25

0.25

0 Mile

White River National Forest

11,325 ft.▲

Shrine Pass Road

Shrine Pass

Shrine Ridge Trail trailhead

START

709

P

Shrine Mountain Inn

11,156 ft.

709

West Tenmile Creek

To I-70

Shrine Ridge Trail

White River National Forest

Turnaround

Shrine Mountain
11,888 ft.

11,602 ft.▲

N

4378000
4377000
4376000

3939000
3940000
3941000
3942000
3943000
3944000

4377000
4378000

often bordered by magenta paintbrush, little red elephants, and Parry primrose, in shades of pink to purple.

Just below the final ascent to the ridge, a dense field of blue lupine blooms below the snowbanks. Watch for flying snowballs as hikers enjoy snowball fights in midsummer. Up on the left side of the ridge heading to Shrine Mountain are fields of red paintbrush and blue lupine with the Sawatch Range and Mount of the Holy Cross for a backdrop. To the right of the ridge are interesting red rock formations, which with some imagination could be shrines of some sort. Rock gardens abound in the area. Watch for marmots and chipmunks scurrying around and crows flying overhead.

Shrine Mountain probably received its name from the view of Mount of the Holy Cross, once a national monument to which people made pilgrimages (See Bowman's Shortcut Trail hike for its history).

Several rock outcroppings on Shrine Mountain are ideal for a picnic with unforgettable views.

Miles and Directions

0.0 Start at the bulletin board at the southeast end of the parking lot. 393374mE 4377891mN Elevation 11,105 feet. Walk south on the road to the Shrine Ridge Trail trailhead.

363 ft Shrine Ridge Trail trailhead. Turn left off the road onto the trail at the sign. 393316mE 4377816mN

0.9 Arrive at the trail junction with the trail from the Shrine Mountain Inn. 392812mE 4376675mN Continue hiking straight ahead.

1.6 Nice views of the Gore Range through the trees to the northeast. 392450mE 4376256mN

1.75 The trail Ys. There might be some snowbanks in this area. 392119mE 4376359mN Take the right fork to the top of the ridge.

1.9 Trail Ys. 391947mE 4376501mN Go straight or a little right here.

2.1 Shrine benchmark, the top of Shrine Mountain. Elevation 11,888 feet. 391799mE 4376721mN

2.3 Great views. 391760mE 4376978mN Return the way you came.

4.5 Arrive back at the parking lot.

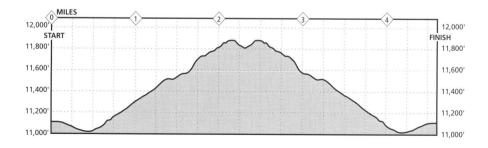

Option: The tundra is fragile on Wingle Ridge so please stay on the designated trail. When the trail disappears, walk on rocks if possible or spread out to avoid damaging the tiny tundra plants with multiple footsteps.

Hike Information

Local Information

Copper Mountain Resort, (866) 841-2481, www.coppercolorado.com
Copper Mountain Resort Chamber, (970) 968-6477, www.copperchamber.com
Frisco Chamber of Commerce, 300 Main Street, (970) 668-5547; Frisco; www.friscocolorado.org
Summit County Chamber of Commerce, (800) 530-3099, www.summitchamber.org
Summit Visitor Information Center, Outlets at Silverthorne, 246 Rainbow Drive, Silverthorne; (970) 262-0817

Local Events/Attractions

Coors Colorado Barbecue Challenge, Frisco, www.townoffrisco.com/bbq.html
Copper Mountain Resort hosts various events throughout the year, (866) 841-2481, www.coppercolorado.com

Accommodations

Several campgrounds are located along the shores of Dillon Reservoir near Frisco. For more information, contact White River National Forest, Dillon Ranger District, (970) 468-5400, www.fs.fed.us/r2/whiteriver, www.dillonrangerdistrict.com.
Gore Creek Campground is just across Gore Creek from the Gore Creek Trail trailhead in

East Vail. For information contact White River National Forest, Holy Cross Ranger District, (970) 827-5175, www.fs.fed.us/r2/whiteriver.

Restaurants

Boatyard Pizzeria and Grill, 304 Main Street, Frisco; (970) 668-4728
Imperial Palace, Village at Copper, (970) 968-6688
MiZuppa, 842 North Summit Boulevard, Frisco; (970) 668-8138
Salsa Mountain Cantina, Village at Copper, (970) 968-6300

Hike Tours

Gore Range Natural Science School, P.O. Box 250, Red Cliff 81649; (970) 827-9725, www.gorerange.org
Vail Nature Center, Vail, (970) 479-2291, www.vailrec.com/venues_naturecenter

Organizations

10th Mountain Division Hut Association, 1280 Ute Avenue, Suite 21, Aspen (970) 925-5775, www.huts.org
Volunteers for Outdoor Colorado, 600 South Marion Parkway, Denver; (303) 715-1010; (800) 925-2220; www.voc.org

22 Bowman's Shortcut Trail

Bowman's Shortcut Trail is often gentle interspersed with a few steep stretches. The trail winds through lodgepole and spruce-fir forest then crosses several open meadows on a gentle ridge with great views of Mount of the Holy Cross and the Sawatch Range to the southwest, the Gore Range to the east, and the Tenmile Range to the south. The meadows are filled with colorful wildflowers in July. In winter, this trail is part of the Commando Run of the U.S. Army's 10th Mountain Division fame.

Start: At the Bowman's Shortcut Trail trailhead
Distance: 5.6 miles out and back
Approximate hiking time: 2.3 to 3.8 hours
Difficulty: Moderate
Elevation gain: 880 feet
Trail surface: Dirt trail
Seasons: Best from late June to early October
Other trail users: Mountain bikers, equestrians
Canine compatibility: Dogs permitted (must be under voice control)
Land status: National forest
Nearest towns: Copper Mountain and Frisco

Fees and permits: No fees or permits required in summer. Daily fee required in winter.
Maps: USGS map: Red Cliff; National Geographic Trails Illustrated: #108 Vail, Frisco, Dillon
Trail contact: White River National Forest, Holy Cross Ranger District, 24747 U.S. Highway 24, Minturn; (970) 827-5715; www.fs.fed .us/r2/whiteriver
Other: This trail is popular with mountain bikers. No water is available along the trail.

Finding the trailhead: From Interstate 70 exit 190, Vail Pass Rest Area, turn left, drive across the bridge and basically straight ahead onto the sometimes rough dirt road marked Shrine Pass and Red Cliff, Forest Development Road (FDR) 709. Drive approximately 3.9 miles over Shrine Pass and past the viewpoint for the Mount of the Holy Cross. Turn right onto Lime Creek Road, FDR 728. Turn left in 0.5 mile when the road Ys. The trailhead is another 0.1 mile on the right. Parking is available on the left. No facilities are available at the trailhead. Vault toilets are available at the top of Shrine Pass and the Mount of the Holy Cross viewpoint known as Julia's Deck. Restrooms and water are available at the rest area if it is open. *DeLorme: Colorado Atlas & Gazetteer:* Page 37 D7

Special considerations: Hunters use this area in the fall. In winter, the Shrine Pass area is a favorite with both snowmobilers and backcountry skiers/snowboarders. The winter trailhead is the Vail Pass Rest Area and a daily fee is charged. A separate ski trail takes off from the first switchback on the Shrine Pass Road. For more information on winter travel, log onto www.huts.org (huts and routes, Shrine Mountain Inn) and call (970) 827-5715, or visit www.fs.fed.us/r2/whiteriver.

The Hike

The best part of Bowman's Shortcut Trail comes along the high, gentle ridge—the great views cover a large section of the central mountains. You can see at least three

The craggy Gore Range from the gentle ridge of Bowman's Shortcut

14,000-foot peaks: Mount Elbert and Mount Massive near Leadville and Mount of the Holy Cross. What appears to be a high meadow above a headwall is really Homestake Reservoir. To the east, the craggy peaks of the Gore Range treat the eye.

In the 1800s various stories about a mountain with a snowy cross circulated around Colorado. As part of the Hayden Survey in the 1870s, William Henry Jackson photographed various areas of Colorado. In 1873, the Survey set a goal to find this mysterious peak. Jackson viewed the mysterious mountain from the top of Grays Peak (see Chihuahua Lake hike). By August the group arrived near present day Minturn. For three days they attempted in vain to find a route to their destination. Fallen trees and thick willows made the going too rough for pack animals, and the group ended up carrying Jackson's one hundred pounds of photographic gear on foot. Jackson used a wet glass plate camera. The "film" glass needed to be developed soon after exposure and Jackson carried a portable darkroom tent with all necessary chemicals and supplies with him. Finally finding an approach, the still-difficult hike took two days with little food and no shelter. (They thought they could do it in one day.) Finally atop Notch Mountain, Jackson found the infamous cross across the valley. He took several pictures in 11x14 and 5x8 format. The nation became enraptured by the photographs. People believed the snow-filled cross to be a sign from God.

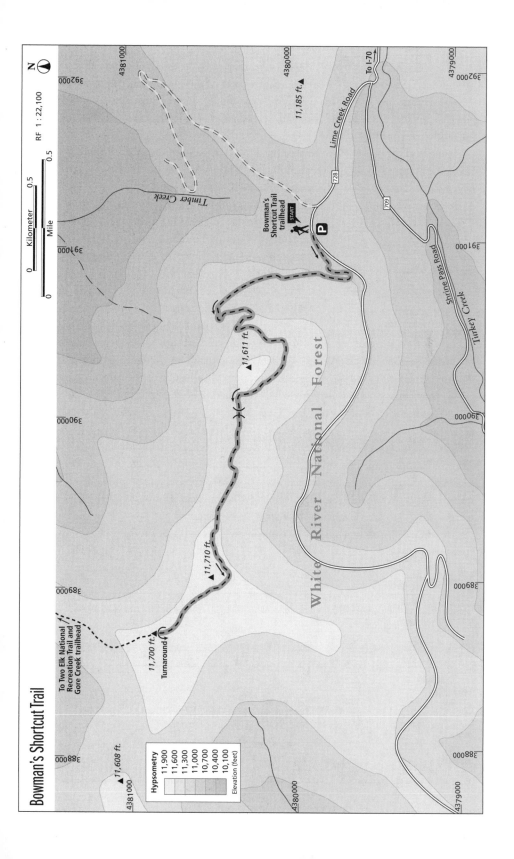

Bowman's Shortcut Trail

RF 1 : 22,100

N

Hypsometry
11,900
11,600
11,300
11,000
10,700
10,400
10,100
Elevation (feet)

11,608 ft.

To Two Elk National
Recreation Trail and
Gore Creek trailhead

11,700 ft.
Turnaround

11,710 ft.

11,611 ft.

White River National Forest

Timber Creek

Bowman's
Shortcut Trail
trailhead
START

P

728

709

Lime Creek Road

Shrine Pass Road

Turkey Creek

To I-70

11,185 ft.

The cross is created by a 1,500-foot vertical gully in the gneiss and schist of the mountain. A 750-foot rock bench across the side of the mountain collects and keeps snow, forming the arms. The right arm supposedly deteriorated due to rockslides, but Jackson admitted that he touched up the right arm for contrast but did not significantly alter his picture.

Annual pilgrimages to Mount of the Holy Cross began in 1927. President Herbert Hoover proclaimed about 1,392 acres around Mount of the Holy Cross as a national monument in 1929. The pilgrimages continued until about 1940. The U.S. Army controlled much of this area between 1938 and 1950, with nearby Camp Hale being a training ground for the famous 10th Mountain Division troops. In 1950 President Harry Truman retracted national monument status and returned the land to the U.S. Forest Service.

▶ The U.S. Army's 10th Mountain Division suffered heavily in routing the Germans—4,888 casualties including 978 killed in action.

The U.S. Army's 10th Mountain Division troops trained at Camp Hale north of Leadville. The troops used this area and that south of Bowman's Shortcut to train for high-altitude missions on skis and commando raids during World War II. In winter, Bowman's Shortcut is part of the backcountry ski route called Commando Run, named in honor of the famous troops.

German lines in the northern Italian Alps had proved nearly impossible to penetrate. Mount Belvedere was a key German position, from which they controlled access to the Po Valley. To protect Mount Belvedere, the German artillery entrenched themselves on nearby Riva Ridge. In February 1945, the 10th Mountain Division Troops, 700 men strong, made a daring night climb of Riva Ridge and captured the German position. They later gained control of Mount Belvedere and other important peaks in the area. By April, the 10th Mountain Division entered the Po Valley. On May 2, 1945, the German Army in Italy surrendered.

Bowman's Shortcut Trail offers a moderate hike with beautiful views in an historic setting.

Miles and Directions

0.0 Start at the Bowman's Shortcut Trail trailhead. 391070mE 4379871mN Elevation 10,820 feet.

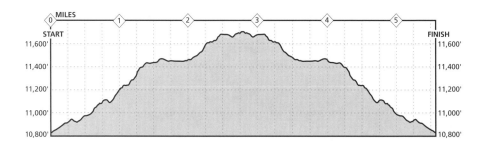

1.2 Enjoy a nice view of the Tenmile Range to the south. 390511mE 4380243mN

1.7 Arrive at a saddle between two little peaks. 389995mE 4380330mN

2.8 Stop at the cairn at the top of Bowman's Shortcut. Enjoy the views of many ranges in central Colorado. 388719mE 4380823mN Elevation 11,700 feet. Return the way you came.

5.6 Arrive back at the trailhead.

Options: Descend from the cairn to another saddle, up a small knoll, then down to Two Elk Pass. From here you can either hike approximately 9 miles west to the Two Elk National Recreation Trail trailhead near Minturn to a waiting vehicle or hike east 1.7 miles to the Vail Pass Recreation Trail then down to the Gore Creek Trail trailhead parking area to a waiting vehicle.

Gore Creek Trail trailhead: From I–70 exit 180, East Vail, head southeast on Big Horn Road (south side of I–70) for approximately 2.2 miles to a little parking area on the left just before Gore Creek Campground.

Hike Information

Local Information
Copper Mountain Resort, (866) 841-2481, www.coppercolorado.com
Copper Mountain Resort Chamber, (970) 968-6477, www.copperchamber.com
Frisco Chamber of Commerce, 300 Main Street; Frisco; (970) 668-5547, www.frisco colorado.org
Summit County Chamber of Commerce, (800) 530-3099, www.summitchamber.org
Vail Valley Chamber & Tourism Bureau, (970) 476-1000, www.visitvailvalley.com

Local Events/Attractions
Coors Colorado Barbecue Challenge, Frisco, www.townoffrisco.com/bbq.html
Copper Mountain Resort hosts various events throughout the year, (866) 841-2481, www.coppercolorado.com

Accommodations
Several campgrounds are located along the shores of Dillon Reservoir near Frisco. For more information, contact White River National Forest, Dillon Ranger District, (970) 468-5400, www.fs.fed.us/r2/whiteriver, www.dillonrangerdistrict.com.
Gore Creek Campground is just across Gore Creek from the Gore Creek Trail trailhead in East Vail. For information, contact White River National Forest, Holy Cross Ranger District, (970) 827-5175, www.fs.fed.us/r2/whiteriver.

Restaurants
Boatyard Pizzeria and Grill, 304 Main Street, Frisco; (970) 668-4728
Butterhorn Bakery, 408 Main Street, Frisco; (970) 668-3997
Imperial Palace, Village at Copper, (970) 968-6688
Salsa Mountain Cantina, Village at Copper, (970) 968-6300

23 Grouse Lake

The hike to Grouse Lake follows Grouse Creek, which could be more aptly named Berry Bush Creek. The trail climbs steadily through spruce-fir forest interspersed with aspen. A few flatter sections provide ample time to restore one's breath. Little creeks along the trail are filled with moss-covered rocks and bordered with flowers. Grouse Peak overlooks a long valley at the end of which sits grass-lined Grouse Lake. The lake lies just within the Holy Cross Wilderness.

Start: At the Grouse Creek Trail trailhead
Distance: 9.2 miles out and back
Approximate hiking time: 4 to 7.7 hours
Difficulty: Most difficult
Elevation gain: 2,865 feet
Trail surface: Dirt road (closed to motorized use) and dirt trail
Seasons: Best from July to early October
Other trail users: Equestrians
Canine compatibility: Dogs must be on leash.
Land status: National forest and wilderness area

Nearest town: Minturn
Fees and permits: Wilderness permit may be required.
Maps: USGS map: Minturn; National Geographic Trails Illustrated: #108 Vail, Frisco, Dillon
Trail contact: White River National Forest, Holy Cross Ranger District, 24747 U.S. Highway 24, Minturn; (970) 827-5175; www.fs.fed.us/r2/whiteriver

Finding the trailhead: From Interstate 70 exit 171, West US 6, East US 24, turn right and head south on US 24 approximately 1.4 miles to the Grouse Creek Trail trailhead parking lot on the right (west) side of US 24. No facilities are available at the trailhead, but the U.S. Forest Service's Holy Cross Ranger District Office is 0.3 mile south of I-70, and Minturn is south of the trailhead. *DeLorme: Colorado Atlas & Gazetteer:* Page 37 D6

Special considerations: This area is popular with hunters in the fall. The first couple of miles are frequently utilized by snowshoers and dog walkers in the winter. The trail is neither marked nor maintained for winter use. Please comply with wilderness regulations.

The Hike

The trail to Grouse Lake is lined with innumerable berry bushes of several varieties, including twinberry, elderberry, gooseberry, currant, and thistleberry. Little creeks run clear and cold, with moss-covered rocks and logs creating exquisite aquatic gardens.

Grouse Lake itself is in the Holy Cross Wilderness. This special area was designated by Congress in the Colorado Wilderness Act of 1980 on December 22. Sometimes referred to as a water wilderness, the Holy Cross contains the headwaters of the Eagle River. Streams, snowmelt, and many alpine lakes provide an abundance of water.

Grass-lined Grouse Lake

Designation of Holy Cross Wilderness was not without conflict. Colorado Springs and Aurora owned water rights in the newly created wilderness area. The Homestake Project, which includes a water-collection system along Homestake Creek and Homestake Reservoir south of Grouse Creek, had already been built in the 1960s to divert about 27,000 acre-feet of water to Colorado Springs and Aurora, cities on the east slope of Colorado. The Colorado Wilderness Act of 1980 specifically stated "Nothing in this act shall be construed to . . . interfere with the construction, maintenance, or repair of [the Homestake Water Development Project of the cities of Aurora and Colorado Springs]." Phase II of the Homestake Project planned to divert water from Cross Creek and Fall Creek. Four small dams would be built in the wilderness area along with a 13-mile underground tunnel to divert about 22,000 acre-feet annually. Concerns arose about the extensive meadows and high-altitude wetlands in the area. Some felt the water to sustain these features came from snow melt while others were convinced the water came from Cross Creek flooding during spring runoff. In 1982, the Holy Cross Wilderness Defense Fund was created to fight the project. Eagle County became involved and denied the permits for the project. Lawsuits were filed, won, lost, and overturned for several years. In 1994, the Colorado Court of Appeals upheld Eagle County's decision to deny the

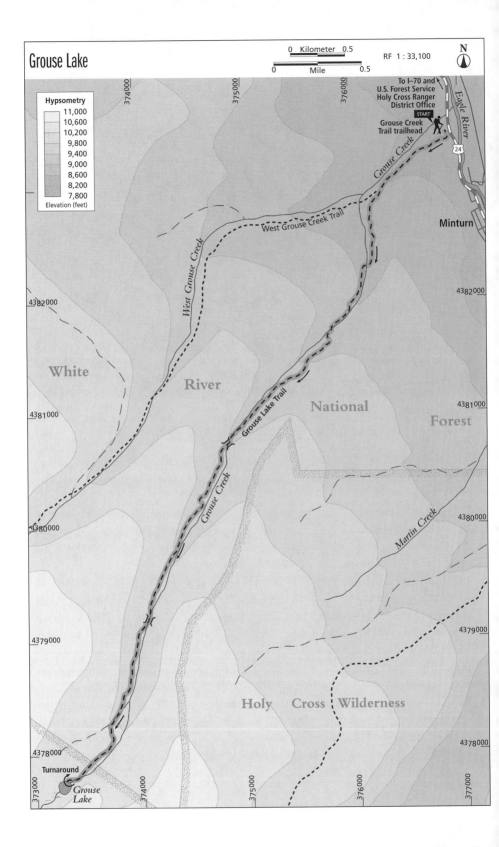

Grouse Lake

0 Kilometer 0.5
0 Mile 0.5
RF 1 : 33,100
N

Hypsometry
11,000
10,600
10,200
9,800
9,400
9,000
8,600
8,200
7,800
Elevation (feet)

To I–70 and
U.S. Forest Service
Holy Cross Ranger
District Office
START
Grouse Creek
Trail trailhead

Eagle River

24

Minturn

West Grouse Creek

West Grouse Creek Trail

Grouse Creek

4382000

4382000

White

River

National

4381000

Grouse Lake Trail

Forest

4381000

Grouse Creek

Martin Creek

4380000

4380000

4379000

4379000

Holy Cross Wilderness

4378000

4378000

Turnaround

Grouse
Lake

373000

374000

375000

376000

377000

construction permits for Homestake II. Both the Colorado Supreme Court and the U.S. Supreme Court declined to hear the case.

The cities still own water rights in Holy Cross Wilderness. They and Eagle County have agreed to cooperate to build a project that will benefit all. Water is precious in Colorado. State water law follows "first-in-time, first-in-right," and water rights are private property. Water is more abundant on the less populated west slope than the drier, heavily populated east slope. Water diversion projects, moving water from west to east, started back in the late 1800s.

The Grouse Creek Trail starts up a dirt road (closed to motorized use) through sagebrush and rabbitbrush. When the trail becomes single track and enters the forest, it winds back and forth over Grouse Creek and other little creeks.

Along the trail after about mile 2.5, watch for trees with patches of bark missing. Porcupine like to eat the outer bark and inner cambium layer. If they get carried away and strip the bark entirely around the tree, the tree will die. The large rodents come back to the same tree, eating above their last dinner because sugar-rich sap collects there. Porcupines like to munch on evergreen trees at night. They also eat berries, nuts, seeds, and flowers. These spiney critters enjoy siestas during the day, snuggled high in tree branches. One porcupine may have as many as 30,000 quills! The slow-moving animal does not throw its quills, but will swing its tail into an enemy's face, leaving quills in its face and maybe mouth—a painful experience indeed. If you see a porcupine, enjoy it from a distance and make sure to keep any pets leashed and away from its tail!

Miles and Directions

0.0 Start at the Grouse Creek Trail trailhead. 376898mE 4383460mN Elevation 7,835 feet. The first part of the trail is a dirt road.

0.1 A trail comes in from the right. Continue straight ahead on the road. 376757mE 4383331mN

0.3 The road goes left and the trail to Grouse Lake goes straight ahead. 376583mE 4383245mN

0.5 Arrive at the junction of West Grouse Creek and Grouse Lake Trails. Take the left fork to Grouse Lake. 376309mE 4382982mN

1.0 Cross Grouse Creek.

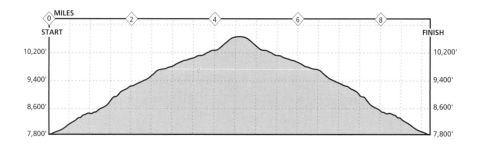

1.5 Cross Grouse Creek and head uphill into the thick forest. 375761mE 4381668mN

2.4 The trail crosses the creek. There's a nice log bridge just beyond the big boulder to the right of the trail. 374836mE 4380733mN

3.5 The trail crosses a mucky area on a puncheon bridge that is disintegrating. Be careful of the spikes sticking up from the bridge. 374122mE 4379293mN Just beyond the bridge the trail curves to the right.

4.1 Cross the little creek and start the final climb to the lake. 373700mE 4378315mN

4.6 Arrive at Grouse Lake. 373261mE 4377783mN Elevation 10,700 feet. Return the way you came.

9.2 Arrive back at the trailhead.

COLORADO OUTDOOR RECREATION SEARCH AND RESCUE (CORSAR) CARD

Every year in Colorado over 1,000 search-and-rescue (SAR) missions are conducted for hikers, hunters, and other outdoor enthusiasts who run into problems in the backcountry. Colorado has many well-trained volunteer SAR groups. They devote numerous hours to training and to actual rescues. Each county sheriff is responsible for search and rescue, yet often lacks a sufficient budget to pay for costs incurred for search helicopters, equipment, and SAR training. Sheriffs seldom charge for rescue efforts except in cases of extreme negligence.

In 1987, the Colorado legislature created the Colorado Search and Rescue Fund (CSRF). Twenty-five cents from each hunting license, fishing license, and snowmobile and off-road vehicle registration finance this fund. The fund's purpose is to help sheriffs recover costs of SAR operations and to provide funding for SAR equipment and training.

As more hikers, mountain bikers, climbers, and backcountry skiers required rescue, the Colorado legislature created the Colorado Outdoor Recreation Search and Rescue (CORSAR) card. The CORSAR card costs only $3.00 per year ($12.00 for five years) with $2.00 going to the CSRF and $1.00 going to the vendor.

If you need rescue in the backcountry, a SAR team will come (depending on where you are), whether you have a CORSAR card or not. The card is NOT insurance and does not pay for medical helicopter evacuation. SAR missions typically cost money when a helicopter is used in the search effort or if a SAR group's equipment is damaged during the mission. Having a CORSAR card or other license mentioned above means certain expenses the SAR group or sheriff accrued during the rescue can be immediately refunded from the CSRF. If you don't have a COR-SAR card or other license and SAR equipment is damaged during your rescue, sheriffs must wait until the end of the year, apply for a grant to replace the equipment, and hopefully receive enough money.

So before starting on your first Summit County or other Colorado hike, buy a CORSAR card and help our volunteer SAR groups stay equipped and prepared!

For more information call (970) 248-7310 or log onto http://dola.colorado.gov/LGS/FA/sar/index.htm. If this URL fails, try http://dola.colorado.gov, then click on site index and look for Search and Rescue. You can buy the CORSAR card online or find a vendor via the Web site.

Hike Information

Local Information

Town of Minturn, (970) 827-5645, www.minturn.org

Vail Valley Chamber & Tourism Bureau, (970) 476-1000, www.visitvailvalley.com

Local Events/Attractions

Betty Ford Alpine Gardens, 183 Gore Creek Drive, Vail; (970) 476-0103; www.betty fordalpinegardens.org

Bravo! Vail Valley Music Festival, Vail and Beaver Creek, (877) 812-5700, www.vail musicfestival.org

Minturn Market, Minturn, (970) 827-5645, www.minturn.org

Vail International Dance Festival, Vail and Beaver Creek, (970) 949-1999, www.vvf.org

Accommodations

Gore Creek Campground is just across Gore Creek from the Gore Creek Trail trailhead in East Vail. For information contact White River National Forest, Holy Cross Ranger District, (970) 827-5175, www.fs.fed.us/r2/whiteriver.

Restaurants

Chilly Willy's, 101 Main Street, Minturn; (970) 827-5887; www.chiliwilly.com

Minturn Saloon, 146 North Main Street, Minturn; (970) 827-5954; www.minturn saloon.com

Hike Tours

Gore Range Natural Science School, P.O. Box 250, Red Cliff 81649; (970) 827-9725; www.gorerange.org

Organizations

Holy Cross Wilderness Defense Fund, 1130 Alpine Avenue, Boulder 80304; (303) 447-1361

Friends of the Eagles Nest Wilderness, www.fenw.org, or call the Dillion Ranger District, (970) 468-5400, for current contact

24 Bear Lake

The hike to Bear Lake ascends the south ridge of Galena Mountain, traveling through lodgepole pine forest. From the top of the ridge, you can see a large part of the upper Arkansas Valley and Colorado's highest peaks. The trail then drops into spruce-fir forest, wandering past several little ponds and lakes. Idyllic Bear Lake sits on a wide flat bench bordered by big boulders on its west side.

Start: At the Timberline Lake Trail trailhead
Distance: 6.5 miles out and back
Approximate hiking time: 3 to 4.5 hours
Difficulty: More difficult
Elevation gain: 1,370 feet
Trail surface: Dirt trail
Seasons: Best from July to early October
Other trail users: Equestrians
Canine compatibility: Dogs must be on leash.
Land status: National forest/wilderness area
Nearest town: Leadville

Fees and permits: Wilderness permit may be required.
Maps: USGS map: Homestake Reservoir; National Geographic Trails Illustrated: #126 Holy Cross/Ruedi Reservoir
Trail contact: San Isabel National Forest, Leadville Ranger District, 810 Front Street, Leadville; (719) 486-0749; www.fs.fed.us/r2/psicc
Other: One section of this trail at the high point is exposed and not a good place to be during a thunderstorm with lightning.

Finding the trailhead: From Interstate 70 exit 195, Copper Mountain/Leadville, drive southwest on Highway 91 to Leadville past the intersection of U.S. Highway 24. At 22.9 miles turn right at the traffic light by Safeway onto Mountain View Drive. Continue 2.8 miles to Lake County Road (CR) 9. Turn right. In 0.1 mile the road curves right onto Lake CR 99. In another 0.4 mile, turn left at the National Recreation Area Turquoise Lake sign (Lake CR 9). Drive another 0.6 miles to a T intersection, then turn left. In 1.8 miles, the road Ts. Turn right and drive over the Sugarloaf Dam. Follow the paved road 5.5 miles to the trailhead turnoff (stay to the right at the Hagerman Pass Road turnoff at 3.5 miles). Turn left and drive 0.1 mile into the parking lot. No facilities are available at the trailhead. *DeLorme: Colorado Atlas & Gazetteer:* Page 47 B6

Special considerations: The Holy Cross Wilderness has a group size limit regulation of fifteen people or a combination of twenty-five people and pack or saddle animals. Hunters use this area during hunting season. The trail is neither marked nor maintained for winter use in wilderness. This trail connects Skinner Hut and Uncle Bud's Hut during the winter, so a trail may be broken. Be aware of avalanche danger in this area.

The Hike

The hike to Bear Lake follows the Colorado Trail and Continental Divide National Scenic Trail, which use the path of the old Main Range Trail. The latter was built by the Civilian Conservation Corps during the Depression in the 1930s for fire protection.

Mount Massive dominates the skyline.

For a change of pace, Bear Lake is not the highest point elevation-wise on this hike. The trail climbs from the parking lot through dense lodgepole-pine forest and some aspen. Whortleberry and Wood's rose bloom, but typical of lodgepole ecosystems, understory vegetation is sparse. In meadowy areas, geraniums, pussytoes, yarrow, and berry bushes grow. Before the trail enters the Holy Cross Wilderness, blue diamonds mark the trail for winter cross-country skiing. Being a sign of man, the blue diamonds are not allowed in wilderness. The lack of signs actually creates a better wilderness experience where route-finding skills are important.

The trail switchbacks up an open meadow on the south ridge of Galena Mountain. Galena is a mineral that is the principal ore of lead. Although gold first brought miners to Leadville, silver enabled the town to grow in the 1880s into a city rivaling Denver. Southeast of Bear Lake the St. Kevins mining district was located. The mines produced ore from fissures of silver ore with some lead, copper, and gold in the 1880s and 1890s. The mining camp called St. Kevin was small, but had a stamp mill and a school.

The fantastic view from the ridge is worth the climb! To the southwest lies Hagerman Pass. Beyond there, Colorado's two highest peaks raise their heads: Mount Elbert at 14,433 feet and aptly named Mount Massive at 14,421 feet. If you take a

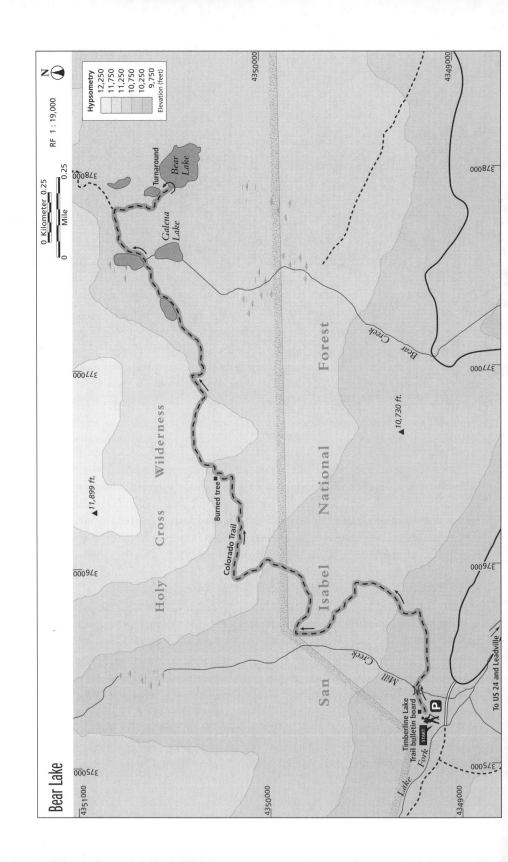

few steps off the trail, you'll find a view of Leadville to the southeast, nestled at the foot of the Mosquito Range.

After dropping down the ridge, the trail passes a little pond and the social trail to little grass-lined Galena Lake. As the trail comes into an open area, look right (southeast) for a fleeting glimpse of Bear Lake.

Bear Creek, whose source is both Galena and Bear Lakes, flows into Turquoise Lake. The reservoir is part of the Fryingpan-Arkansas Project, which uses seventeen different diversion structures on the west slope and nine tunnels to transfer water from the west slope to the east slope. Homestake Reservoir, west of the Continental Divide from West Tennessee Lakes, collects water from Homestake Creek (see the Grouse Lake hike for more information). The water flows through the Homestake Tunnel to Turquoise Lake. Other waters from the Fryingpan and Roaring Fork River basins arrive at Turquoise via the Charles H. Boustead Tunnel. Both tunnels lie beneath the Continental Divide. Water from Turquoise Lake flows downhill through the Mount Elbert Conduit to a forebay (small reservoir). The water is released into the Mount Elbert Pumped-Storage Powerplant next to Twin Lakes. Water released from Twin Lakes heads down the Arkansas River to Pueblo Reservoir, which then feeds thirsty eastern farms and municipalities.

The side trail to Bear Lake stays on the west side of a marshy area and arrives at a boulder field with ample choices of flat rocks for a prime lunch spot. The trail continues through the west boulder field a little farther, where someone placed flat rocks to make an "easier to walk" trail among big lopsided rocks. Nestled below Galena Mountain, Bear Lake is a peaceful location to spend some time watching marmots sunbathing on rocks and little pikas scrambling to stock their hay piles for winter.

Miles and Directions

0.0 Start at the Timberline Lake Trail bulletin board. 375260mE 4349190mN Elevation 10,040 feet. Turn right and follow the Colorado Trail past the fence up the hill. In about 200 feet cross a creek on a bridge and stop to fill out the wilderness permit.

0.6 Arrive at the Holy Cross Wilderness boundary. 375913mE 4349536mN

1.9 From the burned tree, the views are great! 376458mE 4350260mN

2.1 Reach the top of the ridge. Elevation 11,410 feet. 376691mE 4350378mN

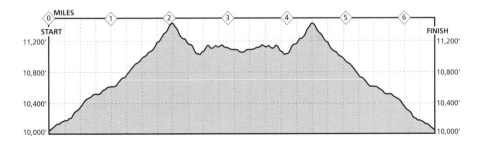

2.8 A little grassy pond is to the left and an unofficial trail to Galena Lake is to the right. 377557mE 4350615mN

3.0 Come to a trail junction. Turn right to go to Bear Lake. 377808mE 4350759mN

3.25 Arrive at Bear Lake. Elevation 11,080 feet. 377903mE 4350472mN Return the way you came.

6.5 Arrive back at the trailhead.

Hike Information

Local Information

Leadville–Twin Lakes Chamber of Commerce, 809 Harrison Avenue, Leadville; (719) 486-3900, (800) 933-3901; www.leadvilleusa.com

Local Events/Attractions

Healy House Museum, 912 Harrison Avenue, Leadville; (719) 486-0487

Leadville, Colorado & Southern Railroad, 326 East 7th Street, Leadville; (719) 486-3936, (866) 386-3936; www.leadville-train.com

Matchless Mine, Leadville, (719) 486-4918

Mount Elbert Pumped-Storage Powerplant, Twin Lakes, (719) 486-2325

National Mining Hall of Fame and Museum, 120 West 9th Street, Leadville; (719) 486-1229; www.mininghalloffame.org

Tabor Opera House, 308 Harrison Avenue, Leadville; (719) 486-3900, (800) 933-3901; www.leadvilleusa.com

Accommodations

Several campgrounds are available in the Turquoise Lake National Recreation Area. For more information, contact Leadville Ranger District, (719) 486-0749, www.fs.fed.us/r2/psicc.

Restaurants

Golden Burro Cafe and Lounge, 710 Harrison Avenue, Leadville; (719) 486-1239

The Grill Bar and Café, 715 Elm, Leadville; (719) 486-9930

Quincy's Steak and Spirits, 416 Harrison Avenue, Leadville; (719) 486-9765

Wild Bill's Hamburgers & Ice Cream, 200 Harrison Avenue, Leadville; (719) 486-0533

Organizations

Colorado Trail Foundation, (303) 384-3729, www.coloradotrail.org

Continental Divide Trail Alliance, (888) 909-CDTA, www.cdtrail.org

Continental Divide Trail Society, (410) 235-9610, www.cdtsociety.org

10th Mountain Division Hut Association, (970) 925-5775, www.huts.org

25 West Tennessee Lakes

The hike to West Tennessee Lakes follows a broad valley as it gently ascends to the base of a headwall. The remains of the Homestake Mine and the tragedy of an avalanche that ended the dreams of its miners lie here. The trail becomes much steeper, but the rewards of the two lakes tucked high in a bowl below the Continental Divide make the extra effort well worth the hike.

Start: On Lily Lake Road at the sign recommending four-wheel drive

Distance: 8.8 miles out and back

Approximate hiking time: 3.5 to 6 hours

Difficulty: More difficult

Elevation gain: 1,410 feet

Trail surface: Dirt road and dirt trail

Seasons: Best from July to early October

Other trail users: Equestrians, vehicles at the very beginning

Canine compatibility: Dogs must be on leash.

Land status: National forest and wilderness area

Nearest town: Leadville

Fees and permits: Wilderness permit may be required.

Maps: USGS map: Homestake Reservoir; National Geographic Trails Illustrated: #109 Breckenridge/Tennessee Pass and #126 Holy Cross/Ruedi Reservoir

Trail contact: San Isabel National Forest, Leadville Ranger District, 810 Front Street, Leadville; (719) 486-0749; www.fs.fed.us/r2/psicc

Other: Some sections of trail have no easily accessible water.

Finding the trailhead: This trail has no official trailhead. From Interstate 70 exit 195, Copper Mountain/Leadville, drive about 22.2 miles southwest on Highway 91 to U.S. Highway 24. Turn right on US 24 and drive north about 7.1 miles to Lake County Road (CR) 19. Turn left here onto a dirt road where an old piece of equipment holds a sign pointing to Webster's Sand & Gravel Pit. Continue past Forest Development Road (FDR) 100 at 0.9 mile and drive onto FDR 131 and Lake CR19A. In another 0.4 mile turn right where the sign says West Tennessee. The road gets rougher here. The unofficial trailhead in this book is about 1.0 mile up this road (FDR 131). After 0.2 mile where you enter public lands (specified by the brown road post on the right side of the road), find a parking place off the road. Most cars can probably make it to the unofficial trailhead. Four-wheel-drive, high-clearance vehicles can make it to the closure gate, 0.5 mile farther. Dispersed camping is available along the road. No facilities are available at the unofficial trailhead. *DeLorme: Colorado Atlas & Gazetteer:* Page 47 B7

Special considerations: The Holy Cross Wilderness has a rule that limits group size to fifteen people or a combination of twenty-five people and pack or saddle animals. Camping is prohibited within 100 feet of lakes, streams, and trails. Please do not build campfires near the West Tennessee Lakes because no wood is available. The krummholz trees above treeline use their dead limbs to protect their living parts. This area is popular with hunters during hunting season. The trail is used in winter by both snowmobilers and cross-country skiers.

Little pond below the remains of the Homestake Mine

The Hike

West Tennessee Creek is a tributary of the Arkansas River, whose main headwaters start near Fremont Pass. The upper Arkansas Valley near Leadville is part of the Rio Grande Rift, land that subsided when forces below uplifted much of Colorado another 5,000 feet between twenty-eight and five million years ago. Periods of glaciation followed, covering the east side of the Sawatch Range. One glacier flowed down the West Tennessee Valley, leaving behind a cirque with two beautiful lakes.

Between about sixty-five and thirty million years ago when the present Rockies were uplifted and during a volcanic period, hot magma full of mineral-rich solutions spread into different cracks and fissures created in rocks. As the magma cooled, it created veins of gold, silver, lead, copper, zinc, molybdenum, uranium, and tungsten. These mineral deposits are concentrated in a 50-mile wide belt, trending northeast from the San Juan Mountains to Boulder. The Colorado Mineral Belt drew miners to the San Juans, Aspen, Leadville, Summit County, and Central City districts.

In 1860, Abe Lee made the first big gold strike near Leadville. In 1874, as the gold dwindled, miners extracted lead carbonate, rich in silver. The silver rush started, turning Leadville and surroundings into a large city, second to Denver.

The Homestake Mine up West Tennessee Creek was discovered in 1872. In 1873, assays of its silver varied from $100 to $800 per ton. Nine men worked the mine, each earning $3.50 per day. The mine owners built a 700-foot tramway to take ore from the mine and to haul lumber for tunnels to the mine. At first the extracted ore was carried by jack train (burros/mules) to South Park and on to smelters in Golden. Other ore went to reduction works in St. Louis. Later the Malta Smelting Works was built near today's intersection of U.S. Highway 24 and Lake County Road 300, southwest of Leadville. Total cost rang in at $125,000, including machines for crushing and sampling the ore and three different types of furnaces. The Homestake Mine was only 8 miles away.

▶ During the winter of 1896, Leadville built a magnificent ice palace, which covered over three acres with two 90-foot Norman towers. Inside, lighted dining rooms and an ice rink provided hours of entertainment. Ice sculptures of miners and prospectors decorated the palace.

In July 1884, the Homestake Mine was leased to parties who couldn't make the mine pay and couldn't pay the miners. Ten miners, ranging in age from twenty-three to thirty-six years of age, who had been working in the mine, subleased it in January 1885 to reimburse themselves for their labor. They bought supplies for the long winter and settled in. Two men would travel to Leadville every few days for mail. The winter of 1884–1885 turned ugly and soon heavy snows made travel impossible. They last trekked to Leadville on February 10. On April 24, two friends of the miners, worried about lack of communication, snowshoed into the mine from Eight Mile House in Tennessee Park. They found the mine cabins covered by a snowslide and no sign of life anywhere. The next day the *Leadville Chronicle* received a message from Frank Sanderson, keeper of Eight Mile House, about the disaster. When townsfolk learned of the tragedy, they formed a rescue party. A train was made available and the equipped party left at 4 A.M., reaching the buried cabins by 8 A.M. They found the first body in early afternoon. By 3 P.M. the other nine bodies had been exhumed from their snowy grave. Judging by a letter dated February 21 and an alarm clock and watch, the snowslide probably occurred after midnight on February 22. A monument to the ten young miners was erected in the Evergreen Cemetery by Leadville's citizens.

Hikers unaware of history would never guess such a tragedy occurred in this beautiful area. The majestic mountains and beautiful lakes carefully guard their past secrets.

Miles and Directions

0.0 Start at the sign recommending four-wheel-drive. 382812mE 4356294mN Elevation 10,433 feet.

0.5 Come to the closure gate near Lily Lake. No motorized vehicles (except snowmobiles in winter) are allowed past this point. 382172mE 4356500mN

1.9 Pass through a split-rail fence. 380262mE 4356939mN

2.4 Come to a ditch—first easily accessible water since Lily Lake. 379572mE 4356723mN

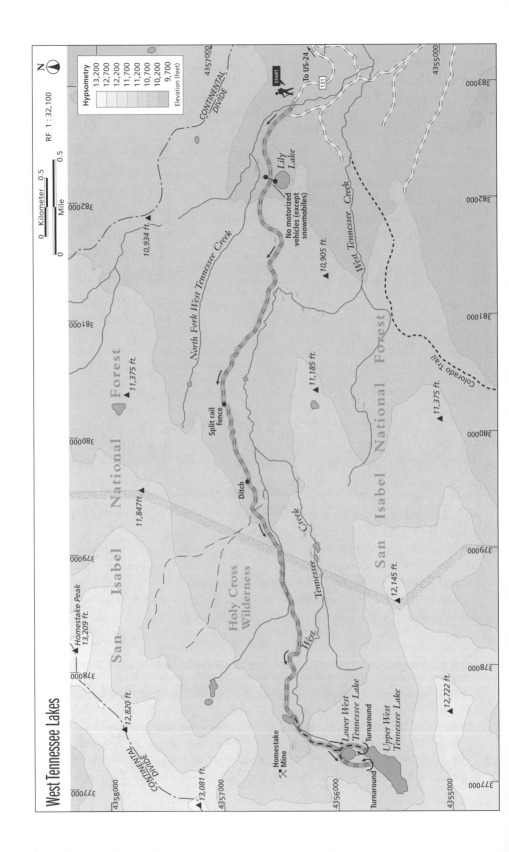

West Tennessee Lakes

RF 1 : 32,100

N

Hypsometry

13,200
12,700
12,200
11,700
11,200
10,700
10,200
9,700

Elevation (feet)

0   Kilometer   0.5

0   Mile   0.5

START

To US-24

131

Lily Lake

No motorized vehicles (except snowmobiles)

▲ 10,905 ft.

West Tennessee Creek

Colorado Trail

▲ 11,375 ft.

San Isabel National Forest

▲ 11,185 ft.

North Fork West Tennessee Creek

▲ 10,934 ft.

San Isabel National Forest

▲ 11,375 ft.

Split rail fence

Ditch

West Tennessee Creek

Holy Cross Wilderness

▲ 12,145 ft.

▲ 11,847 ft.

Homestake Peak
13,209 ft.

CONTINENTAL DIVIDE

▲ 12,820 ft.

▲ 13,081 ft.

CONTINENTAL DIVIDE

West Tennessee Creek

Homestake Mine

Lower West Tennessee Lake

Turnaround

Upper West Tennessee Lake

Turnaround

▲ 12,722 ft.

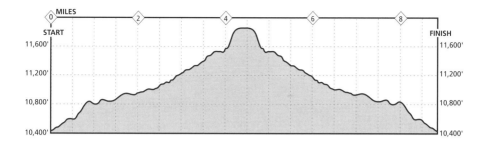

2.8 Arrive at the Holy Cross Wilderness boundary. Stop to fill out the wilderness permit. 379053mE 4356521mN

3.9 Come to a pond near the Homestake Mine and just before the trail climbs up a headwall to the lakes. 377565mE 4356376mN . When the trail Ys, the trail goes right through some trees and into the willows. After crossing the creek, look for the trail to the left hidden in the willows.

4.0 The trail starts to climb. When the trail crosses a rock slab, just go straight up the slab to the trail on the other side. Keep an eye open to the right for a good view of the Homestake Mine.

4.2 Arrive at Lower West Tennessee Lake. 377270mE 4355986mN Trail Ys. Either way works; the left branch might be a little better. Eventually both trails disappear. Make your way up the rise to the upper lake, avoiding any marshy areas. Please remember to spread your party out across the tundra to minimize damage.

4.4 Arrive at Upper West Tennessee Lake. 377269mE 4355754mN 11,844 feet. Return the way you came.

8.8 Arrive back at the trailhead.

Hike Information

Local Information

Leadville–Twin Lakes Chamber of Commerce, 809 Harrison Avenue, Leadville; (719) 486–3900, (800) 933–3901; www.leadvilleusa.com

Local Events/Attractions

Healy House Museum, 912 Harrison Avenue, Leadville; (719) 486-0487
Leadville, Colorado & Southern Railroad, 326 East 7th Street, Leadville; (719) 486-3936, (866) 386-3936; www.leadville-train.com
Matchless Mine, Leadville, (719) 486-4918
National Mining Hall of Fame and Museum, 120 West 9th Street, Leadville; (719) 486-1229; www.mininghalloffame.org
Tabor Opera House, 308 Harrison Avenue, Leadville; (719) 486-3900, (800) 933-3901; www.leadvilleusa.com

Accommodations

Several campgrounds are available in the Turquoise Lake National Recreation Area. For more information, contact Leadville Ranger District, (719) 486-0749, www.fs.fed.us/r2/psicc.

Restaurants

Golden Burro Cafe and Lounge, 710 Harrison Avenue, Leadville; (719) 486-1239
The Grill Bar and Café, 715 Elm, Leadville; (719) 486-9930
Quincy's Steak and Spirits, 416 Harrison Avenue, Leadville; (719) 486-9765
Wild Bill's Hamburgers & Ice Cream, 200 Harrison Avenue, Leadville; (719) 486-0533

Honorable Mentions

A Old Dillon Reservoir Trail

This easy and short trek to the Town of Dillon's old reservoir makes a great hike for the whole family. Hikers and mountain bikers use the trail, which has great views of the surrounding area from either the trail or near the reservoir. Anglers also enjoy fishing in the little lake.

The trail wiggles up the hill then makes a right switchback for an angled climb to a high point at an old road. Elevation 9,180 feet. Continue straight ahead (northeast) to the lakeshore for nice views of Buffalo Mountain to the northwest. Return the way you came for about a 1.2-mile out-and-back hike depending on how far around the lake you walk.

Finding the trailhead: From Interstate 70 exit 203, Frisco/Breckenridge, turn left (northeast) at the first traffic light, and drive past the Holiday Inn for about 1.6 miles to the Old Dillon Reservoir Trail #87 trailhead sign (around the curve past Heaton Bay Campground—watch carefully on the left for the hard-to-see trailhead sign). Turn left (north) into the parking lot. 13S 407736mE 4384379mN Elevation 9,075 feet. No facilities are available at the trailhead.

For more information, contact the Dillon Ranger District, 680 Blue River Parkway, Silverthorne; (970) 468–5456; www.dillonrangerdistrict.com.

B Lenawee Trail

The Lenawee Trail #34 trailhead is near the Chihuahua Gulch Road in Peru Creek. The trail climbs above treeline on Lenawee Mountain to a high point of 12,440 feet, below the summit (12,752 feet). Bring water as none is available along the trail, and start early to avoid the danger of lightning from thunderstorms. Fantastic views of the Continental Divide, Dillon Reservoir, and much of central Summit County are your reward for the steep climb. The hike is a most difficult 7.6-mile out-and-back trail with about a 2,075-foot gain to the high point. The trail is used by hikers and mountain bikers.

Finding the trailhead: From Interstate 70 exit 205, Silverthorne/Dillon, drive 7.9 miles southeast through Dillon and Keystone to the Montezuma exit. Drive on Montezuma Road past Keystone's River Run for 4.5 miles. To the left you will see a big dirt parking area. Turn left into the parking area, which is the start of Forest Development Road 260, Peru Creek Road. The dirt road is narrow and bumpy and gets rougher the farther you drive. Drive on Peru Creek Road for 1.6 miles to the Lenawee Trail trailhead on the left (north). 13S 427317mE 4383672mN Elevation 10,365 feet. Park on the right where there's room for a couple of cars, being careful not to block the road. No facilities are available at the trailhead.

For more information, contact the Dillon Ranger District, 680 Blue River Parkway, Silverthorne; (970) 468–5456; www.dillonrangerdistrict.com.

○ Colorado Trail and Miners Creek Trail

The combination of the Colorado Trail (CT) from Gold Hill Trailhead and the Miners Creek Trail #38 provides an interesting 13.2-mile, most-difficult, point-to-point hike over and along the crest of the Tenmile Range. You can hike in either direction starting at the Gold Hill Trail trailhead or the Wheeler Flats Trailhead near Copper Mountain Resort. This hike offers fantastic views of much of Summit County and a bevy of beautiful wildflowers in July. This trail, especially the lower part near Gold Hill and Miners Creek drainage, is a popular mountain bike route.

From the Gold Hill Trail trailhead, the Colorado Trail humps over Gold Hill then drops into the Miners Creek drainage, where it intersects and joins the Peaks Trail at about 3.3 miles. Turn left and ascend the trail to an intersection with the Miners Creek Trail at mile 3.6. Turn right here on a combination of Miners Creek, Colorado, and Continental Divide National Scenic (CDNST) Trails. The trail climbs below Peaks 3, 4, and 5 as it traverses the east side of the Tenmile Range. The trail then switches at mile 8.3 (elevation about 12,360 feet) to the west side of the range and starts dropping below Peaks 6 and 7 to join the Wheeler National Recreation Trail at about mile 10.1. Turn right (northwest) at that junction and continue downhill about 2.1 miles to the junction of the CT, CDNST, and a trail that heads north along a gas pipeline. Turn right (north) on the flat trail and walk 1.0 mile to the Wheeler Flats Trailhead. When you reach the paved bike path, turn left and walk to the parking lot. Total distance is approximately 13.2 miles, elevation gain 3,155 feet in 8.3 miles. If you start at the Wheeler Flats Trailhead near Copper Mountain, the elevation gain is 2,670 feet in 4.9 miles.

About 3.5 miles of this trail lies above treeline. Be sure to get an early start to avoid thunderstorms and the accompanying lightning.

Finding the trailheads: Gold Hill Trail trailhead: From Interstate 70 exit 203, Frisco/Breckenridge, drive south through Frisco on Highway 9 for approximately 6.1 miles to Gateway Drive, Summit County Road 950. Turn right and then immediately right into the dirt parking lot just off Highway 9. The trail starts across Gateway Drive at the Gold Hill Trail trailhead sign. 13S 410476mE 4377136mN Elevation 9,205 feet. No facilities are available at the trailhead. The Summit Stage (free bus service) has a bus stop just south of the Gold Hill Trail trailhead along Highway 9. For schedule information, contact the Summit Stage, (970) 668–0999, www.summitstage.com.

Wheeler Flats Trailhead: From Interstate 70 exit 195, Copper Mountain/Leadville, drive southwest less than 1 mile on Highway 91 to the entrance to Copper Mountain Resort. Turn left at the traffic signal at the entrance and drive past the Copper Mountain Retail Center about 0.3 mile to the Wheeler Flats Trailhead parking lot. 13S 401850mE 4376702mN. Elevation 9,690 feet. No facilities are available at the trailhead, so be sure to stop at the retail center if you need anything before hiking. The Summit Stage (free bus service) has a bus stop at the entrance to Copper Mountain. For schedule information, contact the Summit Stage, (970) 668–0999, www.summitstage.com.

For more information, contact the Dillon Ranger District, 680 Blue River Parkway, Silverthorne; (970) 468–5456; www.dillonrangerdistrict.com.

D Quandary Peak

At 14,265 feet, Quandary Peak, the thirteenth-highest in Colorado, is a long climb, but well worth the effort not only for the accomplishment but for the view. The Colorado Fourteeners Initiative (CFI), in partnership with the U.S. Forest Service, recently rerouted the trail to make it more environmentally friendly and sustainable. The hike is about 6.6 miles out and back, with an elevation gain of 3,375 feet from the trailhead at 10,890 feet. This hike is considered strenuous (about a 21 percent average grade) although it is considered an "easy" fourteener. Don't be fooled—Summit County Search and Rescue Group rescues many lost and injured hikers and skiers from this peak every year. At about 11,700 feet, CFI has made some modifications and closed the old trail. Please stay on the new trail.

Be sure to start early on this peak and allow at least seven hours round-trip. Bring lots of water and munchies to keep your body fueled. The weather can change quickly and thunderstorms bringing lightning can pose extreme danger. Leave early and return to below treeline before thunderstorms build.

Finding the trailhead: From Interstate 70 exit 203, Frisco/Breckenridge, drive south through Frisco and Breckenridge on Highway 9 for approximately 18.4 miles to just south of mile marker 79 to Blue Lakes Road. Turn right onto Blue Lakes Road and drive 0.1 mile to McCullough Gulch Summit County Road 851. Turn right and drive 0.2 mile to the Quandary Peak Trail #47 trailhead parking on the right of the road. 13S 408611mE 4359830mN Elevation 10,890 feet. This parking area is very small, and you may need to park on the side of the road, being careful not to block it. The bulletin board posters contain a lot of interesting and good information that is worthwhile reading. No facilities are available at the trailhead. The trail starts a little farther up the road on the left.

For current information on this trail, contact the Dillon Ranger District, 680 Blue River Parkway, Silverthorne; (970) 468–5456; www.dillonrangerdistrict.com, or Colorado Fourteeners Initiative, www.coloradofourteeners.org, (303) 278–7525. A Web site containing a good trail description is www.14ers.com.

E Hike across Summit County

By hiking the Wheeler National Recreation Trail (WNRT) #42 from McCullough Gulch to Copper Mountain Resort then connecting with the Gore Range Trail

(GRT) #60, you can hike from almost the southern end of Summit County to Mahan Lake on the far north end. Because of private property issues on the southern end, please access the WNRT from the Quandary Peak Trail. The WNRT is about 11 miles long and the GRT is about 54 miles long. Because vehicle access to Mahan Lake is difficult, you can start at the Eaglesmere Trail trailhead instead and connect to the GRT from there.

Finding the trailheads: Quandary Peak Trail trailhead: From Interstate 70 exit 203, Frisco/Breckenridge, drive south through Frisco and Breckenridge on Highway 9 for approximately 18.4 miles to just south of mile marker 79 to Blue Lakes Road. Turn right onto Blue Lakes Road and drive 0.1 mile to McCullough Gulch Summit County Road 851. Turn right and drive 0.2 mile to the Quandary Peak Trail trailhead parking on the right of the road. 13S 408611mE 4359830mN Elevation 10,890 feet. This parking area is very small and you may need to park on the side of the road, being careful not to block it. No facilities are available at the trailhead. The trail starts a little farther up the road on the left side. Hike up this trail to the intersection with the WNRT and turn right (north).

Wheeler Flats Trailhead by Copper Mountain Resort: At this trailhead, you finish hiking the WNRT and can walk across the Highway 91 bridge over I–70 to access the Gore Range Trail (GRT). This section of the GRT is also known as the Wheeler Lakes Trail. You can get on the GRT on the north side of the bridge and to the left (west) where there are NO PARKING signs. You can also pick up the GRT from the scenic overlook (that doesn't overlook anything) on I–70 at about mile marker 196 (westbound only). This parking lot is the real start of the southern end of the GRT.

Mahan Lake Trail trailhead: The drive to the northern end of the GRT, the Mahan Lake Trail trailhead, requires a high-clearance, four-wheel-drive vehicle. However, you can park at the Elliott Ridge Trail trailhead and walk to the start of the GRT or at the Eaglesmere Trail trailhead (below). Contact the Dillon Ranger District at (970) 468–5400 for access road information because the forest roads can be rough and may require a high-clearance vehicle. From I–70 exit 205, Silverthorne/Dillon, drive north through Silverthorne on Highway 9 for about 27 miles to Spring Creek Road (Grand County Road 10). Turn left (west) and drive 6.8 miles, then bear left at Forest Road (FR) 1830 (Doenz Place). The road becomes FR 23 at this point. Follow FR 23 for about 1.1 miles then take the right fork and follow FR 23/1831 about 5.4 miles. When the road forks here, turn right about 500 feet for the Elliott Ridge Trail trailhead. FR 1831 bears left here, and you can drive down it with the proper vehicle or walk to the Mahan Lake Trail trailhead from where you can also hike to the GRT.

Eaglesmere Trail trailhead: An easier approach to the GRT's northern end, although you'll miss a little of it, is to start at the Eaglesmere Trail trailhead by Lower Cataract Lake and connect to the GRT from there. From Interstate 70 exit 205, Silverthorne/Dillon, drive north through Silverthorne on Highway 9, 16.6 miles to Heeney Road (Summit County Road 30). Turn left and drive on Heeney Road for

5.5 miles to Cataract Creek Road. Turn sharp left (southwest) and follow Cataract Creek Road 2.2 miles to the road to Eaglesmere Trailhead. Turn right and drive 0.3 mile to the Eaglesmere Trail trailhead. Please park only in the few designated spaces. An outhouse is available near the trailhead. Self-pay fee stations are available at both the Eaglesmere and Surprise Lake Trailheads.

For more information, contact the Dillon Ranger District, 680 Blue River Parkway, Silverthorne, (970) 468–5456, www.dillonrangerdistrict.com.

F Summit County and Vail Paved Recreation Path Systems

Summit County has a wonderful system of paved recreational paths, some of which are county owned and maintained while others are maintained by different towns. These mostly nonmotorized trails are used by hikers, bikers, and in-line skaters.

1. Vail Pass Trail links Copper Mountain and Vail over Vail Pass.

2. Tenmile Canyon National Recreation Trail links Frisco and Copper Mountain.

3. Frisco Farmer's Korner Trail and Blue River Pathway links Frisco with Farmer's Korner near Summit High School and on to Breckenridge.

4. Frisco Lakefront Trail and Dillon Dam Trail combine to connect Frisco to Dillon and Silverthorne.

5. Silverthorne's Blue River Trail starts at the Dillon Dam Path and heads through town. Plans to extend the path to just north of Silverthorne Elementary School to a proposed new park are in process.

6. The Dillon-Keystone Pathway connects Dillon to Keystone (and connects with trails to Silverthorne and Frisco).

7. A trail which will connect Farmer's Korner by Summit High School and Summit Cove along the southeast side of Dillon Reservoir is in the planning process. Presently bikers have to ride on the very narrow Swan Mountain Road. The new paved recreation path will be open to nonmotorized users, including hikers.

8. The Gore Valley Trail travels 12 miles from the bottom of Vail Pass (Vail side) to Dowd Junction near Minturn (Interstate 70 and U.S. Highway 24).

9. Other smaller paved paths radiate through the towns from the main recreational path systems.

For more information, contact the Summit Visitor Information Center, Outlets at Silverthorne, 246 Rainbow Drive, Silverthorne; (970) 262–0817, (800) 530–3099; www.summitchamber.org, or the Vail Valley Chamber & Tourism Bureau, (970) 476–1000, www.visitvailvalley.com.

The Art of Hiking

When standing nose to nose with a mountain lion, you're probably not too concerned with the issue of ethical behavior in the wild. No doubt you're just terrified. But let's be honest. How often are you nose to nose with a mountain lion? For most of us, a hike into the "wild" means loading up the SUV with expensive gear and driving to a toileted trailhead. Sure, you can mourn how civilized we've become—how GPS units have replaced natural instinct and Gore-Tex, true-grit—but the silly gadgets of civilization aside, we have plenty of reason to take pride in how we've matured. With survival now on the back burner, we've begun to reason—and it's about time—that we have a responsibility to protect, no longer just conquer, our wild places: that they, not we, are at risk. So please, do what you can. The following section will help you understand better what it means to "do what you can" while still making the most of your hiking experience. Anyone can take a hike, but hiking safely and well is an art requiring preparation and proper equipment.

Trail Etiquette

Zero impact. Always leave an area just like you found it—if not better than you found it. Avoid camping in fragile, alpine meadows and along the banks of streams and lakes. Use a camp stove versus building a wood fire. Pack up all of your trash and extra food. Bury human waste at least 100 feet from water sources under 6 to 8 inches of topsoil. Don't bathe with soap in a lake or stream—use prepackaged moistened towels to wipe off sweat and dirt, or bathe in the water without soap.

Stay on the trail. It's true, a path anywhere leads nowhere new, but purists will just have to get over it. Paths serve an important purpose; they limit impact on natural areas. Straying from a designated trail may seem innocent but it can cause damage to sensitive areas—damage that may take years to recover, if it can recover at all. Even simple shortcuts can be destructive. So, please, stay on the trail.

Leave no weeds. Noxious weeds tend to overtake other plants, which in turn affects animals and birds that depend on them for food. To minimize the spread of noxious weeds, hikers should regularly clean their boots, tents, packs, and hiking poles of mud and seeds. Also brush your dog to remove any weed seeds before heading off into a new area.

Keep your dog under control. You can buy a flexi-lead that allows your dog to go exploring along the trail, while allowing you the ability to reel him in should another hiker approach or should he decide to chase a rabbit. Always obey leash laws and be sure to bury your dog's waste or pack it in resealable plastic bags.

Respect other trail users. Often you're not the only one on the trail. With the rise in popularity of multiuse trails, you'll have to learn a new kind of respect, beyond the nod and "hello" approach you may be used to. First investigate whether you're on a multiuse trail, and assume the appropriate precautions. When you encounter motorized vehicles (ATVs, motorcycles, and 4WDs), be alert. Though they should always yield to the hiker, often they're going too fast or are too lost in the buzz of their engine to react to your presence. If you hear activity ahead, step off the trail just to be safe. Note that you're not likely to hear a mountain biker coming, so be prepared and know ahead of time whether you share the trail with them. Cyclists should always yield to hikers, but that's little comfort to the hiker. Be aware. When you approach horses or pack animals on the trail, always step quietly off the trail, preferably on the downhill side, and let them pass. If you're wearing a large backpack, it's often a good idea to sit down. To some animals, a hiker wearing a large backpack might appear threatening. Many national forests allow domesticated grazing, usually for sheep and cattle. Make sure your dog doesn't harass these animals, and respect ranchers' rights while you're enjoying yours.

Getting into Shape

Unless you want to be sore—and possibly have to shorten your trip or vacation— be sure to get in shape before a big hike. If you're terribly out of shape, start a walking program early, preferably eight weeks in advance. Start with a fifteen-minute walk during your lunch hour or after work and gradually increase your walking time to an hour. You should also increase your elevation gain. Walking briskly up hills really strengthens your leg muscles and gets your heart rate up. If you work in a storied office building, take the stairs instead of the elevator. If you prefer going to a gym, walk the treadmill or use a stair machine. You can further increase your strength and endurance by walking with a loaded backpack. Stationary exercises you might consider are squats, leg lifts, sit-ups, and push-ups. Other good ways to get in shape include biking, running, aerobics, and, of course, short hikes. Stretching before and after a hike keeps muscles flexible and helps avoid injuries.

Preparedness

It's been said that failing to plan means planning to fail. So do take the necessary time to plan your trip. Whether going on a short day hike or an extended backpack trip, always prepare for the worst. Simply remembering to pack a copy of the U.S. Army Survival Manual is not preparedness. Although it's not a bad idea if you plan on entering truly wild places, it's merely the tourniquet answer to a problem. You need to do your best to prevent the problem from arising in the first place. In order to survive—and to stay reasonably comfortable—you need to concern yourself with the basics: water, food, and shelter. Don't go on a hike without having these bases covered. And don't go on a hike expecting to find these items in the woods.

Water. Even in frigid conditions, you need at least two quarts of water a day to function efficiently. Add heat and taxing terrain and you can bump that figure up to one gallon. That's simply a base to work from—your metabolism and your level of conditioning can raise or lower that amount. Unless you know your level, assume that you need one gallon of water a day. Now, where do you plan on getting the water?

Preferably not from natural water sources. These sources can be loaded with intestinal disturbers, such as bacteria, viruses, and fertilizers. *Giardia lamblia,* the most common of these disturbers, is a protozoan parasite that lives part of its life cycle as a cyst in water sources. The parasite spreads when mammals defecate in water sources. Once ingested, Giardia can induce cramping, diarrhea, vomiting, and fatigue within two days to two weeks after ingestion. Giardiasis is treatable with prescription drugs. If you believe you've contracted giardiasis, see a doctor immediately.

Treating water. The best and easiest solution to avoid polluted water is to carry your water with you. Yet, depending on the nature of your hike and the duration, this may not be an option—one gallon of water weighs eight-and-a-half pounds. In that case, you'll need to look into treating water. Regardless of which method you choose, you should always carry some water with you in case of an emergency. Save this reserve until you absolutely need it.

There are three methods of treating water: boiling, chemical treatment, and filtering. If you boil water, it's recommended that you do so for ten to fifteen minutes. This is often impractical because you're forced to exhaust a great deal of your fuel supply. You can opt for chemical treatment, which will kill Giardia but will not take care of other chemical pollutants. Another drawback to chemical treatments is the unpleasant taste of the water after it's treated. You can remedy this by adding powdered drink mix to the water. Filters are the preferred method for treating water. Many filters remove Giardia, organic and inorganic contaminants, and don't leave an aftertaste. Water filters are far from perfect as they can easily become clogged or leak if a gasket wears out. It's always a good idea to carry a backup supply of chemical treatment tablets in case your filter decides to quit on you.

Food. If we're talking about survival, you can go days without food, as long as you have water. But we're also talking about comfort. Try to avoid foods that are high in sugar and fat like candy bars and potato chips. These food types are harder to digest and are low in nutritional value. Instead, bring along foods that are easy to pack, nutritious, and high in energy (e.g., bagels, nutrition bars, dehydrated fruit, gorp, and jerky). If you are on an overnight trip, easy-to-fix dinners include rice mixes with dehydrated potatoes, corn, pasta with cheese sauce, and soup mixes. For a tasty breakfast, you can fix hot oatmeal with brown sugar and reconstituted milk powder topped off with banana chips. If you like a hot drink in the morning, bring along herbal tea bags or hot chocolate. If you are a coffee junkie, you can purchase coffee that is packaged like tea bags. You can prepackage all of your meals in heavy-duty resealable plastic bags to keep food from spilling in your pack. These bags can be reused to pack out trash.

Shelter. The type of shelter you choose depends less on the conditions than on your tolerance for discomfort. Shelter comes in many forms—tent, tarp, lean-to, bivy sack, cabin, cave, etc. If you're camping in the desert, a bivy sack may suffice, but if you're above the treeline and a storm is approaching, a better choice is a three- or four-season tent. Tents are the logical and most popular choice for most backpackers as they're lightweight and packable—and you can rest assured that you always have shelter from the elements. Before you leave on your trip, anticipate what the weather and terrain will be like and plan for the type of shelter that will work best for your comfort level (see Equipment later in this section).

Finding a campsite. If there are established campsites, stick to those. If not, start looking for a campsite early—around 3:30 or 4:00 P.M. Stop at the first decent site you see. Depending on the area, it could be a long time before you find another suitable location. Pitch your camp in an area that's level. Make sure the area is at least 200 feet from fragile areas like lakeshores, meadows, and stream banks. And try to avoid areas thick in underbrush, as they can harbor insects and provide cover for approaching animals.

If you are camping in stormy, rainy weather, look for a rock outcrop or a shelter in the trees to keep the wind from blowing your tent all night. Be sure that you don't camp under trees with dead limbs that might break off on top of you. Also, try to find an area that has an absorbent surface, such as sandy soil or forest duff. This, in addition to camping on a surface with a slight angle, will provide better drainage. By all means, don't dig trenches to provide drainage around your tent—remember you're practicing zero-impact camping.

If you're in bear country, steer clear of creekbeds or animal paths. If you see any signs of a bear's presence (i.e., scat, footprints), relocate. You'll need to find a campsite near a tall tree where you can hang your food and other items that may attract bears such as deodorant, toothpaste, or soap. Carry a lightweight nylon rope with which to hang your food. As a rule, you should hang your food at least 20 feet from the ground and 5 feet away from the tree trunk. You can put food and other items in a waterproof stuff sack and tie one end of the rope to the stuff sack. To get the other end of the rope over the tree branch, tie a good size rock to it, and gently toss the rock over the tree branch. Pull the stuff sack up until it reaches the top of the branch and tie it off securely. Don't hang your food near your tent! If possible, hang your food at least 100 feet away from your campsite. Alternatives to hanging your food are bear-proof plastic tubes and metal bear boxes.

Lastly, think of comfort. Lie down on the ground where you intend to sleep and see if it's a good fit. For morning warmth (and a nice view to wake up to), have your tent face east.

First Aid

I know you're tough, but get 10 miles into the woods and develop a blister and you'll wish you had carried that first-aid kit. Face it, it's just plain good sense. Many companies produce lightweight, compact first-aid kits. Just make sure yours contains at least the following:

- adhesive bandages
- moleskin or duct tape
- various sterile gauze and dressings
- white surgical tape
- an Ace bandage
- an antihistamine
- aspirin
- Betadine solution
- a first-aid book
- antacid tablets

- tweezers
- scissors
- antibacterial wipes
- triple-antibiotic ointment
- plastic gloves
- sterile cotton tip applicators
- syrup of ipecac (to induce vomiting)
- thermometer
- wire splint

Here are a few tips for dealing with and hopefully preventing certain ailments.

Sunburn. Take along sunscreen or sun block, protective clothing, and a wide-brimmed hat. If you do get a sunburn, treat the area with aloe vera gel, and protect the area from further sun exposure. At higher elevations, the sun's radiation can be particularly damaging to skin. Remember that your eyes are vulnerable to this radiation as well. Sunglasses can be a good way to prevent headaches and permanent eye damage from the sun, especially in places where light-colored rock or patches of snow reflect light up in your face.

Blisters. Be prepared to take care of these hike-spoilers by carrying moleskin (a lightly padded adhesive), gauze and tape, or adhesive bandages. An effective way to apply moleskin is to cut out a circle of moleskin and remove the center—like a doughnut—and place it over the blistered area. Cutting the center out will reduce the pressure applied to the sensitive skin. Other products can help you combat blisters. Some are applied to suspicious hot spots before a blister forms to help decrease friction to that area, while others are applied to the blister after it has popped to help prevent further irritation.

Insect bites and stings. You can treat most insect bites and stings by applying hydrocortisone 1% cream topically and taking a pain medication such as ibuprofen or acetaminophen to reduce swelling. If you forgot to pack these items, a cold compress or a paste of mud and ashes can sometimes assuage the itching and discomfort. Remove any stingers by using tweezers or scraping the area with your fingernail or a knife blade. Don't pinch the area as you'll only spread the venom.

Some hikers are highly sensitive to bites and stings and may have a serious allergic reaction that can be life threatening. Symptoms of a serious allergic reaction can include wheezing, an asthmatic attack, and shock. The treatment for this severe type of reaction is epinephrine. If you know that you are sensitive to bites and stings, carry a pre-packaged kit of epinephrine, which can be obtained only by prescription from your doctor.

Ticks. Ticks can carry diseases such as Rocky Mountain spotted fever and Lyme disease. The best defense is, of course, prevention. If you know you're going to be hiking through an area littered with ticks, wear long pants and a long sleeved shirt. You can apply a permethrin repellent to your clothing and a Deet repellent to exposed skin. At the end of your hike, do a spot check for ticks (and insects in general). If you do find a tick, coat the insect with petroleum jelly or tree sap to cut off its air supply. The tick should release its hold, but if it doesn't, grab the head of the tick firmly—with a pair of tweezers if you have them—and gently pull it away from the skin with a twisting motion. Sometimes the mouth parts linger, embedded in your skin. If this happens, try to remove them with a disinfected needle. Clean the affected area with an antibacterial cleanser and then apply triple antibiotic ointment. Monitor the area for a few days. If irritation persists or a white spot develops, see a doctor for possible infection.

Poison ivy, oak, and sumac. These skin irritants can be found most anywhere in North America and come in the form of a bush or a vine, having leaflets in groups of three, five, seven, or nine. Learn how to spot the plants. The oil they secrete can cause an allergic reaction in the form of blisters, usually about twelve hours after exposure. The itchy rash can last from ten days to several weeks. The best defense against these irritants is to wear clothing that covers the arms, legs and torso. For summer, zip-off cargo pants come in handy. There are also nonprescription lotions you can apply to exposed skin that guard against the effects of poison ivy/oak/sumac and can be washed off with soap and water. If you think you were in contact with the plants, after hiking (or even on the trail during longer hikes) wash with soap and water. Taking a hot shower with soap after you return home from your hike will also help to remove any lingering oil from your skin. Should you contract a rash from any of these plants, use an antihistamine to reduce the itching. If the rash is localized, create a light bleach/water wash to dry up the area. If the rash has spread, either tough it out or see your doctor about getting a dose of cortisone (available both orally and by injection).

Snakebites. Snakebites are rare in North America. Unless startled or provoked, the majority of snakes will not bite. If you are wise to their habitats and keep a careful eye on the trail, you should be just fine. When stepping over logs, first step on the log, making sure you can see what's on the other side before stepping down. Though your chances of being struck are slim, it's wise to know what to do in the event you are.

If a *nonpoisonous* snake bites you, allow the wound to bleed a small amount and then cleanse the wounded area with a Betadine solution (10% povidone iodine).

Rinse the wound with clean water (preferably) or fresh urine (it might sound ugly, but it's sterile). Once the area is clean, cover it with triple antibiotic ointment and a clean bandage. Remember, most residual damage from snakebites, poisonous or otherwise, comes from infection, not the snake's venom. Keep the area as clean as possible and get medical attention immediately.

If you are bitten by a poisonous snake, remove the toxin with a suctioning device, found in a snakebite kit. If you do not have such a device, squeeze the wound—DO NOT use your mouth for suction, as the venom will enter your bloodstream through the vessels under the tongue and head straight for your heart. Then, clean the wound just as you would a nonpoisonous bite. Tie a clean band of cloth snugly around the afflicted appendage, about an inch or so above the bite (or the rim of the swelling). This is NOT a tourniquet—you want to simply slow the blood flow, not cut it off. Loosen the band if numbness ensues. Remove the band for a minute and reapply a little higher every ten minutes.

If it is your friend who's been bitten, treat him or her for shock—make the person comfortable, have him or her lie down, elevate the legs, and keep him or her warm. Avoid applying anything cold to the bite wound. Immobilize the affected area and remove any constricting items such as rings, watches, or restrictive clothing—swelling may occur. Once your friend is stable and relatively calm, hike out to get help. The victim should get treatment within twelve hours, ideally, which usually consists of a tetanus shot, antivenin, and antibiotics.

If you are alone and struck by a poisonous snake, stay calm. Hysteria will only quicken the venom's spread. Follow the procedure above, and do your best to reach help. When hiking out, don't run—you'll only increase the flow of blood throughout your system. Instead, walk calmly.

Dehydration. Have you ever hiked in hot weather and had a roaring headache and felt fatigued after only a few miles? More than likely you were dehydrated. Symptoms of dehydration include fatigue, headache, and decreased coordination and judgment. When you are hiking, your body's rate of fluid loss depends on the outside temperature, humidity, altitude, and your activity level. On average, a hiker walking in warm weather will lose four liters of fluid a day. That fluid loss is easily replaced by normal consumption of liquids and food. However, if a hiker is walking briskly in hot, dry weather and hauling a heavy pack, he or she can lose one to three liters of water an hour. It's important to always carry plenty of water and to stop often and drink fluids regularly, even if you aren't thirsty.

Heat exhaustion is the result of a loss of large amounts of electrolytes and often occurs if a hiker is dehydrated and has been under heavy exertion. Common symptoms of heat exhaustion include cramping, exhaustion, fatigue, lightheadedness, and nausea. You can treat heat exhaustion by getting out of the sun and drinking an electrolyte solution made up of one teaspoon of salt and one tablespoon of sugar dissolved in a liter of water. Drink this solution slowly over a period of one hour.

Drinking plenty of fluids (preferably an electrolyte solution/sports drink) can prevent heat exhaustion. Avoid hiking during the hottest parts of the day, and wear breathable clothing, a wide-brimmed hat, and sunglasses.

Hypothermia is one of the biggest dangers in the backcountry, especially for day hikers in the summertime. That may sound strange, but imagine starting out on a hike in midsummer when it's sunny and 80 degrees out. You're clad in nylon shorts and a cotton T-shirt. About halfway through your hike, the sky begins to cloud up, and in the next hour a light drizzle begins to fall and the wind starts to pick up. Before you know it, you are soaking wet and shivering—the perfect recipe for hypothermia. More advanced signs include decreased coordination, slurred speech, and blurred vision. When a victim's temperature falls below 92 degrees, the blood pressure and pulse plummet, possibly leading to coma and death.

To avoid hypothermia, always bring a windproof/rainproof shell, a fleece jacket, tights made of a breathable, synthetic fiber, gloves, and hat when you are hiking in the mountains. Learn to adjust your clothing layers based on the temperature. If you are climbing uphill at a moderate pace you will stay warm, but when you stop for a break you'll become cold quickly, unless you add more layers of clothing.

If a hiker is showing advanced signs of hypothermia, dress him or her in dry clothes and make sure he or she is wearing a hat and gloves. Place the person in a sleeping bag in a tent or shelter that will protect him or her from the wind and other elements. Give the person warm fluids to drink and keep him awake.

Frostbite. When the mercury dips below 32 degrees, your extremities begin to chill. If a persistent chill attacks a localized area, say, your hands or your toes, the circulatory system reacts by cutting off blood flow to the affected area—the idea being to protect and preserve the body's overall temperature. And so it's death by attrition for the affected area. Ice crystals start to form from the water in the cells of the neglected tissue. Deprived of heat, nourishment, and now water, the tissue literally starves. This is frostbite.

Prevention is your best defense against this situation. Most prone to frostbite are your face, hands, and feet, so protect these areas well. Wool is the material of choice because it provides ample air space for insulation and draws moisture away from the skin. Synthetic fabrics, however, have recently made great strides in the cold weather clothing market. Do your research. A pair of light silk liners under your regular gloves is a good trick for keeping warm. They afford some additional warmth, but more importantly they'll allow you to remove your mitts for tedious work without exposing the skin.

If your feet or hands start to feel cold or numb due to the elements, warm them as quickly as possible. Place cold hands under your armpits or bury them in your crotch. If your feet are cold, change your socks. If there's plenty of room in your boots, add another pair of socks. Do remember, though, that constricting your feet in tight boots can restrict blood flow and actually make your feet colder more quickly. Your socks need to have breathing room if they're going to be effective.

Dead air provides insulation. If your face is cold, place your warm hands over your face, or simply wear a head stocking.

Should your skin go numb and start to appear white and waxy, chances are you've got or are developing frostbite. Don't try to thaw the area unless you can maintain the warmth. In other words, don't stop to warm up your frostbitten feet only to head back on the trail. You'll do more damage than good. Tests have shown that hikers who walked on thawed feet did more harm, and endured more pain, than hikers who left the affected areas alone. Do your best to get out of the cold entirely and seek medical attention—which usually consists of performing a rapid rewarming in water for twenty to thirty minutes.

The overall objective in preventing both hypothermia and frostbite is to keep the body's core warm. Protect key areas where heat escapes, like the top of the head, and maintain the proper nutrition level. Foods that are high in calories aid the body in producing heat. Never smoke or drink when you're in situations where the cold is threatening. By affecting blood flow, these activities ultimately cool the body's core temperature.

Altitude sickness (AMS). High lofty peaks, clear alpine lakes, and vast mountain views beckon hikers to the high country. But those who like to venture high may become victims of altitude sickness (also known as Acute Mountain Sickness—AMS). Altitude sickness is your body's reaction to insufficient oxygen in the blood due to decreased barometric pressure. While some hikers may feel lightheaded, nauseous, and experience shortness of breath at 7,000 feet, others may not experience these symptoms until they reach 10,000 feet or higher.

Slowing your ascent to high places and giving your body a chance to acclimatize to the higher elevations can prevent altitude sickness. For example, if you live at sea level and are planning a weeklong backpacking trip to elevations between 7,000 and 12,000 feet, start by staying below 7,000 feet for one night, then move to between 7,000 and 10,000 feet for another night or two. Avoid strenuous exertion and alcohol to give your body a chance to adjust to the new altitude. It's also important to eat light food and drink plenty of nonalcoholic fluids, preferably water. Loss of appetite at altitude is common, but you must eat!

Most hikers who experience mild to moderate AMS develop a headache and/or nausea, grow lethargic, and have problems sleeping. The treatment for AMS is simple: stop heading uphill. Keep eating and drinking water and take meds for the headache. You actually need to take more breaths at altitude than at sea level, so breathe a little faster without hyperventilating. If symptoms don't improve over twenty-four to forty-eight hours, descend. Once a victim descends about 2,000 to 3,000 feet, his signs will usually begin to diminish.

Severe AMS comes in two forms: High Altitude Pulmonary Edema (HAPE) and High Altitude Cerebral Edema (HACE). HAPE, an accumulation of fluid in the lungs, can occur above 8,000 feet. Symptoms include rapid heart rate, shortness of breath at rest, AMS symptoms, dry cough developing into a wet cough, gurgling sounds, flu-like or bronchitis symptoms, and lack of muscle coordination. HAPE is life threatening so descend immediately, at least 2,000 to 4,000 feet. HACE usually occurs above 12,000 feet but sometimes occurs above 10,000 feet. Symptoms are similar to HAPE but also include seizures, hallucinations, paralysis, and vision disturbances. Descend immediately—HACE is also life threatening.

Hantavirus Pulmonary Syndrome (HPS). Deer mice spread the virus that causes HPS, and humans contract it from breathing it in, usually when they've disturbed an area with dust and mice feces from nests or surfaces with mice droppings or urine. Exposure to large numbers of rodents and their feces or urine presents the greatest risk. As hikers, we sometimes enter old buildings, and often deer mice live in these places. We may not be around long enough to be exposed, but do be aware of this disease. About half the people who develop HPS die. Symptoms are flu-like and appear about two to three weeks after exposure. After initial symptoms, a dry cough and shortness of breath follow. Breathing is difficult. If you even think you might have HPS, see a doctor immediately!

Natural Hazards

Besides tripping over a rock or tree root on the trail, there are some real hazards to be aware of while hiking. Even if where you're hiking doesn't have the plethora of poisonous snakes and plants, insects, and grizzly bears found in other parts of the United States, there are a few weather conditions and predators you may need to take into account.

Lightning. Thunderstorms build over the mountains almost every day during the summer. Lightning is generated by thunderheads and can strike without warning, even several miles away from the nearest overhead cloud. The best rule of thumb is to start leaving exposed peaks, ridges, and canyon rims by about noon. This time can vary a little depending on storm buildup. Keep an eye on cloud formation and don't underestimate how fast a storm can build. The bigger they get, the more likely a thunderstorm will happen. Lightning takes the path of least resistance, so if you're the high point, it might choose you. Ducking under a rock overhang is dangerous as you form the shortest path between the rock and ground. If you dash below treeline, avoid standing under the only or the tallest tree. If you are caught above treeline, stay away from anything metal you might be carrying, Move down off the ridge slightly to a low, treeless point and squat until the storm passes. If you have an insulating pad, squat on it. Avoid having both your hands and feet touching the ground at once and never lay flat. If you hear a buzzing sound or feel your hair standing on end, move quickly as an electrical charge is building up.

Flash floods. On July 31, 1976, a torrential downpour unleashed by a thunderstorm dumped tons of water into the Big Thompson watershed near Estes Park. Within hours, a wall of water moved down the narrow canyon killing 139 people and causing more than $30 million in property damage. The spooky thing about flash floods, especially in western canyons, is that they can appear out of nowhere from a storm many miles away. While hiking or driving in canyons, keep an eye on the weather. Always climb to safety if danger threatens. Flash floods usually subside quickly, so be patient and don't cross a swollen stream.

Bears. Most of the United States (outside of the Pacific Northwest and parts of the Northern Rockies) does not have a grizzly bear population, although some rumors exist about sightings where there should be none. Black bears are plentiful, however. Here are some tips in case you and a bear scare each other. Most of all, avoid scaring a bear. Watch for bear tracks (five toes) and droppings (sizable with leaves, partly digested berries, seeds, and/or animal fur). Talk or sing where visibility or hearing are limited. Keep a clean camp, hang food, and don't sleep in the clothes you wore while cooking. Be especially careful in spring to avoid getting between a mother and her cubs. In late summer and fall bears are busy eating berries and acorns to fatten up for winter, so be extra careful around berry bushes and oakbrush. If you do encounter a bear, move away slowly while facing the bear, talk softly, and avoid direct eye contact. Give the bear room to escape. Since bears are very curious, it might stand upright to get a better whiff of you, and it may even charge you to try to intimidate you. Try to stay calm. If a bear does attack you, fight back with anything you have handy. Unleashed dogs have been known to come running back to their owners with a bear close behind. Keep your dog on a leash or leave it at home.

Mountain lions. Mountain lions appear to be getting more comfortable around humans as long as deer (their favorite prey) are in an area with adequate cover. Usually elusive and quiet, lions rarely attack people. If you meet a lion, give it a chance to escape. Stay calm and talk firmly to it. Back away slowly while facing the lion. If you run, you'll only encourage the curious cat to chase you. Make yourself look large by opening a jacket, if you have one, or waving your hiking poles. If the lion behaves aggressively throw stones, sticks, or whatever you can while remaining tall. If a lion does attack, fight for your life with anything you can grab.

Moose. Because moose have very few natural predators, they don't fear humans like other animals. You might find moose in sagebrush and wetter areas of willow, aspen, and pine, or in beaver habitats. Mothers with calves, as well as bulls during mating season, can be particularly aggressive. If a moose threatens you, back away slowly and talk calmly to it. Keep your pets away from moose.

Other considerations. Hunting is a popular sport in the United States, especially during rifle season in October and November. Hiking is still enjoyable in those months in many areas, so just take a few precautions. First, learn when the different hunting seasons start and end in the area in which you'll be hiking. During this time frame, be sure to wear at least a blaze orange hat, and possibly put an orange vest over your pack. Don't be surprised to see hunters in camo outfits carrying bows or muzzleloading rifles around during their season. If you would feel more comfortable without hunters around, hike in national parks and monuments or state and local parks where hunting is not allowed.

Navigation

Whether you are going on a short hike in a familiar area or planning a weeklong backpack trip, you should always be equipped with the proper navigational equipment—at the very least a detailed map and a sturdy compass.

Maps. There are many different types of maps available to help you find your way on the trail. Easiest to find are Forest Service maps and BLM (Bureau of Land Management) maps. These maps tend to cover large areas, so be sure they are detailed enough for your particular trip. You can also obtain National Park maps as well as high quality maps from private companies and trail groups. These maps can be obtained either from outdoor stores or ranger stations.

U.S. Geological Survey topographic maps are particularly popular with hikers—especially serious backcountry hikers. These maps contain the standard map symbols such as roads, lakes, and rivers, as well as contour lines that show the details of the trail terrain like ridges, valleys, passes, and mountain peaks. The 7.5-minute series (1 inch on the map equals approximately ⅖ mile on the ground) provides the closest inspection available. USGS maps are available by mail (U.S. Geological Survey, Map Distribution Branch, P.O. Box 25286, Denver, CO 80225), or at mapping.usgs.gov/esic/to_order.html.

If you want to check out the high-tech world of maps, you can purchase topographic maps on CD-ROM. These software-mapping programs let you select a route on your computer, print it out, then take it with you on the trail. Some software mapping programs let you insert symbols and labels, download waypoints from a GPS unit, and export the maps to other software programs.

The art of map reading is a skill that you can develop by first practicing in an area you are familiar with. To begin, orient the map so the map is lined up in the correct direction (i.e. north on the map is lined up with true north). Next, familiarize yourself with the map symbols and try and match them up with terrain features around you such as a high ridge, mountain peak, river, or lake. If you are practicing with a USGS map, notice the contour lines. On gentler terrain these contour lines are spaced further apart, and on steeper terrain they are closer together. Pick a short loop trail, and stop frequently to check your position on the map. As you practice map reading, you'll learn how to anticipate a steep section on the trail or a good place to take a rest break, and so on.

Compasses. First off, the sun is not a substitute for a compass. So, what kind of compass should you have? Here are some characteristics you should look for: a rectangular base with detailed scales, a liquid-filled housing, protective housing, a sighting line on the mirror, luminous alignment and back-bearing arrows, a luminous north-seeking arrow, and a well-defined bezel ring.

You can learn compass basics by reading the detailed instructions included with your compass. If you want to fine-tune your compass skills, sign up for an orienteering class or purchase a book on compass reading. Once you've learned the basic skills of using a compass, remember to practice these skills before you head into the backcountry.

If you are a klutz at using a compass, you may be interested in checking out the technical wizardry of the GPS (Global Positioning System) device. The GPS was developed by the Pentagon and works off twenty-four NAVSTAR satellites, which were designed to guide missiles to their targets. A GPS device is a handheld unit that calculates your latitude and longitude with the easy press of a button. The Department of Defense used to scramble the satellite signals a bit to prevent civilians (and spies!) from getting extremely accurate readings, but that practice was discontinued in May 2000, and GPS units now provide nearly pinpoint accuracy (within 30 to 60 feet).

There are many different types of GPS units available and they range in price from $100 to $400. In general, all GPS units have a display screen and keypad where you input information. In addition to acting as a compass, the unit allows you to plot your route, easily retrace your path, track your travelling speed, find the mileage between waypoints, and calculate the total mileage of your route.

Before you purchase a GPS unit, keep in mind that these devices don't pick up signals indoors, in heavily wooded areas, on mountain peaks, or in deep valleys.

Pedometers. A pedometer is a small, clip-on unit with a digital display that calculates your hiking distance in miles or kilometers based on your walking stride. Some units also calculate the calories you burn and your total hiking time. Pedometers are available at most large outdoor stores and range in price from $20 to $40.

Trip Planning

Planning your hiking adventure begins with letting a friend or relative know your trip itinerary so they can call for help if you don't return at your scheduled time. Your next task is to make sure you are outfitted to experience the risks and rewards of the trail. This section highlights gear and clothing you may want to take with you to get the most out of your hike.

Day Hikes

- camera/film
- compass/GPS unit
- pedometer
- daypack
- first-aid kit
- food
- guidebook
- headlamp/flashlight with extra batteries and bulbs
- hat
- insect repellent
- knife/multipurpose tool
- map
- matches in waterproof container and fire starter
- fleece jacket
- rain gear
- space blanket
- sunglasses
- sunscreen
- swimsuit
- watch
- water
- water bottles/water hydration system

Overnight Trip

- backpack and waterproof rain cover
- backpacker's trowel
- bandanna
- bear repellent spray
- bear bell
- biodegradable soap
- pot scrubber
- collapsible water container (2–3 gallon capacity)
- clothing—extra wool socks, shirt and shorts
- cook set/utensils
- ditty bags to store gear
- extra plastic resealable bags
- gaiters
- garbage bag
- ground cloth
- journal/pen
- nylon rope to hang food
- long underwear
- permit (if required)
- rain jacket and pants
- sandals to wear around camp and to ford streams
- sleeping bag
- waterproof stuff sack
- sleeping pad
- small bath towel
- stove and fuel
- tent
- toiletry items
- water filter
- whistle

Equipment

With the outdoor market currently flooded with products, many of which are pure gimmickry, it seems impossible to both differentiate and choose. Do I really need a tropical-fish-lined collapsible shower? (No, you don't.) The only defense against the maddening quantity of items thrust in your face is to think practically—and to do so before you go shopping. The worst buys are impulsive buys. Since most name brands will differ only slightly in quality, it's best to know what you're looking for in terms of function. Buy only what you need. You will, don't forget, be carrying what you've bought on your back. Here are some things to keep in mind before you go shopping.

Clothes. Clothing is your armor against Mother Nature's little surprises. Hikers should be prepared for any possibility, especially when hiking in mountainous areas. Adequate rain protection and extra layers of clothing are a good idea. In summer, a wide-brimmed hat can help keep the sun at bay. In the winter months the first layer you'll want to wear is a "wicking" layer of long underwear that keeps perspiration away from your skin. Wear long underwear made from synthetic fibers that wick moisture away from the skin and draw it toward the next layer of clothing, where it then evaporates. Avoid wearing long underwear made of cotton as it is slow to dry and keeps moisture next to your skin.

The second layer you'll wear is the "insulating" layer. Aside from keeping you warm, this layer needs to "breathe" so you stay dry while hiking. A fabric that provides insulation and dries quickly is fleece. It's interesting to note that this one-of-a-kind fabric is made out of recycled plastic. Purchasing a zip-up jacket made of this material is highly recommended.

The last line of layering defense is the "shell" layer. You'll need some type of waterproof, windproof, breathable jacket that will fit over all of your other layers. It should have a large hood that fits over a hat. You'll also need a good pair of rain pants made from a similar waterproof, breathable fabric. Some Gore-Tex jackets cost as much as $500, but you should know that there are more affordable fabrics out there that work just as well.

Now that you've learned the basics of layering, you can't forget to protect your hands and face. In cold, windy, or rainy weather you'll need a hat made of wool or fleece and insulated, waterproof gloves that will keep your hands warm and toasty. As mentioned earlier, buying an additional pair of light silk liners to wear under your regular gloves is a good idea.

Footwear. If you have any extra money to spend on your trip, put that money into boots or trail shoes. Poor shoes will bring a hike to a halt faster than anything else. To avoid this annoyance, buy shoes that provide support and are lightweight and flexible. A lightweight hiking boot is better than a heavy, leather mountaineering boot for most day hikes and backpacking. Trail running shoes provide a little extra cushion and are made in a high-top style that many people wear for hiking. These running shoes are lighter, more flexible, and more breathable than hiking boots. If you know you'll be hiking in wet weather often, purchase boots or shoes with a Gore-Tex liner, which will help keep your feet dry.

When buying your boots, be sure to wear the same type of socks you'll be wearing on the trail. If the boots you're buying are for cold weather hiking, try the boots on while wearing two pairs of socks. Speaking of socks, a good cold weather sock combination is to wear a thinner sock made of wool or polypropylene covered by a heavier outer sock made of wool. The inner sock protects the foot from the rubbing effects of the outer sock and prevents blisters. Many outdoor stores have some type of ramp to simulate hiking uphill and downhill. Be sure to take advantage of this test, as toe-jamming boot fronts can be very painful and debilitating on the downhill trek.

Once you've purchased your footwear, be sure to break them in before you hit the trail. New footwear is often stiff and needs to be stretched and molded to your foot.

Hiking poles. Hiking poles help with balance, and more importantly take pressure off your knees. The ones with shock absorbers are easier on your elbows and knees. Some poles even come with a camera attachment to be used as a monopod. And heaven forbid you meet a mountain lion, bear, or unfriendly dog, the poles can make you look a lot bigger.

Backpacks. No matter what type of hiking you do you'll need a pack of some sort to carry the basic trail essentials. There are a variety of backpacks on the market, but let's first discuss what you intend to use it for. Day hikes or overnight trips?

If you plan on doing a day hike, a daypack should have some of the following characteristics: a padded hip belt that's at least 2 inches in diameter (avoid packs with only a small nylon piece of webbing for a hip belt); a chest strap (the chest strap helps stabilize the pack against your body); external pockets to carry water and other items that you want easy access to; an internal pocket to hold keys, a knife, a wallet, and other miscellaneous items; an external lashing system to hold a jacket; and a hydration pocket for carrying a hydration system (which consists of a water bladder with an attachable drinking hose).

For short hikes, some hikers like to use a fanny pack to store just a camera, food, a compass, a map, and other trail essentials. Most fanny packs have pockets for two water bottles and a padded hip belt.

If you intend to do an extended, overnight trip, there are multiple considerations. First off, you need to decide what kind of framed pack you want. There are two backpack types for backpacking: the internal frame and the external frame. An internal frame pack rests closer to your body, making it more stable and easier to balance when hiking over rough terrain. An external frame pack is just that, an aluminum frame attached to the exterior of the pack. An external frame pack is better for long backpack trips because it distributes the pack weight better and you can carry heavier loads. It's easier to pack, and your gear is more accessible. It also offers better back ventilation in hot weather.

The most critical measurement for fitting a pack is torso length. The pack needs to rest evenly on your hips without sagging. A good pack will come in two or three sizes and have straps and hip belts that are adjustable according to your body size and characteristics.

When you purchase a backpack, go to an outdoor store with salespeople who are knowledgeable in how to properly fit a pack. Once the pack is fitted for you, load the pack with the amount of weight you plan on taking on the trail. The weight of the pack should be distributed evenly and you should be able to swing your arms and walk briskly without feeling out of balance. Another good technique for evaluating a pack is to walk up and down stairs and make quick turns to the right and to the left to be sure the pack doesn't feel out of balance. Other features that are nice to have on a backpack include a removable day pack or fanny pack, external pockets for extra water, and extra lash points to attach a jacket or other items.

Sleeping bags and pads. Sleeping bags are rated by temperature. You can purchase a bag made of synthetic fiber, or you can buy a goose down bag. Goose down bags are more expensive, but they have a higher insulating capacity by weight and will keep their loft longer. You'll want to purchase a bag with a temperature rating that fits the time of year and conditions you are most likely to camp in. One caveat: The techno-standard for temperature ratings is far from perfect. Ratings vary from manufacturer to manufacturer, so to protect yourself you should purchase a bag rated 10 to 15 degrees below the temperature you expect to be camping in. Synthetic bags are more resistant to water than down bags, but many down bags are now made with a Gore-Tex shell that helps to repel water. Down bags are also more compressible than synthetic bags and take up less room in your pack, which is an important consideration if you are planning a multiday backpack trip. Features to look for in a sleeping bag include a mummy style bag, a hood you can cinch down around your head in cold weather, and draft tubes along the zippers that help keep heat in and drafts out.

You'll also want a sleeping pad to provide insulation and padding from the cold ground. There are different types of sleeping pads available, from the more expensive self-inflating air mattresses to the less expensive closed-cell foam pads. Self-inflating air mattresses are usually heavier than closed-cell foam mattresses and are prone to punctures.

Tents. The tent is your home away from home while on the trail. It provides protection from wind, snow, rain, and insects. A three-season tent is a good choice for backpacking and can range in price from $100 to $500. These lightweight and versatile tents provide protection in all types of weather, except heavy snowstorms or high winds, and range in weight from four to eight pounds. Look for a tent that's easy to set up and will easily fit two people with gear. Dome type tents usually offer more headroom and places to store gear. Other tent designs include a vestibule where you can store wet boots and backpacks. Some nice-to-have items in a tent include interior pockets to store small items and lashing points to hang a clothesline. Most three-season tents also come with stakes so you can secure the tent in high winds. Before you purchase a tent, set it up and take it down a few times to be sure it is easy to handle. Also, sit inside the tent and make sure it has enough room for you and your gear.

Cell phones. Many hikers are carrying their cell phones into the backcountry these days in case of emergency. That's fine and good, but please know that cell phone coverage is often poor to nonexistent in valleys, canyons, and thick forest. More importantly people have started to call for help because they're tired or lost. Let's go back to being prepared. You are responsible for yourself in the backcountry. Use your brain to avoid problems, and if you do encounter one, first use your brain to try to correct the situation. Only use your cell phone, if it works, in true emergencies.

Hiking with Children

Hiking with children isn't a matter of how many miles you can cover or how much elevation gain you make in a day; it's about seeing and experiencing nature through their eyes.

Kids like to explore and have fun. They like to stop and point out bugs and plants, look under rocks, jump in puddles, and throw sticks. If you're taking a toddler or young child on a hike, start with a trail that you're familiar with. Trails that have interesting things for kids, like piles of leaves to play in or a small stream to wade through during the summer, will make the hike much more enjoyable for them and will keep them from getting bored.

You can keep your child's attention if you have a strategy before starting on the trail. Using games is not only an effective way to keep a child's attention, it's also a great way to teach him or her about nature. Play hide and seek, where your child is the mouse and you are the hawk. Quiz children on the names of plants and animals. If your children are old enough, let them carry their own daypack filled with snacks and water. So that you are sure to go at their pace and not yours, let them lead the way. Playing follow the leader works particularly well when you have a group of children. Have each child take a turn at being the leader.

With children, a lot of clothing is key. The only thing predictable about weather is that it will change. Especially in mountainous areas, weather can change dramatically in a very short time. Always bring extra clothing for children, regardless of the season. In the winter, have your children wear wool socks, and warm layers such as long underwear, a fleece jacket and hat, wool mittens, and good rain gear. It's not a bad idea to have these along in late fall and early spring as well. Good footwear is also important. A sturdy pair of high top tennis shoes or lightweight hiking boots are the best bet for little ones. If you're hiking in the summer near a lake or stream, bring along a pair of old sneakers that your child can put on when he wants to go exploring in the water. Remember when you're near any type of water, always watch your child at all times. Also, keep a close eye on teething toddlers who may decide a rock or leaf of poison oak is an interesting item to put in their mouth.

From spring through fall, you'll want your kids to wear a wide-brimmed hat to keep their face, head, and ears protected from the hot sun. Also, make sure your children wear sunscreen at all times. Choose a brand without Paba—children have sensitive skin and may have an allergic reaction to sunscreen that contains Paba. If you are hiking with a child younger than six months, don't use sunscreen or insect repellent. Instead, be sure that their head, face, neck, and ears are protected from the sun with a wide-brimmed hat, and that all other skin exposed to the sun is protected with the appropriate clothing.

Remember that food is fun. Kids like snacks so it's important to bring a lot of munchies for the trail. Stopping often for snack breaks is a fun way to keep the trail interesting. Raisins, apples, granola bars, crackers and cheese, cereal, and trail mix all make great snacks. If your child is old enough to carry her own backpack, fill it with treats before you leave. If your kids don't like drinking water, you can bring boxes of fruit juice.

Avoid poorly designed child-carrying packs—you don't want to break your back carrying your child. Most child-carrying backpacks designed to hold a forty-pound child will contain a large carrying pocket to hold diapers and other items. Some have an optional rain/sun hood.

Hiking with Your Dog

Bringing your furry friend with you is always more fun than leaving him behind. Our canine pals make great trail buddies because they never complain and always make good company. Hiking with your dog can be a rewarding experience, especially if you plan ahead.

Getting your dog in shape. Before you plan outdoor adventures with your dog, make sure he's in shape for the trail. Getting your dog into shape takes the same discipline as getting yourself into shape, but luckily, your dog can get in shape with you. Take your dog with you on your daily runs or walks. If there is a park near your house, hit a tennis ball or play Frisbee with your dog.

Swimming is also an excellent way to get your dog into shape. If there is a lake or river near where you live and your dog likes the water, have him retrieve a tennis ball or stick. Gradually build your dog's stamina up over a two- to three-month period. A good rule of thumb is to assume that your dog will travel twice as far as you will on the trail. If you plan on doing a 5-mile hike, be sure your dog is in shape for a 10-mile hike.

Training your dog for the trail. Before you go on your first hiking adventure with your dog, be sure he has a firm grasp on the basics of canine etiquette and behavior. Make sure he can sit, lie down, stay, and come. One of the most important commands you can teach your canine pal is to "come" under any situation. It's easy for your friend's nose to lead him astray or possibly get lost. Another helpful command is the "get behind" command. When you're on a hiking trail that's narrow, you can have your dog follow behind you when other trail users approach. Nothing is more bothersome than an enthusiastic dog that runs back and forth on the trail and disrupts the peace of the trail for others. When you see other trail users approaching you on the trail, give them the right of way by quietly stepping off the trail and making your dog lie down and stay until they pass.

Equipment. The most critical pieces of equipment you can invest in for your dog are proper identification and a sturdy leash. Flexi-leads work well for hiking because they give your dog more freedom to explore but still leave you in control. Make sure your dog has identification that includes your name and address and a number for your veterinarian. Other forms of identification for your dog include a tattoo or a microchip. You should consult your veterinarian for more information on these last two options.

The next piece of equipment you'll want to consider is a pack for your dog. By no means should you hold all of your dog's essentials in your pack—let him carry his own gear! Dogs that are in good shape can carry 30 to 40 percent of their own weight.

Most packs are fitted by a dog's weight and girth measurement. Companies that make dog packs generally include guidelines to help you pick out the size that's right for your dog. Some characteristics to look for when purchasing a pack for your dog include a harness that contains two padded girth straps, a padded chest strap, leash attachments, removable saddle bags, internal water bladders, and external gear cords.

You can introduce your dog to the pack by first placing the empty pack on his back and letting him wear it around the yard. Keep an eye on him during this first introduction. He may decide to chew through the straps if you aren't watching him closely. Once he learns to treat the pack as an object of fun and not a foreign enemy, fill the pack evenly on both sides with a few ounces of dog food in resealable plastic bags. Have your dog wear his pack on your daily walks for a period of two to three weeks. Each week add a little more weight to the pack until your dog will accept carrying the maximum amount of weight he can carry.

You can also purchase collapsible water and dog food bowls for your dog. These bowls are lightweight and can easily be stashed into your pack or your dog's. If you are hiking on rocky terrain or in the snow, you can purchase footwear for your dog that will protect his feet from cuts and bruises.

Always carry plastic bags to remove feces from the trail. It is a courtesy to other trail users and helps protect local wildlife.

The following is a list of items to bring when you take your dog hiking: collapsible water bowls, a comb, a collar and a leash, dog food, plastic bags for feces, a dog pack, flea/tick powder, paw protection, water, and a first-aid kit that contains eye ointment, tweezers, scissors, stretchy foot wrap, gauze, antibacterial wash, sterile cotton tip applicators, antibiotic ointment, and cotton wrap.

First aid for your dog. Your dog is just as prone—if not more prone—to getting in trouble on the trail as you are, so be prepared. Here's a rundown of the more likely misfortunes that might befall your little friend.

Bees and wasps. If a bee or wasp stings your dog, remove the stinger with a pair of tweezers and place a mudpack or a cloth dipped in cold water over the affected area.

Porcupines. One good reason to keep your dog on a leash is to prevent it from getting a nose full of porcupine quills. You may be able to remove the quills with pliers, but a veterinarian is the best person to do this nasty job because most dogs need to be sedated.

Heat stroke. Avoid hiking with your dog in really hot weather. Dogs with heat stroke will pant excessively, lie down and refuse to get up, and become lethargic and disoriented. If your dog shows any of these signs on the trail, have him lie down in the shade. If you are near a stream, pour cool water over your dog's entire body to help bring his body temperature back to normal.

Heartworm. Dogs get heartworms from mosquitoes which carry the disease in the prime mosquito months of July and August. Giving your dog a monthly pill prescribed by your veterinarian easily prevents this condition.

Plant pitfalls. One of the biggest plant hazards for dogs on the trail are foxtails. Foxtails are pointed grass seed heads that bury themselves in your friend's fur, between his toes, and even get in his ear canal. If left unattended, these nasty seeds can work their way under the skin and cause abscesses and other problems. If you have a long-haired dog, consider trimming the hair between his toes and giving him a summer haircut to help prevent foxtails from attaching to his fur. After every hike, always look over your dog for these seeds—especially between his toes and his ears.

Other plant hazards include burrs, thorns, thistles, and poison oak. If you find any burrs or thistles on your dog, remove them as soon as possible before they become an unmanageable mat. Thorns can pierce a dog's foot and cause a great deal of pain. If you see that your dog is lame, stop and check his feet for thorns. Dogs are immune to poison oak but they can pick up the sticky, oily substance from the plant and transfer it to you.

Protect those paws. Be sure to keep your dog's nails trimmed so he avoids getting soft tissue or joint injuries. If your dog slows and refuses to go on, check to see that his paws aren't torn or worn. You can protect your dog's paws from trail hazards such as sharp gravel, foxtails, lava scree, and thorns by purchasing dog boots.

Sunburn. If your dog has light skin he is an easy target for sunburn on his nose and other exposed skin areas. You can apply a nontoxic sunscreen to exposed skin areas that will help protect him from overexposure to the sun.

Ticks and fleas. Ticks can easily give your dog Lyme disease, as well as other diseases. Before you hit the trail, treat your dog with a flea and tick spray or powder. You can also ask your veterinarian about a once-a-month pour-on treatment that repels fleas and ticks.

Mosquitoes and deer flies. These little flying machines can do a job on your dog's snout and ears. Best bet is to spray your dog with fly repellent for horses to discourage both pests.

Giardia. Dogs can get giardia, which results in diarrhea. It is usually not debilitating, but it's definitely messy. A vaccine against giardia is available.

Mushrooms. Make sure your dog doesn't sample mushrooms along the trail. They could be poisonous to him, but he doesn't know that.

When you are finally ready to hit the trail with your dog, keep in mind that national parks and many wilderness areas do not allow dogs on trails. Your best bet is to hike in national forests, BLM lands, and state parks. Always call ahead to see what the restrictions are.

Organizations

Clubs

Colorado Mountain Club

Colorado's main hiking/climbing club is the Colorado Mountain Club. The state offices are located in Golden, but groups exist in many parts of the state.

State Office

710 10th Street #200, Golden 80401; (303) 279–3080, (800) 633–4417; www.cmc.org

Boulder Group

Table Mesa Shopping Center, 633 South Broadway, Unit N, Boulder 80305; (303) 554–7688; www.cmcboulder.org

Denver Group

Same number as state office

Gore Range Group

Members of this group live in Summit and Eagle Counties and surrounding areas.

Contact the state office for membership information.

Trail Groups (Education, Trail Maintenance, Advocacy)

Friends of the Eagles Nest Wilderness, P.O. Box 4504, Frisco 80443-4504; www.fenw.org; or contact the Dillon Ranger District at (970) 468–5400 for the current contact. FENW helps the U.S. Forest Service maintain trails and preserve wilderness values in the Eagles Nest, Holy Cross, and Ptarmigan Peak Wilderness areas. Volunteer opportunities include trail projects, the Volunteer Wilderness Steward program, and fundraising. See sidebar in Hike 11, Buffalo Mountain, for more information.

Friends of Dillon Ranger District, P.O. Box 1648, Silverthorne 80498-1648; www.fdrd.org; or contact the Dillon Ranger District at (970) 468–5400 for the current contact. FDRD helps the U.S. Forest Service maintain trails and works on other forest-related projects in nonwilderness, multiple-use national forest lands in Summit County. This new group focuses on trail maintenance and construction, conservation education, invasive weeds, and wildland fire mitigation. See Hike 13, Masontown/Mount Royal, for more information.

Friends of Breckenridge Trails, Town of Breckenridge Open Space & Trails, P.O. Box 168, Breckenridge 80424; (970) 547–3155; www.townofbreckenridge.org (click on Leisure then Volunteer Opportunities). This group helps the Town of Breckenridge build and maintain trails in Breckenridge.

Volunteers for Outdoor Colorado, 600 South Marion Parkway, Denver 80209; (303) 715–1010 or (800) 925–2220; www.voc.org. Volunteers for Outdoor Colorado (VOC) is a nonprofit organization that sponsors work projects throughout Colorado from April to October, partnering with various land management agencies. See Hike 9, Dillon Peninsula, for more information.

The Colorado Fourteeners Initiative, 710 10th Street #220, Golden 80401; (303) 278–7525; www.coloradofourteeners.org. "The mission of the Colorado Fourteeners Initiative is to protect and preserve the natural integrity of Colorado's 14,000-foot peaks through active stewardship and public education."

Colorado Trail Foundation, 710 10th Street #210, Golden 80401; (303) 384–3729; www.coloradotrail.org. CTF works in partnership with the U.S. Forest Service to maintain the Colorado Trail with volunteer work crews and educational materials. See Hike 20, Colorado Trail from Wheeler Flats to Guller Creek, for more information.

Continental Divide Trail Alliance, P.O. Box 628 Pine 80470; (303) 838–3760 or (888) 909–CDTA; www.cdtrail.org. "The Continental Divide Trail Alliance (CDTA) was formed in 1995 to assist the federal land management agencies in the completion, management and protection of the Trail."

Continental Divide Trail Society, 3704 North Charles Street #601, Baltimore, MD 21218; (410) 235–9610; www.cdtsociety.org. "The mission of the Society is to help in the planning, development, and maintenance of the CDT as a silent trail and to assist users plan and enjoy their experiences along the route."

Conservation Groups

Town and County Volunteer Advisory Groups

Breckenridge Open Space Advisory Commission (BOSAC), Town of Breckenridge Open Space & Trails, P.O. Box 168, Breckenridge 80424; (970) 547–3110

Frisco Recreation, Open Space and Trails Committee (FROST), Town of Frisco, P.O. Box 4100, Frisco 80443; (970) 668–5276

Silverthorne Parks, Open Space, Recreation, and Trails (SPORT), Town of Silverthorne Recreation & Culture, P.O. Box 1309, Silverthorne 80498; www .silverthorne.org

The ECO Eagle Valley Trails Committee, P.O. Box 850, Eagle 81631-0850; (970) 328–3523; www.eaglecounty.us (click on County Services then ECO Trails)

Summit County Open Space Advisory Council (OSAC), Open Space & Trails Department, P. O. Box 5660, Frisco 80443; (970) 668–4060

Other Conservation Groups

Continental Divide Land Trust, P.O. Box 4488, Frisco 80443; (970) 453–3875; www.cdlt.org. "The Continental Divide Land Trust (CDLT) is a local nonprofit organization dedicated to preserving unique open space values on private and public lands."

Friends of the Lower Blue River, P.O. Box 2007, Silverthorne 80498; www.folbr.org. "FOLBR is a group of volunteers who share a concern for maintaining the rural character, quality of life and the environment of the Lower Blue River Valley."

Sierra Club, Blue River Group, www.rmc.sierraclub.org/brg/

Leave No Trace Center for Outdoor Ethics, P.O. Box 997, Boulder 80306; (303) 442–8222 or (800) 332–4100; www.LNT.org. "The Leave No Trace Center for Outdoor Ethics is a national nonprofit organization dedicated to promoting and inspiring responsible outdoor recreation through education, research and partnerships."

Further Reading

For very interesting reading check out Colorado's Historic Newspaper Collection online at www.cdpheritage.org/collection/chnc.cfm. Newspapers published in various Colorado towns and cities between about 1859 and 1928 have been scanned. You can search on a topic, pick an appropriate newspaper(s), and see the world through the writer's eyes in the actual format of yesteryear. Information from old newspapers was obtained from this collection.

History

Bollinger, Edward T. *Rails That Climb: A Narrative History of the Moffat Road*. Boulder: Johnson Publishing 1979.

Bollinger, Edward T., and Frederick Bauer. *The Moffat Road*. Chicago: Sage Books, 1962.

Brown, Robert L. *Colorado Ghost Towns—Past and Present*. Caldwell: Caxton Printers, 1972.

Brown, Robert L. *Holy Cross—The Mountain and the City*. Caldwell: Caxton Printers, 1970.

Clarke, Charlotte. *The Mines of Frisco: A Self-Guided Tour*. Self-publishing, 2004.

Clawson, Janet Marie. *Echoes of the Past: Copper Mountain, Colorado*. Denver: Copper Mountain Resort, 1986.

Eberhart, Perry. *Guide to the Colorado Ghost Towns and Mining Camps*. Chicago: Swallow Press, 1959.

Emore, Anna. *Dillon, the Blue River Wonderland*. Dillon: Summit Historical Society, 1983.

Fiester, Mark. *Blasted Beloved Breckenridge*. Boulder: Pruett, 1973.

Foster, Jack. *Adventures at Timberline*. Denver: Monitor Publications, 1963.

Gardiner, Harvey N. *Mining Among the Clouds: The Mosquito Range and the Origins of Colorado's Silver Boom*. Denver: Colorado Historical Society, 2002.

Gaug, Maryann. *The History of the Land: The Giberson Preserve*. Continental Divide Land Trust, 2005.

Gilliland, Mary Ellen. *Frisco! A Colorful Colorado Community*. Silverthorne: Alpenrose Press, 1984.

Gilliland, Mary Ellen. *Summit: A Gold Rush History of Summit County, Colorado*. Silverthorne: Alpenrose Press, 1980.

Griswold, Don L., and Jean Harvey. *History of Leadville and Lake County, Colorado: From Mountain Solitude to Metropolis*. 2 vols. Denver: Colorado Historical Society, 1996.

Howe, Hazel M. *The Story of Silver Plume*. Idaho Springs: Sander Graphics Printing, 1960.

Kramarsic, Joseph D. *Mountaineering in the Gore Range: A Record of Explorations, Climbs, Routes, and Names*. Self-published, 1989.

McConnell, Virginia. *Bayou Salado: The Story of South Park*. Chicago: Sage Books, 1966.

McTighe, James. *Roadside History of Colorado*. Boulder: Johnson Publishing, 1984.

Parkhill, Forbes. *Mister Barney Ford: A Portrait in Bistre*. Denver: Sage Books, 1963.

Pritchard, Sandra F. *Dillon—Denver and the Dam*. Dillon: Summit Historical Society, 1994.

Pritchard, Sandra F. *Roadside Summit. Part II, The Human Landscape*. Dillon: Summit Historical Society, 1992.

Roberts, Jack. *The Amazing Adventures of Lord Gore: A True Saga from the Old West*. Silverton: Sundance, 1977.

Roller, Elizabeth Rice. *Memoirs from Montezuma, Chihuahua, and Sts. John*. Dillon: Summit Historical Society.

Sharp, Verna. *A History of Montezuma, Sts. John, and Argentine: Early Mining Camps of Summit County*. Dillon: Summit Historical Society, 1971.

Wolle, Muriel Sibell. *Stampede to Timberline*. Denver: Sage Books, 1949.

Natural History

Benedict, Audrey DeLella. *A Sierra Club Naturalist's Guide: The Southern Rockies*. San Francisco: Sierra Club, 1991.

Cassells, E. Steve. *The Archaeology of Colorado*. Boulder: Johnson Books, 1983.

Chronic, Halka. *Roadside Geology of Colorado*. Missoula: Mountain Press, 1980.

Mutel, Cornelia Fleisher, and John C. Emerick. *From Grassland to Glacier: The Natural History of Colorado and the Surrounding Region*. Boulder: Johnson Books, 1992.

Pritchard, Sandra F. *Roadside Summit. Part I, The Natural Landscape*. Dillon: Summit Historical Society, 1988.

West, Michael W. "Quaternary Geology and Reported Surface Vaulting Along East Flank of Gore Range, Summit, Colorado." Master's Thesis, Colorado School of Mines, 1978.

Zwinger, Ann H., and Beatrice E. Willard. *Land Above the Trees*. Boulder: Johnson Books, 1996.

Hiking Guides

The Colorado Mountain Club. *Guide to the Colorado Mountains.* With Robert M. Ormes. 9th ed. Denver: The Colorado Mountain Club, 1992.

Colorado Trail Foundation. *The Colorado Trail: The Official Guidebook.* Denver: Colorado Mountain Club Press, 2002.

Fielder, John, and Mark Pearson. *The Complete Guide to Colorado's Wilderness Areas.* Englewood: Westcliffe, 1994.

Irwin, Pamela D. *Colorado's Best Wildflower Hikes. Vol. 2, The High Country.* Englewood: Westcliffe, 1999.

Jones, Tom Lorang. *Colorado's Continental Divide Trail: The Official Guide.* Englewood: Westcliffe, 1997.

To find articles referenced from the *Summit Daily News,* log onto www.summit daily.com and choose Archives.

Alphabetical Order by Title

Foster, Jack. *Adventures at Timberline.* Denver: Monitor, 1963.

Roberts, Jack. *The Amazing Adventures of Lord Gore: A True Saga from the Old West.* Silverton: Sundance, 1977.

Cassells, E. Steve. *The Archaeology of Colorado.* Boulder: Johnson Books, 1983.

McConnell, Virginia. *Bayou Salado: The Story of South Park.* Chicago: Sage Books, 1966.

Fiester, Mark. *Blasted Beloved Breckenridge.* Boulder: Pruett Publishing Company, 1973.

Brown, Robert L. *Colorado Ghost Towns—Past and Present.* Caldwell: Caxton Printers, 1972.

Colorado Trail Foundation. *The Colorado Trail: The Official Guidebook.* Denver: Colorado Mountain Club Press, 2002.

Irwin, Pamela D. *Colorado's Best Wildflower Hikes. Vol. 2, The High Country.* Englewood: Westcliffe, 1999.

Jones, Tom Lorang. *Colorado's Continental Divide Trail: The Official Guide.* Englewood: Westcliffe, 1997.

Fielder, John, and Mark Pearson. *The Complete Guide to Colorado's Wilderness Areas.* Englewood: Westcliffe, 1994.

Pritchard, Sandra F. *Dillon—Denver and the Dam.* Dillon: Summit Historical Society, 1994.

Emore, Anna. *Dillon, the Blue River Wonderland*. Dillon: Summit Historical Society, 1983.

Clawson, Janet Marie. *Echoes of the Past: Copper Mountain, Colorado*. Denver: Waldo Litho, 1986.

Gilliland, Mary Ellen. *Frisco! A Colorful Colorado Community*. Silverthorne: Alpenrose Press, 1984.

Mutel, Cornelia Fleisher, and John C. Emerick. *From Grassland to Glacier: The Natural History of Colorado and the Surrounding Region*. Boulder: Johnson Books, 1992.

Eberhart, Perry. *Guide to Colorado Ghost Towns and Mining Camps*. Chicago: Swallow Press, 1959.

The Colorado Mountain Club. *Guide to the Colorado Mountains*. With Robert M. Ormes. 9th ed. Denver: The Colorado Mountain Club, 1992.

Griswold, Don L., and Jean Harvey. *History of Leadville and Lake County, Colorado: From Mountain Solitude to Metropolis*. 2 vols. Denver: Colorado Historical Society, 1996.

Sharp, Verna. *A History of Montezuma, Sts. John, and Argentine: Early Mining Camps of Summit County*. Dillon: Summit Historical Society, 1971.

Gaug, Maryann. *The History of the Land: The Giberson Preserve*. Continental Divide Land Trust, 2005.

Brown, Robert L. *Holy Cross—The Mountain and the City*. Caldwell: Caxton Printers, 1970.

Zwinger, Ann H., and Beatrice E. Willard. *Land Above the Trees*. Boulder: Johnson Books, 1996.

Roller, Elizabeth Rice. *Memoirs from Montezuma, Chihuahua, and Sts. John*. Dillon: Summit Historical Society.

Clarke, Charlotte. *The Mines of Frisco: A Self-Guided Tour*. Self-published, 2004.

Gardiner, Harvey N. *Mining Among the Clouds: The Mosquito Range and the Origins of Colorado's Silver Boom*. Denver: The Colorado Historical Society, 2002.

Parkhill, Forbes. *Mister Barney Ford: A Portrait in Bistre*. Denver: Sage Books, 1963.

Bollinger, Edward T., and Frederick Bauer. *The Moffat Road*. Chicago: Sage Books, 1962.

Kramarsic, Joseph D. *Mountaineering in the Gore Range: A Record of Explorations, Climbs, Routes, and Names*. Self-published, 1989.

West, Michael W. "Quaternary Geology and Reported Surface Vaulting Along East Flank of Gore Range, Summit, Colorado." Master's Thesis, Colorado School of Mines, 1978.

Bollinger, Edward T. *Rails That Climb: A Narrative History of the Moffat Road.* Boulder: Johnson Publishing, 1979.

Chronic, Halka. *Roadside Geology of Colorado.* Missoula: Mountain Press, 1980.

McTighe, James. *Roadside History of Colorado.* Boulder: Johnson Publishing, 1984.

Pritchard, Sandra F. *Roadside Summit. Part I, The Natural Landscape.* Dillon: Summit Historical Society, 1988.

Pritchard, Sandra F. *Roadside Summit. Part II, The Human Landscape.* Dillon: Summit Historical Society, 1992.

Benedict, Audrey DeLella. *A Sierra Club Naturalist's Guide: The Southern Rockies.* San Francisco: Sierra Club Books, 1991.

Wolle, Muriel Sibell. *Stampede to Timberline.* Denver: Sage Books, 1949.

Howe, Hazel M. *The Story of Silver Plume.* Idaho Springs: Sander Graphics Printing, 1960.

Gilliland, Mary Ellen. *Summit: A Gold Rush History of Summit County, Colorado.* Silverthorne: Alpenrose Press, 1980.

To find articles referenced from the *Summit Daily News,* log onto www.summitdaily.com and choose Archives.

Hike Index

About the Author

A native of Colorado, Maryann Gaug was born in Denver and spent much of her youth dreaming about living in the mountains. While working on a B.S. degree in mathematics at Gonzaga University in Spokane, Washington, she started backpacking and downhill skiing. Missing the Colorado mountains, she returned and earned an M.S. in computer science at the University of Colorado Boulder. She joined the Boulder group of the Colorado Mountain Club and graduated from their mountaineering school. The Colorado Mountain Club and the Rocky Flats Mountaineering Group gave Maryann plenty of opportunities to continue her hiking, backpacking, backcountry skiing, and other favorite mountain-oriented activities.

After twenty years at Rocky Flats, she took a voluntary separation plan and moved to Silverthorne, Colorado. She worked as a cross-country ski instructor at Copper Mountain Resort, completed a wilderness studies certificate at Colorado Mountain College, and became a Master of Leave No Trace. She also started following another dream—to write about the mountains and canyons that she loves.

Maryann has written articles for several Summit County newspapers and *Cyberwest* e-zine on topics ranging from her outdoor adventures to natural history. Her first book for Globe Pequot's FalconGuides series, *Hiking Colorado III,* now titled *Hiking Colorado* (2nd edition), contains fifty hikes around Colorado. Other books include *The History of the Land: The Fiester Preserve, The History of the Land: The Giberson Preserve,* and *Colorado High Country Anthology,* which she co-authored. She is a board member of Friends of the Eagles Nest Wilderness. Writing this hiking guide is her latest adventure, one which involved hiking over 180 miles in four months, revisiting favorite haunts and discovering new ones close to her home.